TOUGH WITHOUT A GUN

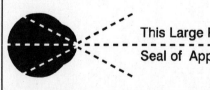

This Large Print Book carries the
Seal of Approval of N.A.V.H.

TOUGH WITHOUT A GUN

THE LIFE AND EXTRAORDINARY AFTERLIFE OF HUMPHREY BOGART

STEFAN KANFER

THORNDIKE PRESS

A part of Gale, Cengage Learning

GALE
CENGAGE Learning

Detroit • New York • San Francisco • New Haven, Conn • Waterville, Maine • London

GALE
CENGAGE Learning™

LIBRARY OF CONGRESS CATALOGING-IN-PUBLICATION DATA

Kanfer, Stefan.
   Tough without a gun : the life and extraordinary afterlife of
Humphrey Bogart / by Stefan Kanfer.
      p. cm.
   Includes bibliographic references.
   ISBN-13: 978-1-4104-3704-4 (lg. print : hardcover)
   ISBN-10: 1-4104-3704-3 (lg. print : hardcover)
   1. Bogart, Humphrey, 1899–1957. 2. Motion picture actors
and actresses—United States—Biography. I. Title.
PN2287.B48K36 2011b
791.4302'8092—dc22
   [B]   2011000805

Published in 2011 by arrangement with Alfred A. Knopf, Inc.

FOR LYNN HENSON

*Those friends thou hast,
and their adoption tried,
Grapple them to thy soul
with hoops of steel.*

CONTENTS

INTRODUCTION

JOE GILLIS: You're Norma Desmond.
You used to be big.
NORMA DESMOND: I am big. It's the
pictures that got small.

Sunset Boulevard has it in reverse. Toward
the end of the twentieth century, it was the
pictures that got big. They got enormous.
They offered surround sound, high-density
images, computerized special effects, wide-
screen galactic epics.

It's the stars that got small.

This has nothing to do with ability. But it
does have to do with quality — with the
kinds of films that are being made, the green
and undemanding audiences who see them,
the bottom-lining studios that produce
them, and, finally, the actors who appear in
them.

Modern leading men are well trained,
skilled in their craft, buff, manipulated by

9

powerhouse publicists. What they don't have is singularity. Impersonators don't "do" Tobey Maguire or Brad Pitt or Leonardo DiCaprio or Christian Bale et al. because these actors don't have imitable voices or faces. This is in sharp contrast to the leading men of the past. Men like Cary Grant, Gary Cooper, James Cagney, Edward G. Robinson, and Humphrey Bogart provided field days — and nights — for comedians and impressionists. And first among those equals was Bogart, the most imitated movie actor of all time. His unique, almost musical sibilance, his creased frown and rare, infectious smile gave him a quality that was at once dangerous and sympathetic. Which is why, more than fifty years after his death, he attained a summit no other actor had ever reached. The American Film Institute ranked him as the greatest male legend in cinema history. It is impossible to imagine anyone supplanting him.

The reasons are numerous and irreversible. For one thing, films are no longer the centerpieces of American culture, the artifacts that everyone goes out to see at the same time. Not only is the attention of the young fractured by Twitter, TiVo, Facebook, YouTube, iPhones, and iPods; now there are also ways for them to catch up with new

10

movies within months of their national release.

For another, the collapse of the studio system in the 1960s meant that promising actors could no longer be brought along slowly. As we'll see, Bogart began as a heavy and was slain in some twenty-seven films before he was offered a major romantic role. ("I played more scenes writhing around on the floor," he once recalled, "than I did standing up.")

Demographics also play a part. Today, young viewers constitute some 70 percent of the filmgoing audience. Understandably, they want to see actors closer to their own ages. When Bogart broke through, he was forty-two.

Finally, a Humphrey Bogart can come along once in a century: someone who isn't conventionally handsome or particularly versatile (he couldn't dance like his contemporary James Cagney, he looked out of place in Gary Cooper–style Westerns, and comedy was never his long suit) but who can convince an audience that whatever character he's playing is of great importance, because he represents something vital about themselves and their time.

"Bogie," as he came to be called, was a legend when alive, much admired in the

United States and imitated internationally by Yves Montand, Jean-Paul Belmondo, and many others. Yet, as far as stature and persona went, something even more dramatic happened after he passed away in 1957. There would be no more Humphrey Bogart pictures, and audiences had a hard time accepting the fact. They would not, *could* not let go of him, and their fanatical devotion made him bigger in death than he had been in life.

In a memoir about his father, Stephen Bogart comments on the first days of that phenomenon. The eight-year-old sat in a limousine with his mother, Lauren Bacall, staring at the hundreds of mourners and onlookers assembled for the funeral.

" 'I hate them,' I said.

" 'No you don't, Stephen. You don't hate them.'

" 'He's my father, not theirs. They don't even know him.' "

But, as Stephen subsequently acknowledged, they *did* know him. They still do. The actor has been gone for more than five decades, but to millions he remains a singular and ageless representative of two cities: old New York, with its gritty avenues and rude wit, its hard-nosed gin joints and occasional grace notes; and old Hollywood, with its big-studio glamour, shadowy film noirs, and tight-lipped, uncompromisingly male superstars. His outstanding characteristics — integrity, stoicism, a sexual charisma accompanied by a cool indifference to women — are never out of style when he's on-screen, and he is still on-screen all the time.

Humphrey Bogart was born in 1899; thus his life and posthumous reputation span three centuries. That claim could be made for only two other iconic Hollywood figures: Charlie Chaplin, born in 1889, and Fred Astaire, born the same year as Bogart. But the former was a director as well as a performer; and the latter was, of course, a dancer first and an actor second. Bogart had only one string on his bow. Yet he has provided the most enduring mark and remains the most forceful presence. Why is that true after all these years? The reasons could make a book.

CHAPTER 1
THE END DEPENDS ON THE BEGINNING

I

In the 150-year history of cinema, few performers have arrived with a more impressive résumé of monetary privilege and social distinction. Humphrey Bogart's father, Belmont DeForest Bogart, was a high-toned graduate of Phillips Andover prep school and Columbia University; his medical degree came from Yale. Belmont rarely failed to inform classmates and colleagues that the Bogarts of Holland were among the earliest settlers in New York, and that one of *their* ancestors was the first "European" child to be born in that state.

Actually, the Bogarts had been a line of burghers and truck farmers until Belmont's father, Adam, came along. He married late, became an innkeeper to support his wife and child, and compulsively tinkered in his off-hours. Lithography — etching on large, unwieldy stones — had become popular in the later nineteenth century; Adam seized the day, creating a process for transfering lithographs to portable sheets of tin. Printers wanted in on this new invention, and the sales made him a rich man. It was a classic case of an old family with new money, very much in the spirit of the nineteenth century. Adam relocated to Manhattan, taking comfort in the knowledge that many a New York City plutocrat had humble beginnings: Jacob Astor started out as a fur trapper; Peter Schermerhorn as a ship chandler; Frederick and William Rhinelander as bakers; Peter Lorillard as a tobacco merchant.

Adam maneuvered the family name into the Blue Book of New York City society and, after his wife died, concentrated all his energy and ambition on his only son. There would be no hayseed in this boy's hair; no scent of the carbolic acid used to clean hotel rooms would cling to his clothes as it had to his father's. Adam was sharply aware of *Power of Personality,* a book by the business writer Orison Swett Marden. "In this fiercely competitive age," warned the author, "when the law of the survival of the fittest acts with seemingly merciless rigor, no one can afford to be indifferent to the smallest detail of dress, or manner, or appearance, that will add to his chance of suc-

cess."
right v
schools
and pro
world,
made up
biology,
School,
as a phys
gart had
staffs of t
tals: Belle

During
wholly alt
horse-draw

most Belmont's height, not
but striking, with russet ha
jaw, and a slender, shape
also famous. At the a
prodigy had sold
After studying i
caught on as
children's
Ivory s
ance
he

...g in a
...ance when the animal got spooked in traffic, reared, and overturned the vehicle. Belmont's leg was broken, badly set, and then reset to correct the original errors. Morphine and other drugs were prescribed to lessen the misery. He leaned on them to get through the nights.

Still, he was tall, slim, and attractive; sporting a cane, he continued to make his professional rounds and attend parties, customarily introduced as one of the city's most eligible bachelors. It was at one of those preaccident fêtes that the thirty-year-old medical man had met the twenty-nine-year-old daughter of a Rochester, New York, stove salesman. Maud Humphrey was al-

beautiful,
a determined
y figure. She was
ge of sixteen the art
rawings to magazines.
Paris and New York she
an illustrator of calendars,
books, and advertisements for
ap and Metropolitan Life Insur-
Everywhere Belmont looked, he saw
pictures.

In their intelligent study, *Maud Humphrey: Her Permanent Imprint on American Illustration,* Karen Choppa and Paul Humphrey suggest that, skilled as she was, Maud owed much of her early success to industrial timing. Just as Enrico Caruso came along when single-sided wax recordings were being mass-produced, so Maud's meticulous watercolor technique turned out to be ideal for the brand-new methods of lithographic reproduction. Her renderings of moppets and misses were sentimental without being cloying, and expertly done; they made her the best-known illustrator of her time. When she and Belmont Bogart first met, he was drawing a yearly salary of twenty thousand dollars, an excellent sum in those days. Maud Humphrey was already earning more than twice as much.

A liaison began, interrupted by Maud's militant feminism: Belmont's nineteenth-century, male-centered view made the suffragist uncomfortable. They broke off. Two years later she heard about his accident and dropped by to express her sympathy. She paid another call, and another, and another. During one rendezvous the pair abruptly decided that personal politics be damned, they could not live without each other. A week later an item appeared in the *Ontario County Times* of June 15, 1898. It explained that in view of Dr. Bogart's indisposition,

Miss Humphrey thought she would rather nurse her husband through his trial than visit him duly chaperoned at stated intervals, so about the middle of the week the young couple announced casually that they were going to be married Saturday, and they were, with only a handful of cousins to give away the orphaned artist. The honeymoon will be spent in a hospital. Mrs. Bogart, nee Humphrey, is a connection of Admiral Dewey, and is also related to the Churchills and the Van Rensselaers.

The newlyweds bought a four-story town house at 245 West 103rd Street, between

Riverside Drive and West End Avenue, then a toney address. Down the hill was Riverside Park, leading to the mile-wide Hudson River and the picturesque craggy Palisades; across the street was the Hotel Marseille, city home of folks like Sara Roosevelt, mother of the future president Franklin Delano Roosevelt. The Bogarts had four live-in help (two maids, a cook, and a laundress); their combined salaries added up to less than twenty dollars a week. In 1899, Maud gave birth to the Bogarts' first child and only son. He had something of his father's dark coloring, modified by his mother's delicate bone structure. The boy was christened with her maiden name, and there was great rejoicing. Before Humphrey was out of swaddling clothes Belmont made plans to enter him at Phillips Andover, predicting that someday young Bogart would become a doctor, like his old man. Over the next five years two daughters were added to the family. In keeping with Maud's progressive outlook, all three children were instructed to address her by her first name. None of them ever called her "Mother." She was not a great believer in hugs, either. A pat on the back or a soft clip on the shoulder was her way of showing affection. Belmont was undemonstrative as well, but this was in keeping with a man of his class and period. Thus he had enormous expectations of his handsome son; thus he assumed that Frances and Catherine would simply marry well and raise their own families. Maud demurred. They could have lives and jobs of their own; a new day was dawning for women. It was the beginning of many arguments about the family, and about life itself.

For more than a decade the three little Bogarts enjoyed an atmosphere of ostentatious comfort, surrounded by reproductions of classical statues, heavy tapestries, and overstuffed horsehair couches and chairs. They played with the latest toys, were luxuriously togged, and ate the best food money could buy. When Maud and Belmont dined out, it was at stylish restaurants like Delmonico's and the Lafayette, but those occasions were rare; they were around the house much of the time. The doctor received patients in a mahogany-lined office on the first floor, and the artist did her work in a studio at the top of the house. On many occasions she sketched and painted until after midnight, when the only sound was the cooing of pigeons on the roof. Belmont raised them in his spare time; it was one of his many hobbies. His favorite avocation was sailing, something he had done as a youth.

To that end, the Bogarts acquired an estate on the exclusive shore of Canandaigua Lake, one of the long, wide Finger Lakes in upstate New York. Willow Brook's fifty-five acres contained a working farm, an ice-house, and broad lawns leading down to the dock where Belmont kept a yacht he called the *Comrade.*

So far, so Edwardian. Yet there were cracks in this grand façade, imperceptible to most outsiders but sadly apparent to Humphrey, Frances, and Catherine. For Maud and Belmont were running out of mutual affection. It was not a question of lovers or mistresses. They had gradually, and then not so gradually, grown apart, vanishing into their professional obligations and political beliefs, into alcohol, and, in Belmont's case, into morphine addiction. They fought much of the time, usually behind closed doors. But in hot weather secrets could not be kept so easily. Maud suffered from migraine headaches, and through the open windows her throaty voice could be overheard by neighbors, bawling out the children for some trivial misbehavior. Her outbursts were often followed by Belmont's own tantrums. Those could lead to harsh corporal punishment; like his father before him, Belmont was a believer in the razor strop as an instrument of moral instruction. At Willow Brook the children's lives veered between the terror of evening quarrels and the delights of lyrical summer afternoons.

For Humphrey, some of the pleasure came from his newfound role as leader of the Seneca Point Gang. This was a self-styled group of adolescent boys who addressed him as "Hump," a nickname he found congenial. They skinny-dipped in local streams, built their own clubhouse of spare planks, played war with lead soldiers, and put on amateurish stage plays at the lakefront beach. There was nothing remarkable about these productions except for the costumes. They were the real thing, Broadway discards donated by William Aloysius Brady, a patient of Dr. Bogart's.

Despite his Irish-sounding name, Bill Brady was a Jewish theatrical producer. At a time when New York society referred to Jews by such code references as NOKD (Not Our Kind, Darling) and restrictive covenants barred "Hebrews" from certain city neighborhoods, the Bogarts displayed few of the standard social biases. Maud was uncomfortable with Jews, but she considered herself a freethinker and a realist. One had to get along with all sorts of people these days. Belmont liked the idea of befriending a man who had managed two undisputed heavyweight champions, James Corbett and James Jeffries, bankrolled touring companies, married the glamorous actress Grace George, and owned the Playhouse Theater on 48th Street. Brady's son, Bill Jr., was an occasional houseguest and honorary gang member; more often he and Humphrey formed their own mini-gang back in the city, where they checked out Sarah Bernhardt and W. C. Fields at the Palace, broke up at the antics of Chaplin and Keaton, and gazed approvingly at the manly images of John Barrymore and Francis X. Bushman in nickelodeons. Bill Sr. had little use for movies — he told the boys they were a passing fad, full of exaggerated gestures by overemoting hambones. He was fond of quoting the director Marshall Neilan: "The sooner the stage people who have come into pictures get out, the better for the pictures."

II

Vaudeville and silent-movie houses were Humphrey's oases in the city. In the country, the *Comrade* became his sanctuary. He had an innate ability to read the wind, and the silence and beauty of the flat water gave him a sense of calm he had never felt before.

When Belmont let him steer, he seemed to take control not only of the vessel, but of his whole being.

There was an additional reason to enjoy puttering around the dock and the lake: Canandaigua was three hundred miles from school. Humphrey had found his first private academy, Delancey, a pain. He was even more restive at the all-male Trinity, an institution of learning founded in 1709, and since that day attended by offspring of the well-connected. In a magazine interview many years later, one of his classmates confessed that "the fact that he posed for his mother's 'pretty' illustrations helped earn him a sissy reputation. We always called him 'Humphrey' because we considered that a sissy name. We must have made life miserable for Bogart."

Underachievers often make themselves popular by excelling in sports. But Humphrey only looked like an athlete. In fact he had no gift for any game except chess. Nor had he any for concentrating on his studies. He was bright enough, and his erect posture and fine features gave him the look of the customary WASP Trinitarian. But, like the Bogart estate, it was all for show. Easily distracted, unhappy at home, he got into fights with classmates and quarreled with teachers. His grades hovered at C level. The headmaster confronted him: "This endless flouting of authority. Why do you do these things?" The adolescent was sullen but unresponsive. Only after decades was he able to supply an answer: "I always liked stirring up things, needling authority. I guess I got it from my parents. They needled everyone, including each other."

In Humphrey's junior year, Maud was offered a position as art director of the *Delineator,* a prominent ladies' magazine. The hours would be long, the vacations brief. On the other hand, the pay and expense account were generous. She signed on. The new arrangement meant that Willow Brook would be a rarely used, and therefore prohibitively expensive, family retreat. It was sold, effectively ending Humphrey's long summer idylls. Belmont acquired a smaller place on Fire Island, but nothing was the same after the five Bogarts stopped summering upstate.

Resentful of circumstances over which he had no control, Humphrey played hooky and affected an indifference to achievement of any kind. Upperclassmen were required to wear blue suits to school; he topped his with a black derby, giving him the air of a racetrack tout. His behavior made Maud edgy, and he was the absolute despair of Belmont. Here was his only son, the one who would carry on the family name, given the best of material comforts, the finest schooling. And what was he turning out to be? A scapegrace, a bottom-of-the-class wastrel. It would never do. Using all the pull he could muster, Belmont got the wayward boy into his old alma mater, Phillips Andover, gateway to Yale.

The oldest boarding school in the United States, Phillips, in Andover, Massachusetts, had been established two years after the Declaration of Independence. John Hancock signed the institution's papers of incorporation, Paul Revere created its seal, and Frederick Law Olmsted, designer of Central Park and himself a graduate, laid out much of the campus grounds. Understandably, an aura of privilege has been part of the school's tradition since the day George Washington's nephews were admitted. This has caused the predictable hostility from outsiders, encapsulated by Holden Caulfield in *The Catcher in the Rye:* "I sort of hated old Sally by the time we got in the cab, after listening to that phony Andover bastard for about ten hours." Within its walls there have also been dissidents who failed to catch the school spirit summarized by its motto, *Finis Origine Pendet* (The End Depends on the Beginning). Humphrey was one of the surliest.

The year was 1917, and the end of the old world was at hand. The tsar of Imperial Russia had just abdicated. The Great War inflamed Europe. U.S. president Woodrow Wilson, who had campaigned on the slogan "He kept us out of war," steered his nation into the conflict. Conscription began. Thousands of American boys were put in uniform and given basic training; they would shortly be sent to join the decimated Allied troops in Belgium and France. Yet in the leafy little town in Massachusetts, all were sheltered and secure, even though a handful of students did recite the popular ditty "If He Can Fight Like He Can Love, Good Night Germany," and sang a spirited version of George M. Cohan's new tune "Over There," with its warning to beware because the Yanks were coming, to the accompaniment of drums rum-tumming everywhere. For most of them this was merely an upbeat lark; what fool would want to wear puttees and carry a rifle when he could be enjoying a cloistered life behind these ivied walls? Study was the main thing; as long as you kept up your grades, you were immune from the draft.

But safety was the last thing Humphrey wanted. It was the old story in a new setting: he had applied himself for the first month, and his grades showed the effect, gratifying his parents. And then, as before, things fell apart. He tested poorly and hardly ever participated in class discussions. By the end of the academic year he was failing geometry, English, French, and Bible study. Belmont examined the report card. Fuming, he gave Humphrey a lecture on responsibility and self-discipline. In a letter to the Andover headmaster he adopted a cooler tone, advising him that "Humphrey is a good boy with no bad habits, who has simply lost his head temporarily." A line was appended: "The harder the screws are put on the better it will be for my son."

The screws were applied — and they completely closed Humphrey's mind. The only times he experienced anything like enlightenment came during after-hours bull sessions at Bishop Hall dorm. The most popular talker was Floyd Furlow, whose father ran the Otis Elevator Company. Floyd was up on world affairs as well as local scuttlebutt, and he had a generous allowance with which he bought luxurious snacks to share with his fellow students. One of them spoke about his origins in

South Africa; another, to Humphrey's transparent envy, let everyone know he had worked on a ship before returning to school. Arthur Sircom, a frequent attendee, was to remember young Bogart sitting on the floor, irritable and melancholy, as out of place as a porcupine in a herd of colts. It was Arthur who ran across Humphrey packing up his belongings. It was a Thursday afternoon near the end of the spring term. Arthur inquired about the early departure; was Humphrey planning a long family weekend at Fire Island? "No," came the reply. "I'm leaving this fucking place! For good! It's just a waste of time here." Arthur shook his head. Humphrey never did understand the meaning of *Finis Origine Pendet.* He had cut himself off from his future. He would be drafted now, made into cannon fodder, perhaps maimed or killed overseas.

As Humphrey packed, he explained his departure to the other boys in the dorm: "The bastards threw me out." The faculty and staff had done exactly that, not because of Humphrey's disposition or his demerits. Or, as Andover legend still has it, because he had thrown grapefruits through the headmaster's window. It was because his grades had fallen so precipitously. He came home in disgrace to find Belmont icy and

30

Maud sulfurous: the boy had had every chance, she said, and he failed both himself and his parents. She went on like that for four days straight. Finally Belmont broke his silence. He had arranged with a friend, a naval architect, to employ the wayward youth in a Manhattan shipyard. At least Humphrey could contribute to the war effort, like a decent able-bodied male.

Humphrey had a better idea, though he left it unexpressed. In his life he would journey to Europe and Africa, and he would make his home three thousand miles from the house on 103rd Street. But he would never take a longer journey than the one he made on May 28, 1918, when he dropped a nickel in the subway turnstile and headed for Brooklyn.

III

The recruiting officer aboard the SS *Granite State* was pleased to receive him, as he was pleased to receive all volunteers for the U.S. Navy. Enlistment had been brisk since May 7, 1915. On that date a German U-boat torpedoed the British ocean liner RMS *Lusitania,* killing 1,198 of the passengers aboard, many of them Americans. The incident turned U.S. opinion against Germany and prompted scores to volunteer for naval

31

service. Now, two years later, the nation had joined the Allies in the fight to save civilization, and men were lined up by the thousands, ready to go to battle against the Hun.

Looking back, Humphrey saw that in the eyes of an eighteen-year-old dropout, "The war was great stuff. Paris! French girls! Hot damn!" He was given a physical on board the ship, checking in at five feet, eight inches in height, weighing 136 pounds, with brown eyes and hair and no remarkable scars. He had, in effect, run away from home, but when his parents learned of the enlistment they expressed pride and euphoria. Now Maud saw her boy as something of a hero, an American in uniform ready to do his duty for his country. Belmont thought the navy might teach him a thing or two about discipline, and make a man of him in the process. School wasn't everything; didn't Herman Melville write "A whaleship was my Yale college and my Harvard"?

The enlistee received his basic training at the Naval Reserve Training Station at Pelham, New York, graduating with rank of coxswain. Like most of the class, he was assigned to the *Leviathan,* a troop transport. According to Humphrey's own version, his father got what he wanted on the second day out, when Coxswain Bogart received a direct order to carry out an assignment and told his superior, "Not my detail." This was the old navy, and infractions were dealt with directly; Humphrey was decked with a right to the jaw. From above him he heard the command, "Don't say that again when you're given an order." He never got in an officer's face after that. But neither did he become a model sailor. Various infractions landed him in the brig several times; he got demoted to seaman second class, lost a month's pay in a crap game, and never saw any action overseas — the war ended on November 11, 1918, five and a half months after he had signed up. He also got into a disfiguring accident that year, one that would turn out to be the stuff of legend.

In later years movie publicists would churn out a story about the mark on Humphrey Bogart's upper lip: just as he had taken the wheel of the *Leviathan,* a U-boat fired at the ship and an errant piece of shrapnel hit the valorous young Bogart in the face. This was a total fiction. Darwin Porter's scabrous and dubiously referenced *The Secret Life of Humphrey Bogart* claims that a drunken Belmont Bogart savagely struck his fourteen-year-old son, loosening two front teeth and smashing his upper lip. The beating was supposed to have come after the boy used an air rifle to shoot out some red lanterns on the grounds of the Delancey school. Sober, says Porter, Belmont might have sewed up the lip leaving a minimum trace, but he was drunk and botched the job. Nathaniel Benchley, a confidant and early biographer, seems a more reliable source. He swore that the scar came from a stateside non-domestic incident. Humphrey had been assigned to guard a navy prisoner being transferred from a docked ship to Portsmouth Naval Prison, in New Hampshire. The captive's wrists were cuffed to each other, and he was quiet and obedient as they made their way north. When they changed trains in Boston he pleaded for a smoke, and Humphrey amiably handed over a cigarette. He even supplied a light. As the prisoner bent over the match he suddenly put his hands together, struck the guard's mouth with the manacles, and fled. Humphrey was stunned, but not disabled. He took his .45 from its holster and fired away, hitting the running man in the leg. After the prisoner was locked up in Portsmouth, a doctor tended to the lip. He sewed up the wound badly, and left a small disfiguring cicatrix.

The incident made Seaman Bogart suspicious of prisoners in particular and the navy in general. And then he became a jailbird himself. It happened in 1919, five months after the armistice. He had just been transferred to the USS *Santa Olivia,* a small troopship assigned to pick up American soldiers in Europe and ferry them home. On April 13, the night before she was due to sail, Humphrey and a few other servicemen tied one on. A game began: Who would be the last to board the *Olivia*? One by one they clambered aboard. At the very last minute they looked around. No Bogart. There was an iron law about sailing time, and the ship left Hoboken without him. He was marked down as a deserter. Panicked, he turned himself in to the authorities. He had not deserted, he pleaded; he had merely overslept. He was wrong, he admitted, he was contrite, he would suffer any punishment for his neglect of duty, just as long as the authorities understood that he was not a traitor, only a sailor who'd gone absent without leave. The U.S. Navy let him dangle for weeks, and then accepted his plea.

All the same, AWOL was not a crime without punishment. Humphrey was put behind bars for three days, confined to solitary and restricted to bread and water. A few weeks later he was demobilized and given an honorable discharge. Seaman Bogart was astonished to see his performance sheet: some forgiving officer had given him the highest possible marks in Sobriety and Obedience.

IV

In 1919 Humphrey faced a problem common to every war veteran: how to reenter civilian society. But he had special problems for a man of his class and upbringing. He possessed no degree in anything, no seagoing skills that could be adapted for peacetime use. And there was one other impediment. While he was gone, Belmont, his judgment clouded by morphine addiction, had made some unwise investments in the timber industry. The end of the war had meant the end of shipbuilding, and there was an unpredicted slump in housing. The Bogarts had lost a fortune. En route, Belmont also lost many of his important patients. To hold up his end of the family finances, the doctor agreed to become the official physician on ocean liners. This kept him away for weeks at a time, an arrangement agreeable to Maud. But not to Humphrey. Whatever his father's faults, he still had business connections; his mother had none, and when he moved back to his room at 103rd Street he found her as critical and as cold as she had been before he enlisted. "There was no running down the stairs with arms outstretched," he remembered ruefully, "no 'My darling son!' Only 'Good job, Humphrey!' or something like that." The lack of affection between mother and son could only have intensified Humphrey's feelings of dislocation and self-doubt.

He turned to his father. To his surprise, Belmont came through. On one of the doctor's shore leaves he spoke to businessman clients and friends, calling in chips for his wayward boy. In later years Humphrey claimed to have been an entry-level executive for the National Biscuit Co., a tugboat inspector, and a Pennsylvania Railroad worker. He left the last job, according to his own account, "when I found that there were 50,000 employees between me and the president." Finally he became a runner for a major Wall Street firm, S. W. Strauss & Co. None of it added up to a career. As far as he could see, making whoopee was about all he was good at. He threw himself into Manhattan's raucous nightclub scene, refusing to look back, unwilling to peer into the future.

The Volstead Act of 1920, forbidding the sale of alcohol, had become the law of the land. Warren G. Harding had replaced

Woodrow Wilson in the White House and, harrumphing about a "Return to Normalcy," did nothing as the stock market went wild and the liquor business boomed. With broad winks and nudges from the police, speakeasies were set up throughout the city, and Humphrey and his short-skirted, hair-bobbed dates were frequent visitors to the hot ones. He wasn't a hit with everyone, though. A local girl, Lenore Strunsky, later the wife of lyricist Ira Gershwin, was to remember the twenty-year-old Bogart as "an attractive boy," but not very popular with her crowd. "For one thing, he ate onions, and he didn't write poetry. In fact, he didn't do anything interesting that I can recall."

Humphrey was all too aware that he was a slacker in real life, a wise guy with no future. Everybody seemed to be getting on, in the media, in show business, on Wall Street — everyone except Humphrey Bogart. He griped to friends who listened, but did nothing. In the company of Bill Brady Jr. he was particularly down. His pal had a show business future ahead of him; all he had to do was follow Bill Sr.'s trail. But what chance did Humphrey have? Junior thought about it. He convinced his married half sister, Alice, to work on their father, persuade him to give Humphrey a job doing something, anything, backstage. It was during this time that the senior Brady changed his mind about cinema. One look at the profit sheets at Fox and Universal had been enough to persuade him that a man could make a nice living in the picture business — *if* he got the right people in front of the camera. To that end, he founded a company, World Film Corporation, in Fort Lee, New Jersey; hired two proven stars, Nita Naldi and Arlene Pretty, for one movie; and signed a director to develop another, provisionally entitled *Life.* He needed an office boy — or said that he did — and took Humphrey on. The kid had something, God knew what; better to give Junior's pal a job than let it go to a stranger.

A few months into production, William Brady Sr. decided that the director of *Life* had no talent and fired him. Senior prided himself on his seat-of-the-pants instincts about people and tapped Humphrey to finish the picture. This was the young man's big chance. He turned the opportunity into amateur night. In too many scenes the camera recorded Humphrey's gesticulations, reflected in the windows of storefronts as he directed the actors. The footage had to be thrown away. Brady took over and finished the picture himself. Humiliated, Humphrey regarded the experience as strike one and expected to be dismissed.

But Brady Sr. didn't want to upset his children. They liked Humphrey and, for that matter, so did he. The young man was encouraged to try another branch of show business: writing. He sat down before a typewriter and in a few weeks came up with a script. Brady thought it was a bit too violent for his studio, but that the dialogue showed promise. He gave the pages to Jesse L. Lasky, head of a burgeoning new film company. Lasky was busy and handed them to his assistant. Walter Wanger said Humphrey's script was just about the worst thing he had ever seen, pitched it in a wastebasket, and let everybody know what he had done. Strike two.

By now Humphrey was certain that he had no value, no skills worth developing, no way of distinguishing himself from the crowd of faceless veterans. And still he wasn't fired. Alice Brady had no designs on him; she simply thought the young man was intelligent and trustworthy, and that there ought to be a place for him in her father's business, somewhere, somehow. She enlisted her stepmother, actress Grace George, in the campaign to make Humphrey Bogart a stage manager. Why not? She argued. What was it but a sort of glorified gofer in charge of props and costumes? Her mother gave way. Together, the two women worked on Brady Sr. until he assented. But he mischievously added a proviso. Grace was about to tour in *The Ruined Lady*. If young Bogart was so good, why didn't he stage-manage *her* company? To his surprise, Grace said she'd be pleased to have Humphrey aboard.

The novice had no trouble with the usual requirements of the job. He saw to it that there was a place for everything, and everything was in its place. What threw him was the additional assignment: to earn his fifty-dollar weekly salary, the stage manager had to understudy every male role. As long as the actors stayed healthy, all was well. Humphrey did his job, and stayed so loose that he took to needling the juvenile lead, Neil Hamilton, about being overpaid for reciting a few lines and bowing at curtain time. Hamilton took the remarks in good spirits, but on the last night of the tour he arranged to succumb to a heavy cold. Humphrey called for a rehearsal, got into costume, and went onstage. "It was awful," he remembered. "I knew all the lines of all the parts because I had heard them from out front about a thousand times. But I took one look at the emptiness where the audience would be that night and I couldn't remember anything."

No one thought this would be the making of Humphrey Bogart — least of all Humphrey Bogart. He had never considered an acting career. You had to prepare long years for such a vocation. And you needed the gift for performance, for imitation, for climbing inside the skin of another person. He sensed no such gift, had attended no acting school, studied no master of the art, and couldn't be anybody but himself. All the young man could do was keep from embarrassing himself and everyone else in the cast. That seemed unlikely.

Watching this catastrophe in the making, Grace George charitably decided that she, too, was suffering from a sore throat, and the performance was canceled. Audiences would have to wait until the following year to see Humphrey Bogart make his stage debut.

V

An army veteran named Stuart Rose had started to call on Frances Bogart and, after winning the approval of Maud and Belmont, became a familiar presence around the house. Maud was otherwise occupied on

Memorial Day 1921, so Stuart bought three tickets to a show at the Fulton Theater in Brooklyn and treated Frances and Belmont to Humphrey's first performance. Humphrey, never the introspective sort, tended to dismiss his early roles as minuscule and insignificant. Yet even the smallest part seemed to encapsulate his time and place.

In this long-forgotten play, for example, he did some doubling in crowd scenes, but had only one line: "Drinks for my lady and her most honored guests." He delivered it dressed in livery and wearing thick yellow face powder. The corners of his eyes were marked with heavy black lines. It was the makeup man's way of turning Humphrey into a Japanese butler. He was supposed to represent the customary image of the Mysterious Easterner of the 1920s: smiling, servile, and asexual, with a vaguely conspiratorial air.

Stuart recalled his future brother-in-law entering tentatively, carrying a tray of cocktails and speaking with a stagy accent. "He said his line and he embarrassed me it was so bad." Belmont leaned over and burbled, "The boy's good, isn't he?" Stuart choked out, "Yes, he is." Yet Brady Sr. liked it well enough; a few months later he offered Humphrey a part in a melodrama. The actor was billed as H. D. Bogart, and completely ignored by the Broadway critics. Brady kept using him anyway. This was Broadway's heyday; it had gone from prewar tawdry to postwar vibrant, alive with the dazzle of electric lights, theater marquees, and immense signs advertising Lucky Strike and Pepsi-Cola. French novelist Paul Morand cheerfully noted that in the theater district, "it is a glowing summer afternoon all night: one might almost wear white trousers and a straw hat. Theaters, night clubs, movie palaces, restaurants are all lighted at every porthole. Undiscovered prisms, rainbows squared." Tourists flooded the place; optimism and booze were everywhere. There were often more than one hundred openings a year in the early 1920s, and an untried actor could be hidden in a large cast with no damage done to the overall production.

Grace, Alice, and Bill Jr. kept working on Bill Sr., and in 1922, the impresario surrendered, casting Humphrey as the worthless "young sprig of the aristocracy" in *Swifty.* This melodrama starred Neil Hamilton and a soubrette named Frances Howard, fiancée of silent-film producer Sam Goldwyn. The part of a high-toned seducer was Humphrey's most demanding role and

Senior was taking no chances. One day he overheard his protégé asking the director, "Which way do I face — toward the audience or toward the other actors?" That was all Brady needed. In his view there were but two kinds of actors, professionals and bums, and he wanted everyone who worked for him to be a pro. During rehearsals he sat in the balcony, battering the sprig, shouting "What?" every time the actor failed to enunciate clearly. It was here that the distinctive Bogart delivery was born — the sudden rictus, the lips pulled back after a statement, the unique sibilance that sometimes made him sound tentative and boyish, and at other times gave him a vaguely malevolent air.

Swifty was roundly panned. The bad news was conveyed to Humphrey by his mother the next day when she entered his room with the morning papers. Sitting on the edge of the bed, Maud briskly quoted the critics. Heywood Broun of the *New York World* had found the play "cheap and implausible," and Alan Dale of the *New York American* said that Humphrey Bogart gave a "rather trenchant example of bad acting." Most of the notices depressed Humphrey, but one angered him. That column he preserved, as if to toughen his resolve. For the rest of Humphrey's life, Alexander Woollcott's words occupied a central place in his scrapbook, turning yellow with the years. It read, "The young man who embodies the aforesaid sprig is what is usually and mercifully described as inadequate."

Humphrey interpreted Woollcott's words as a challenge, and urged Brady to give him bigger and better roles. Instead, the boss kept casting him in play after play as a juvenile wearing striped jacket and white ducks, vigorously entering with a racket or a cocktail in hand. Some journalists claimed to have heard Bogart make the hallowed inquiry, "Tennis anyone?," among them Hearst columnist Louella Parsons and *New York Post* critic Richard Watts Jr. But no such documentary evidence exists. Humphrey did swear to Nathaniel Benchley that he had said "It's forty–love outside — anyone care to watch?" and claimed to have spoken every stage cliché except "Give me the ball, coach, and I'll get you a touchdown."

Actually, the role of a sprig was a technical necessity. In the era of large casts, playwrights often needed to clear the stage to get to the next scene. Hence the device of the young man who invites everyone outside to watch a game or have some tea.

Quite a few of these male ingenues were gay and made no attempt to hide their inclinations. This was not only the New York theater with its reputation for liberality, it was also the 1920s with its new emphasis on nontraditional lifestyles and deportment. Yet even the tolerant world of Broadway found itself confused by the jumble of gender roles being pushed by fashion and music. Eventually those feelings erupted in the novelty number "Masculine Women, Feminine Men":

Girls were girls and boys were boys when I was a tot.
Now we don't know who is who, or even what's what!

For all his rebellions against Maud and Belmont, for all his drunken sprees and surly postures, Humphrey could not escape the central fact of his life. He was the scion of straitlaced parents whose roots were in another time. Their customs and attitudes may have become outmoded, but they were deeply ingrained in their son no matter how hard he tried to escape them. They showed in his upright carriage and in his careful manner of speaking, in his courtesy to women and frank dealing with men. He came to recognize that he gave "the impression of a Nineteenth Century guy," no matter how hard he tried to be au courant. But it worked in his favor. In the 1920s many dramas and comedies looked back to the Edwardian era. Humphrey became a favorite of casting directors during the time William Brady Sr. kept him out of plays he regarded as "Grade A."

At last, in 1923, Senior finally rewarded Humphrey with a major part in *Meet the Wife*. The comedy starred two highly polished professionals, Clifton Webb and Mary Boland, and gave them clever lines and situations. For the first time Humphrey read an unqualified, if brief, approval of his own work. "Bogart," said the *World* review, "is a handsome and nicely mannered reporter, which is refreshing." Humphrey was in his first bona fide Broadway hit; *Wife* ran thirty weeks. With the guarantee of a steady salary, a modicum of fame, and the knowledge that he only had to work three hours out of every twenty-four, he began to lose his bearings.

With his date of choice — and he changed women nearly as often as he changed shirts — Humphrey visited the Cotton Club in Harlem, heard Texas Guinan shout "Hello, suckers!" to her patrons, watched Jimmy

Durante caper at the Dover Club, and drank at Chumley's in the Village before heading home at sunrise. This kind of behavior led to the inevitable hangovers, and one evening, shortly before the close of the long run, he showed up onstage with glazed eyes and liquor-scented breath. He groped for his lines and came up empty, leaning against a wall to regain his composure. Boland was forced to improvise a monologue on the spot. At length Humphrey recalled his line and they got through the rest of the act without further incident. But as soon as the curtain fell she rounded on him: "Get this, Bogart — you'll never work in another play with me!"

It was shameful conduct, and he knew it. *There were but two kinds of actors, professionals and bums.* And Humphrey Bogart had just behaved like a bum. He resolved never to repeat the incident, and went at his next assignment with the self-discipline of an old trouper. In the 1924 season, *Nerves,* the story of a flying squadron going from the halls of Yale to the skies of France, was given a first-class production by Bill Brady Jr. Co-written by the poet Stephen Vincent Benét, it featured a set by the gifted designer Jo Mielziner and starred a group of emerging actors. They included Humphrey,

Mielziner's brother Kenneth, who had changed his last name to MacKenna, and a pretty female lead named Mary Philips. Alas, in the theater as elsewhere, timing is everything, and *Nerves* could not have chosen a more inauspicious moment to open. The night before, the antiwar comedy-drama *What Price Glory* ("Stop the blood! Stop the blood!") had debuted at the Plymouth Theater and used up all the oxygen on Broadway.

Nerves expired twenty-three days later, but not before Humphrey received the best notices of his career. In Heywood Broun's opinion Humphrey Bogart gave "the most effective performance" in an unsatisfactory play. The *Times* critic agreed: Bogart "was dry and fresh, if that be possible." The notices went into Humphrey's scrapbook, and the judgments, he recalled, went to his "badly swelled head." In a key scene Philips was supposed to walk away silently as Humphrey spoke. "I noticed," he said, "that she was putting a lot of *that* in her walk." So much, in fact, that he could feel the audience's eyes leave him in order to follow her. He confronted Mary and was met with a saucy reply: "Suppose you try to stop me." He didn't accept the challenge because "while I was talking I was suddenly aware that here was a girl with whom I could very easily fall in love."

VI

He put Mary Philips out of his mind the moment the show closed. But that was typical of Humphrey in those days. Freud's influence was only beginning to be felt in the 1920s, yet it didn't take a psychoanalyst to see how a cold, remote mother could shape her son's attitude toward the female of the species. Maud's influence, coupled with the hell-with-it mind-set of the flappers, kept him from caring deeply about women — an indifference that seemed to color his general outlook.

So Humphrey's friends were astonished by his next move: he forsook acting and took a step backward to stage-managing. The action was motivated by fear and shame. In the first place, he had never quite shaken off his stage fright and wondered whether he had it in him to become a professional player. In the second place, he had been smarting ever since his disgraceful behavior in *Meet the Wife.* Playing the good soldier in William Brady's outfit might help everyone forget — or at least forgive — his missteps.

It turned out to be a wise move. Brady

expressed his gratitude early and often. For the touring company of *Drifting,* headed by his daughter, Alice, had just run into trouble. Alice was pregnant and doctors predicted the child would be born prematurely. Just how premature they would find out on a Saturday night, immediately after the show. The Sunday performance was canceled, giving the staff of *Drifting* two days to find a new female lead. The following afternoon an assistant stage manager ran through the lines onstage with one actress, while in an office upstairs Humphrey did the same thing with another. Her name was Helen Menken; after a brief consultation, the two men decided that she was by far the better candidate.

Menken had to memorize the lines overnight, and she went through the blocking on Monday. Her opening was a disaster. *Drifting* had eight scene changes, and she could hardly be blamed for colliding with the scenery a few times. One divider actually fell on her. Somehow she managed to get through the night without blowing a line. After the final bows, though, she aimed a stream of invective at Humphrey. He conceded that Miss Menken had done her best under arduous conditions, but then again, so had he. His protestations only seemed to make her more irritable. She got louder and hotter. "I guess I shouldn't have done it," he remembered ruefully, "but I booted her. She, in turn, belted me and ran to her dressing room to cry." Willful, short-tempered, sharp-tongued — in brief, Humphrey's kind of woman.

Within a week they were dating; within a month they had taken out a wedding license. Smitten though they were, no nuptials followed. Helen was older and more established and drew a higher salary than Humphrey. That would never do. The last thing he wanted was a repeat of his parents' financial situation. On this point he stood firmly with Belmont: the husband, not the wife, should be the breadwinner. To that end, Humphrey went back to acting. Stuart Rose was to remember that his brother-in-law had no innate gift for performance. What he had was determination. He would make himself into a leading man by dint of "observation, integrity and brains. He had a very strong character." While Helen returned to the road, Humphrey moved on to *Hell's Bells,* a comedy co-starring Shirley Booth, one of the critics' favorite actresses. The comedy got so-so reviews but enjoyed a decent run. Better still, from Humphrey's point of view, the critic for the *American* said that his part was "gorgeously acted." That notice helped him get his next assignment.

Mary Boland ("Get this, Bogart") personified the show business adage "I'll never speak to you again — until I need you." She interviewed player after player for her new show, *Cradle Snatchers*, a slam-bang farce about three society wives who acquire their own private gigolos. They also acquire a hideout in a bordello, only to find their husbands seeking comfort at the same place. No actor seemed to have the right combination of good looks and discernible sense of humor. At the end of the day Boland turned to her producer and sighed, "Oh, all right then. Get Bogart. I know it's what you have in mind."

It was indeed. Boland said nothing about Humphrey's gaffe in *Meet the Wife*, nor did he, and they got along splendidly through the long and lucrative run. Everyone got good notices, but Amy Leslie, who covered New York for the *Chicago Tribune*, only had eyes for Humphrey. She said he was "as young and handsome as Valentino . . . elegant in comedy . . . as graceful as any of our best actors." Whatever private doubts Humphrey had about his ability vanished forever. He had found a vocation — or a vocation had found him. He was no longer one of the postwar drifters bereft of purpose or direction. All right, he acknowledged, this was unplanned; he had been the beneficiary of a series of happy accidents. So what? The important thing was the Latin phrase he had learned in prep school, even though he had learned little else there: *Carpe diem.* Seize the day. Humphrey forswore stage-managing without a backward glance and thereafter devoted himself to three main pursuits: the theater, romance, and alcohol.

The 1925–26 season was to have a profound significance for Humphrey. While he basked in critical appreciation, a versatile, twinkling Briton, Leslie Howard, was starring in *The Green Hat,* and a short, dynamic ex-hoofer named James Cagney was featured in *Outside Looking In.* Along the Rialto three actresses were hard at work: Helen Menken in *Makropoulos Secret,* Mary Philips in *The Wisdom Tooth,* and Mayo Methot in *Alias the Deacon.* All would mold the Bogart image; all were regulars at midtown speakeasies. Humphrey's favorite was Tony's, a joint patronized by the Broadway elite. Among the regulars were columnist Heywood Broun and producer Mark Hellinger, who became a close friend. Also present was the influential critic, gossip, and show-off Alexander Woollcott — the one who had witheringly described Humphrey's debut as "inadequate." He was accorded a wary tip of the Bogart fedora.

By now Stuart Rose had married Humphrey's sister Frances, and Humphrey thought about heading for the altar himself. In theory Helen Menken would make an ideal bride. In reality, however, too much had happened since their whirlwind engagement. During the past year, Helen had become a Broadway diva. Currently starring in the hit play *Seventh Heaven,* she received nightly ovations at the theater, and then again when she entered the lobby at her place of residence, the Gramercy Park Hotel. Again Humphrey had visions of Maud and Belmont redivivus. What to do? In wine, Humphrey confessed to Bill Brady Jr. that he really didn't want to get married. Bill knew the politics of theater and journalism far better than his friend. Alexander Woollcott, who had no romantic interest in women, was nonetheless an admirer and close friend of Helen's. Bill gave it to his buddy straight: he was in too deep now, and if he didn't marry Helen he'd never work on Broadway again; Alex would take care of that. Bill urged Humphrey to consider the situation: with Helen, he could crack the big time; without her he was, face it, one more superannuated juvenile.

To test Bill's verdict, Humphrey had only to look in the mirror. Louise Brooks, the silent-movie star who had turned her back on Hollywood, was in New York City at the time, and her memoir speaks of him as "a slim boy with charming manners, who was extraordinarily quiet for an actor. His handsome face was made extraordinary by a most beautiful mouth. It was very full, rosy, and perfectly modeled. To make it completely fascinating, at one corner of his upper lip a scarred quilted piece hung down in a tiny scallop." All very charming, but hardly the stuff of which icons are made.

At winter's end Humphrey talked himself into abandoning the single life. It cannot have been easy. In essence this was an arrangement, something he was forced to do in order to advance his career. He liked Helen well enough, but love was something else entirely. Was he even capable of such an emotion? He considered the example of his parents' own marriage and its many difficulties. Marriage was not for him. Not now, anyway; not to Helen. Yet the single life would condemn him to obscurity. That was intolerable. So wedding plans were made, and in late May 1926 he and Helen were wed in her hotel apartment. The nuptials were witnessed by the press, a group of prominent actors, and Helen's parents, both stone-deaf. The Episcopal minister was himself deaf, but he had learned to speak in a high-pitched singsong manner, creaking out the words as an assistant echoed them in sign language. It was a weird ceremony, made weirder when Helen faced a reporter, suddenly became hysterical, and had to be led to an adjoining room. Several hours passed before she granted the interview. It was not the happiest way to begin.

Serenity remained in short supply. "We quarreled over the most inconsequential things," Humphrey ruefully admitted later. Those things included a battle royal over the right of their pet dog to have caviar when people were starving in Europe. "I contended that the dog should eat hamburger and like it. She held out for caviar." Customarily, these bouts ended with one of them storming out in a rage. Although the couple would reconcile within a day or two, the ceasefires grew shorter as 1926 wore on. At last *Seventh Heaven* closed after a forty-two-week run, the longest of the season. For the first time, Helen told friends, she was free to work on the marriage. But Humphrey was too busy to do any heavy lifting. First he took over for an ailing player in Maxwell Anderson's comedy *Saturday's Children.* Then he got a large part in another comedy, *Baby Mine,* starring Roscoe "Fatty" Arbuckle. Arbuckle, the silent-film comedian who mentored Chaplin and gave Buster Keaton his first film role, had been ruined by one of Hollywood's first sex scandals. In 1921 he and two friends drove north, checked into the St. Francis Hotel in San Francisco, and enticed several women to their suite. During the course of the evening Arbuckle's date, thirty-year-old actress Virginia Rappe, ran a high fever and complained of sharp abdominal pain. She died three days later of peritonitis, caused by a ruptured bladder. Subsequently, one of the other women claimed that the three-hundred-pound Arbuckle had raped the young woman, piercing her bladder in the process. Rappe's manager went further: he claimed that the comedian had used a piece of ice to simulate sex with her. In vain Arbuckle protested that he had only used the ice on her skin, hoping to ease the young lady's distress. The papers in America and Europe got hold of the news, and Arbuckle found himself endlessly pilloried in columns and editorials. The San Francisco district attorney, hungry for publicity, hauled him into court. The first trial ended in a hung jury; so did a second. The DA persisted. The third jury found the defendant innocent of all charges. They were was too late; the damage had been done. Arbuckle was washed up in movies. Six years down the road, *Baby Mine* was supposed to provide a second act for one of the funniest men in America.

Some actors shied away from an appearance with the fat man. Humphrey made a point of telling Arbuckle how glad he was to be working with a comic genius. The New York papers attempted to be broad-minded, and no mention was made of *l'affaire Rappe*. But the public no longer had any interest in the ruined star; he was old news. The show closed after just two weeks. No matter: Humphrey was promptly offered a role in Chicago, playing the lead in the touring company of *Saturday's Children*. An idea occurred to him: Why didn't Helen come along? They could be a couple of tourists in the Windy City. Mrs. Bogart said no, thank you; she preferred to hang around Broadway until the right play came along.

In fact, neither partner had ever really invested emotion or time in the marriage, and from that point on they agreed on only one matter: separation. Helen did accompany her husband to Chicago, but only to file for divorce. She charged neglect and cruelty, although her lawyers were instructed not to ask for alimony. Later she summed up the eighteen-month union to a reporter: "I was deeply interested in acting, but I felt that the managing of a home was something greater." Unfortunately, her husband "did not want a home. He regarded his career as more important than married life." This was half true at best. Indeed, Humphrey was more interested in professional advancement than in settling down. But so was Helen; the ink had hardly dried on the divorce agreement when she sailed off to London to be the lodestar in the West End version of *Seventh Heaven.* In time Menken was to admit that she was "to blame for the breakup of our marriage. I put my career first." There is no evidence that Humphrey cared much for the marriage, or about its breakup. He just didn't want any trouble. In a letter to a colleague he protested, "I have tried my very best to keep my mouth shut — and be discreet. Any talking has come from my so-called friends and not from me. . . ." The prep school rebel gave way to the gentleman. He acknowledged that the marriage with Helen had

61

been a mistake, but even so, "she's a wonderful girl."

Now that he was free, Humphrey celebrated for a couple of weeks — and then again fell into the tender trap. To his friends it seemed an odd thing for him to do. The public failure of his first marriage should have been a chastening experience. What was the rush to repeat — especially with another actress? But when they thought about it later, Humphrey's move made sense. He was uncomfortable with "civilians," women outside show business who never quite understood what he did for a living. And then there was the hidden careerist in Bogart, a man still looking for the main chance. He knew a lot about Mary Philips; she was not only attractive, she was a comer, someone who might give him a boost. He called her up out of the blue. "I had had enough women by the time I was twenty-seven," he remembered, "to know what I was looking for in a wife next time I married." After a few weeks of dating, he decided that Mary was his belle ideal. And when he learned that Kenneth MacKenna was also wooing the actress, his desire for her became unappeasable. He plied Mary with boxes of candy, bouquets of roses, dinners in expensive restaurants, always decorous, never forcing the issue. Philips remembered the Bogart of 1927: "He was a strangely puritanical man with very old fashioned virtues. He had class as well as charm" — the nineteenth-century guy on display. She fell for him, casting aside a cruelly disappointed MacKenna. In the spring of 1928 the twenty-five-year-old became the second Mrs. Humphrey Bogart at a wedding at the home of her widowed mother in Hartford, Connecticut.

The marriage could not have had a better beginning. The attractive couple hung out in after-hours clubs and attended parties. She was known for her winning smile, he for consuming vast quantities of booze without slurring his words or losing his appeal. For a time the Bogarts were cast opposite each other in *Skyrocket,* a drama about a married couple who fall in love when they're indigent — and out of love when they strike it rich. In the last act they reconcile for good when they lose all their money and become poor again. The run was brief, but critics praised the leading actor and actress. Humphrey caught on again in Bill Brady Jr.'s production of *A Most Immoral Lady,* and following that, in the comedy hit of the 1929 season, *It's a Wise Child.*

And then, on October 30, everything

changed for everyone. WALL ST. LAYS AN EGG, said *Variety*'s cheeky headline. The story added some melancholy details. The paper spoke of a "vaudeville producer, elderly, who was found weeping like a child on the street having lost $75,000," and added, "Many people of Broadway are known to have been wiped out." Matters got dire in a hurry. A week later, the front page read: "Market cataclysm echoed in New York's nite clubs, speaks & dives — Afterdark rounders limp, in dough & spirit."

After the Crash, the New York theater shrank to half its size. Productions were canceled; actors, directors, choreographers, musicians, set and lighting designers were thrown out of work. Everyone's eyes turned west, where jobs were said to be available. Now that sound had come in, what the town wanted was stage actors who knew how to project, not silent-film stars like John Gilbert, whose fluting voices failed to match their macho screen images.

Humphrey had paid little attention to his sister's husband, Stuart Rose. But now Stuart was of great interest: he had gone to work for Fox Films. The studio owned a property titled *The Man Who Came Back,* and the moguls had an idea about casting. Instead of using such established names as

Janet Gaynor and Charles Farrell, they thought of employing newcomers, people they could get on the cheap and build into stars. But which newcomers? The casting department gave screen tests to more than fifty Broadway actors. None seemed right. The front office didn't want to put Humphrey before the cameras; they were not hiring sprigs in 1930. They wanted men, real men, with bass voices and animal magnetism. Stuart pulled some strings and got his brother-in-law an audition. Humphrey surprised the Fox executives with his precise diction and on-screen personality; they offered him a contract of $750 a week and offered to pay his way to the coast.

The money was more than the Bogarts had ever been offered, singly or together. Even so, Mary was uncertain. She was currently in a straight play, *The Tavern,* and it was thriving in a bad time. If she went west now she would forsake Broadway to be in her husband's shadow. Times were bad; she might never find work again. The odds were weighted in his favor, she continued, not in hers. It was the Helen Menken story all over again. In the end Mary refused to leave New York and Humphrey insisted on going to Hollywood. They did agree on one thing: the Bogarts would have an open marriage

— not an uncommon arrangement in the early 1930s. Discreetly, it was agreed, Humphrey would see other women while in California. Mary would date in Manhattan.

For all the studio talk about new faces, Fox decided to use Charles Farrell and Janet Gaynor. Humphrey's first assignment in Hollywood was not as an actor but as a vocal coach. He was there, said the Fox front office, to teach silent-film star Farrell how to articulate with authority. Humphrey hated his job and let everyone around him know it — particularly Farrell. To mollify the newcomer, Fox cast him in two pictures. The first was an inconsequential bit of fluff, *A Devil with Women,* in which he played yet another juvenile; the second, a comedy titled *Up the River,* had no box office impact at all. Nonetheless, it contained two assets: director John Ford, then learning his trade with great alacrity, and Spencer Tracy, a young, versatile, hard-drinking actor. Humphrey immediately took to both of them.

Professionally, however, Humphrey appeared to be on a treadmill. In 1931 he was cast in the World War I aviation drama *Body and Soul.* The male lead was Charles Farrell, and in one scene the two men shared a cockpit. Humphrey needled him and Farrell, who never thought he needed a vocal coach, especially one with such a pronounced sibilance, needled back. When the film wrapped, Humphrey decided to have it out with the arrogant star. Farrell, who was at least six inches taller and far more muscular, asked if Bogart knew how to fight. Humphrey's blood was up and he agreed to do battle. Before they began, the gentlemanly Farrell thought it only fair to inform his opponent of a vital fact: he had been a boxing champion at Boston University. Ah well, Humphrey concluded, that was different. Perhaps they could talk things over peaceably. And so they did, concluding with an amiable voyage on Farrell's boat, where Humphrey showed off his navigation skills.

It was a brief hiatus during an unhappy time. In the sixteen months between his arrival and departure, Hollywood was either indifferent or openly hostile to Bogart's prep school pugnacity. He made casting directors uneasy, and they looked elsewhere for male talent. But Humphrey refused to change. Indeed, he began to go public with his contradictory persona, mixing elevated manners with a surly disdain for authority. The inner conflict of wellborn New Yorker and insubordinate actor was never more apparent than on the day he and a buddy were out on a local golf course. They tried to finish their nine holes quickly, only to find themselves stuck behind a stuffy foursome. Humphrey inquired whether they might play through. One of the quartet harrumphed that they could do no such thing. And who the hell was asking, anyway?

"I'm nobody," Humphrey informed him. "My name is Humphrey Bogart; I work at Fox, and what are you doing playing a gentleman's game at a gentleman's club?"

The gentleman in question identified himself as the first vice president at Fox.

Humphrey expected the ax to fall that afternoon. Instead he was hired as the second lead in *The Bad Sister.* He went unnoticed; it was Bette Davis's film debut. ("Even when I had a gun," Humphrey said about his co-star, "she scared the be-Jesus out of me.") He was also ignored in a handful of other movies. In *Big City Blues* his name was at the bottom of the cast list. In *Three on a Match* he played a gangster for the first time. No one seemed impressed, least of all the studio executives. *Holy Terror* was his first Western. "I was too short to be a cowboy," he remembered, "so they gave me elevator shoes and padded out my shoulders. I walked around as though I were on stilts, and felt like a dummy." When Fox failed to renew his contract he was disappointed but not surprised, and he headed directly back to Broadway.

As Humphrey unpacked he learned that Mary had fallen in love more than once during his absence. His ego was badly bruised, but no sympathy came from his informant: by agreeing to the open marriage, he had opened the door to mutual infidelity. Then and there Humphrey determined to get Mary back and, in his traditionally courteous but newly attentive manner, wooed and won her all over again. A month after his return the Bogarts renewed their vows. He swore to return to the Broadway stage for good, and began auditioning.

His timing was execrable. The Depression had battered the Broadway theater, usually immune to stock market tergiversations. Openings dipped from more than four hundred per year to well under two hundred. Humphrey had enough of a name to get work in five plays in the 1932–33 season, but not one of them lasted more than seven days. Producers of the last one, *Our Wife,* guaranteed him a percentage of the gross. It opened on March 4, 1933 — the day the new president, Franklin D. Roosevelt, declared a bank holiday in order to bring some order to the nation's finances. There were ten people in the opening-night audience. *Our Wife* closed after twenty performances, assuring the star a grand total of fifty-six dollars.

Mary picked up some work in summer stock, and Humphrey kept her company. Edith Oliver, an actress who would leave show business to become *The New Yorker*'s off-Broadway critic, ran into them in New England. She remembered that he was often inebriated, but always beguiling ("Bogart had class — he was such a gent") and that Mary could match him drink for drink. One night a policeman in Cohasset, Massachusetts, arrested both Bogarts for disorderly conduct, along with another young actor, Broderick Crawford, the troubled son of a leading stage comedienne, Helen Broderick. The police chief failed to recognize any of them, and Humphrey wondered aloud if he had chosen the wrong profession.

The younger Bogarts returned to the city with only a few hundred dollars in their bank account. They had hoped for a loan from the elder Bogarts, but Belmont and Maud's dwindling investments had crashed with the market. The couple had sold the house on 103rd Street and taken a floor in an East 56th Street brownstone. Dr. Bogart had given up his practice. He was ill and apathetic, wholly dependent on drugs and alcohol. Maud, as strong-willed as before, paid the bills and kept order. It was a full-time job. Humphrey's younger sister, Catherine, called Kay, had started out as a clothes model. Now she was unemployed and alcoholic. Her older sister, Frances, had been unable to shake the postpartum blues that began with the birth of her son in 1930.

The autumn of 1933 brought no relief. Frances remained in the slough of despond and Kay kept drinking. Belmont got sicker. Mary and Humphrey were unemployed. He brought in some money by playing chess for fifty cents a game at the arcades along Sixth Avenue. He was a shrewd, audacious opponent, and frequently returned to their East Side apartment with enough funds to bankroll dinner and a few drinks. But it was a precarious life, and each week their meager savings dwindled a little more.

With the new year came two breaks, allowing Humphrey to believe that his moribund career might get jump-started after all. Early in 1934 he won a meaty part as a gangster in *Midnight,* a film hastily shot, edited, and released in New York. It was just as hastily dismissed by the movie critics. In the fall he got a major role in a Broadway melodrama, *Invitation to a Murder,* playing the part of an aristocrat whose fortune is derived from criminal enterprises. It also failed. Bitterly, Humphrey returned to the chess tables. In the middle of a match, Mary telephoned with bad news: Belmont had suffered a stroke. An ambulance conveyed him to the unpleasantly named Hospital for the Ruptured and Crippled. As the seventy-eight-year-old man took his last breaths, his son held him close.

"It was only at that moment," Humphrey was to recall, "that I realized how much I loved him and needed him and never really told him. Just before he died I said, 'I love you, Father.' He heard me, because he looked at me and smiled. Then he died. He was a real gentleman." This summary was in sharp contrast to his portrait of Maud. Told about Belmont's death, she "doubled up momentarily, as if she had the wind knocked out of her, then straightened up and said, 'Well, that's done.'"

Belmont DeForest Bogart left ten thousand dollars' worth of debts. Here the other Humphrey, the son of well-bred, accomplished people, emerged to meet the crisis. He resolved to pay off the IOUs to the final dollar, stepping into the role of dignified and enlightened person — Belmont before his fall from grace. The burden of that role was heavier than he imagined. The more Humphrey thought about the money he owed, the sadder he got. And the sadder he got, the more he imbibed. His wife and friends worried about him because he had assumed a quiet, fatalistic air, as if the dying man was going to be his next role. Among the friends were convivial journalists and writers who gathered at familiar drinking holes. Playwright Robert Emmet Sherwood, the most successful of the bunch, had taken to Humphrey from the day they first clinked classes. Like the others, he was disturbed by the actor's profound melancholia. But unlike the others, he was in a position to do something about it. Sherwood's producer-director, Arthur Hopkins, was in the process of auditioning actors for *The Petrified Forest.* The writer had an idea. His play had a cast of twenty-one. What if Humphrey were to take one of the smaller roles? The job might get him back on track. Sherwood put in a word with Hopkins.

The male lead was already signed. Leslie Howard had made his mark on the West End and Broadway, and in the last few years he had conquered Hollywood as well. In his latest film, *The Scarlet Pimpernel,* he had demonstrated a unique talent for swashbuckling and comedy. Audiences couldn't get enough of him. But there would be very little humor in *Petrified Forest.* Howard, né Steiner, a man of Hungarian-Jewish background, had journeyed to Germany after Hitler came to power in 1933. He saw for himself that Winston Churchill's warning was not an exaggeration: a threatening militant force had taken over Deutschland and war lay dead ahead. What interested Howard now was not the brittle, lighthearted work he did with such ease. He wanted to be part of a committed theater, expressing the pervasive sense of dread that characterized the era. He looked enviously at the Federal Theater downtown, the dark exploratory work of Eugene O'Neill, the fireworks of the Group Theater, with its exciting new talents, Elia Kazan, Stella Adler, Clifford Odets, Marc Blitzstein.

In *The Anxious Years: America in the Nineteen Thirties,* Louis Filler observes, "Numerous writers hoped to build careers upon their understanding of the world's needs and conditions, and, in fact, to no small degree did so. What they had in common was their belief that their writing constituted a contribution to the world's work, rather than to 'mere' personal expression." Sherwood was among that number, and he found his ideal surrogate in Howard. The

Englishman was going to play Alan Squier, a doomed intellectual marooned with a group of foundlings, wastrels, and criminals in a lunchroom at the edge of the Arizona desert. Sherwood imagined that with a little swagger and a few more pounds, Humphrey might play Boze Hertzlinger, a dreamy ex–football player.

Arthur Hopkins had a better idea. The fifty-six-year-old writer-director-producer had dominated the New York theater since the 1920s. He had introduced Ibsen and O'Neill plays to Broadway; produced *Hamlet* and *Richard III,* both starring John Barrymore; directed hit comedies, dramas, and musicals. His vita was long and his instincts reliable. So when he turned down Humphrey for the part of Boze, Sherwood could only bow to his wisdom and experience. But Hopkins was not through talking. Every season he made a point of seeing everything on Broadway, the flops as well as the smashes, and he had been impressed with Humphrey's performance as the villain of *Invitation to a Murder.* In that play his silences seemed more impressive than his speeches; when he was quiet, said Hopkins, "time seemed to stand still." In his biography of Sherwood John Mason Brown goes into considerable detail about the producer's reasoning. At that moment, Humphrey was wearing his personal tribulations on his face. "Hopkins thought of more than Bogart's masculinity." He thought of his "driven power, his anguished dark eyes, the puffs of pain beneath them, and the dangerous despair which lined his face." That despair was both a personal matter and a general one; in his speech and demeanor, Humphrey had caught the spirit of the Aspirin Age.

The producer asked Sherwood and his colleagues a question: What about casting Bogart as Duke Mantee, the escaped convict? They were uncertain, hemmed and hawed, asked for a delay. First among equals, Hopkins refused to take maybe for an answer and made a declaration. Bogart would be Mantee and that was that. The stage was literally set for an epoch-making performance. The run would begin on January 17, 1935, a key date in the history of American theater, and, as it turned out, also in the story of American cinema.

CHAPTER 2
LET ME KNOW WHEN YOU
WANT TO BE KILLED

I

Robert Sherwood had left Harvard before graduation, romantically eager for battle. Journeying north, the New Yorker enlisted and trained with the Canadian Black Watch before sailing off to France in 1917, appropriately kilted and armed, towering (six feet, six inches), proud and fervent. Private Sherwood's tour of duty opened his eyes in a way he could not have foreseen. The enlisted man witnessed most of the horrors the Great War had to offer, from the ineptitude of the generals to the slaughter of the troops who obeyed them. In the process he was choked with mustard gas and pierced with shrapnel. Sherwood was invalided home early in 1918, a troubled veteran of twenty-two. For him, as for most of his contemporaries, the armistice signaled more than the end of the war. It meant the end of his world.

Ernest Hemingway caught the zeitgeist in *A Farewell to Arms:* "I was always embarrassed by the words sacred, glorious and sacrifice. . . . I had seen nothing sacred, and the things that were glorious had no glory and the sacrifices were like the stockyards at Chicago if nothing was done with the meat except to bury it."

John Dos Passos had also been at the front. "How damned ridiculous it all is!" he wrote. "My God what a time. All the cant and hypocrisy . . . all the vestiges of old truths now putrid and false infect the air, choke you worse than German gas."

To these returning Americans, everything they knew seemed to be tainted or senseless. Even small pleasures circled the drain. "The idea staggered me," says Nick Carraway, narrator of F. Scott Fitzgerald's *The Great Gatsby,* when he sees Meyer Wolfsheim, the racketeer who brought down baseball. "I remembered, of course, that the World Series had been fixed in 1919, but if I had thought of it at all I would have thought of it as something that merely *happened,* the end of an inevitable chain. It never occurred to me that one man could start to play with the faith of fifty million people — with the singlemindedness of a burglar blowing a safe."

As the Roaring Twenties proceeded, gangsters took over the distribution of alcohol. Extortion, violence, and slaughter became a part of city life. The Teapot Dome scandal revealed that Warren Harding's White House was in the pay of Big Oil. Its companies had been allowed to plunder public land, and would have gone on plundering if their crimes had not been inadvertently exposed. Science took a beating during the 1925 Scopes trial in Tennessee, where it was forbidden to teach evolution in the state schools. Nicola Sacco and Bartolomeo Vanzetti, two anarchists accused of participating in a holdup despite a paucity of evidence, were railroaded to the electric chair in August 1927. That month, President Harding's successor, Calvin "Silent Cal" Coolidge, conveniently arranged to be on a Montana fishing trip.

Sherwood's literary comment on the sham and greed of the 1920s, followed by the scarifying Depression of the early 1930s, was *The Petrified Forest*. Within the four walls of the Black Mesa Bar-B-Q, he sought to represent America's enervated intellectuals, selfish capitalists, obsolete partisans, violent crooks, and malleable citizens. It was a tall order, and the playwright's ambitions outreached his talent. Yet he was a professional theater man, and with Arthur Hopkins's help and a sterling cast he brought off the illusion of profundity.

Leslie Howard offered an amalgam of pathos and charm, accurately described as Chaplin in a Savile Row suit. He was never less than elegant, but in every role Howard hinted at an undertow of vulnerability and melancholia. Fellow actors admired his gift; women found him irresistible. In the role of Alan Squier, Howard portrayed a failed writer, formerly kept by a rich lady but now on his own, hitchhiking across the southwestern desert. Squier's knapsack contains a shirt, underwear, socks, toothbrush, passport, and a copy of *Modern Man in Search of a Soul* by Carl Jung. "Call it gypsying," the wanderer explains. "I had a vague idea that I'd like to see the Pacific Ocean, and perhaps drown in it."

As he chats with the daughter of the garrulous old owner, Squier becomes captivated by her innocence and artistic yearnings. Gabby (short for Gabrielle) admires the poetry of François Villon (whose name she touchingly mispronounces) and longs to study painting in France, an unattainable goal since her family is stone broke. Others traverse this bleak emotional landscape, including a former college athlete, a callous

80

industrialist, his wife and their black servant, linemen, lawmen, and, fulcrum of the play's action, Duke Mantee, a gangster on the run, accompanied by his small and fearsome entourage.

On the page, Mantee is a dime-store sociopath ("Just keep in mind that I and the boys are candidates for hanging, and the minute anybody makes the wrong move, I'm going to kill the whole lot of you"). As Humphrey played him, though, he became much more than a desperado on the lam. Something about Duke's unshaven, lived-in face suggested a renegade, but also a man of his time, a time that has bent and disfigured him. Mantee, in Sherwood's stage description, is "well-built but stoop-shouldered, with a vaguely thoughtful, saturnine face." If he "hadn't elected to take up banditry, he might have been a fine left-fielder." Duke has "one quality of resemblance to Alan Squier: he too is unmistakably condemned." In *Petrified Forest,* Broadway theatergoers got their first glimpse at two modern existential figures, long before those words became fashionable. Squier longs for death — but death with a purpose. Gabby provides that purpose; with a bold stroke of the pen, he makes her the beneficiary of his five-thousand-dollar life insurance policy. The money will provide a ticket to France and a new life. Squier considers his options aloud. If he commits suicide, the policy will be invalid. But there's another option. What if Duke were to shoot him? The insurance company would have to pay in full. Mantee's side-of-the-mouth response masks a new respect for Squier: "Let me know when you want to be killed." As the authorities close in, the gang heads for the doors, but not before Duke makes good on his promise, ennobling Squier by gunning him down. Duke's fatalistic exit line was soon to be echoed along Broadway: "O.K., pal. I'll be seeing you soon."

Critics showered the play with raves. In the *Times,* Brooks Atkinson called Sherwood's new play "a peach" and "a roaring Western melodrama." Howard was, as always, exemplary, and Humphrey Bogart did "the best work of his career as the motorized guerilla." In the *News* Robert Garland wrote that "Humphrey Bogart is gangster Mantee to the tip of his sawed-off shotgun."

Cast against type, Humphrey had thrown himself into this role as never before. In the process, he showed the world that he had outgrown his white flannels forever. As Duke Mantee, everything about him was different. His diction, his gait, his attitude, his prison pallor all spoke of a life outside the law. A man like that would not have the time or inclination to shave, so Humphrey's beard was the real thing, carefully maintained at a quarter-inch length. When Duke made his first entrance there were audible gasps, in part because he was so dark and menacing, in part because John Dillinger, America's most wanted fugitive, had recently escaped from jail. The real-life gangster seemed, in the play's edgiest moments, to have materialized onstage. Humphrey Bogart, the eternal upper-class twit, had turned himself into the new villain du jour, and the play's strongest attraction. Indeed, according to the *Post,* wealthy ticket buyers were demanding seats close enough to see Bogart's facial hair. In those first few weeks Humphrey learned something that would stay with him all his life: "When the heavy, full of crime and bitterness, grabs his wounds and talks about death and taxes in a husky voice, the audience is his and his alone."

The play ran from January to June, allowing Humphrey to pay off his father's debts and put a thousand dollars aside for himself. He referred to the bank account as his F.Y. fund — money that would give him the freedom to spurn trivial roles from now on. He took joy in every night and every matinee. One tragic incident did occur during the run: Bill Brady Jr. had been relaxing in his summer bungalow in Colt's Neck, New Jersey. Perhaps he had been smoking; in any case, the wooden house caught fire and burned to the ground. Humphrey's boyhood pal died in the blaze. At his funeral, the seventy-one-year-old Bill Brady Sr. put his hand on Humphrey's shoulder and told him how glad he was to see his protégé get on. "I always knew one day you would be a great actor."

Throughout the run Humphrey made a special point of being courtly offstage, in direct contrast to Mantee's snarling persona, as if to show that he could inhabit a part without allowing it to affect his private life. His dressing room was next to the one occupied by Esther Leeming, who played a Mexican cook. She was to remember him fondly as quiet and gentle, scrupulous in his behavior toward her and all the other actresses. That, too, was in direct contrast to the shenanigans of Howard, a notorious skirt chaser. For despite Humphrey's checkered scholastic career, it was now apparent to all who knew him that he was truly old school. He never believed in totally immersing himself in a character; there was no fusing of the performer and the part that was to mark film and stage acting in the decades to come.

No doubt *Petrified Forest* could have gone on and on — there were still long lines at the Broadhurst Theater when the final curtain rang down. But Howard was not only the star, he was a co-producer, and he had no taste for going on the road. Nor did he want another actor to take the role with which he had become so strongly identified. Humphrey accepted the star's decision philosophically; it was time to move on. Besides, Warner Bros. had bought the play. It would go before the cameras next year, with Leslie Howard repeating as Squier. Backstage at the last performance, Howard told Humphrey that no one else could possibly play Mantee.

Unencumbered, reassured, Humphrey made plans to enjoy married life to the full. His wife had other ideas. If Humphrey was idle, she had no intention of joining him on the sidelines. Mary tried out for the female lead in *A Touch of Brimstone,* a new comedy. She got the part, playing opposite Roland Young, one of the slyest comic actors in town, and busied herself with rehearsals and then with out-of-town tryouts. All along, she insisted on being billed as Mary Philips, and in newspaper interviews Miss Philips omitted the fact that she was the wife of Humphrey Bogart. That was not good news, and there were more disappointments in the air. Anxious to get away from the stifling New York summer, Humphrey went north to Maine, appearing in a regional production of Somerset Maugham's *Rain*. The money was good, but he was really in it for a lark, well aware that the melodrama's big draw was the fan-dancing artiste Sally Rand. When he got home he learned that Warners had cast their film adaptation of *The Petrified Forest*. Howard would be Squier. The part of Duke Mantee would be assumed by a studio favorite, Edward G. Robinson.

II

To comprehend the Warner decision is to understand the Warner studio. It was founded by four brothers whose family fled the ghettos of Poland for the sanctuary and promise of Ontario, Canada. From the beginning, Harry, Albert, Sam, and Jack Warner had big ideas. After a few false starts as butchers and bicycle salesmen, they started projecting silent films in nickelodeons. When this venture met with success, the brothers expanded their activities, acquiring theaters in the United States. They became American citizens and, in 1918, relocated to Hollywood. Five years later they officially incorporated as Warner Bros., with the avowed intention of becoming big-league film producers. Few took the quartet seriously; they were regarded as the new boys on the block, upstarts who had little chance against powerhouses like MGM, Universal, and Fox. And, in fact, following a profitable start with movies starring the heroic German shepherd Rin-Tin-Tin and the Broadway matinee idol John Barrymore, Warners floundered.

And then came sound.

Their 1927 picture *The Jazz Singer* starred Al Jolson in the world's first singing, talking film. A global sensation, it revolutionized the movie business and put the studio on the map. No one could afford to ignore Warners now. A great flow of Warner Bros. musicals followed, from *Fifty Million Frenchmen* to *42nd Street.* But by the mid-1930s the public had wearied of pop tunes, and profits fell off. It was at this point that the studio found its true mission. By then Sam had died, Albert had become the company treasurer, and the day-to-day functions were in the hands of Jack, Harry, and a Rin-Tin-

Tin writer turned executive, Darryl F. Zanuck.

Unlike their more elegant and financially secure competitors, the brothers were still bitter about the hard climb from the ghettos of Eastern Europe to the gated communities of Southern California. Nor had they overlooked the way they had been ostracized and mocked when they first hit town. Since then the Warners had acquired money and influence, but they continued to nourish a deep-seated sympathy for the powerless — as long as the powerless didn't work for the brothers. Jack and Harry suffered from an ethical myopia when it came to their own employees. Actors chafed under restrictive, long-term contracts; writers, in Jack's view, were "schmucks with Underwoods," typists who punched a clock and turned out the requisite number of pages per week.

Yet in other ways, the Warner brothers did what no other studio dared to do: they showed the American underside. MGM specialized in elegance and high production values, as in *Gone with the Wind,* as well as optimistic small-town stories like the adventures of the teenaged Andy Hardy. Paramount concentrated on sophisticated comedies, RKO on the sparkling Astaire-Rogers musicals. Columbia showcased Frank Capra's directorial touch, and Twentieth Century Fox made a mint with Shirley Temple vehicles. Warner Bros. took a different road. In his study of Jewish filmmakers, *An Empire of Their Own,* historian Neil Gabler observes that the Warners' conscience became palpable by the mid-thirties, "in dozens of films that embraced the losers and the loners, the prizefighters, the meat packers, truck drivers, coal miners, cardsharps, gumshoes, racketeers, con artists, and the rest of what might have seemed like the detritus of Depression America."

Warners made a star of the Yiddish theater crossover Paul Muni (né Muni Weisenfreund) by casting him as James Allen, a good man victimized by the prison system in *I Am a Fugitive from a Chain Gang* and, more advantageously, as the crime kingpin Tony Camonte in *Scarface.* That film was so graphic Warners added a subtitle, *The Shame of the Nation,* to assure viewers that the studio was condemning, not glorifying, the gangster life. The studio also elevated James Cagney from supporting player to leading man with an electric performance in his fifth film, *The Public Enemy.* At the same time, Edward G. Robinson entered the mainstream with his stark portrayal of Caesar Enrico Bandello — clearly modeled after Al Capone — in *Little Caesar.* All of these films made use of a new combination: irony and social criticism. In the last scene of *Fugitive,* the protagonist's girlfriend spots him in the shadows. "How do you live?" she asks. Whispers the innocent escapee: "I steal."

As *Public Enemy*'s street-smart crook with an oedipal fixation on his kindly old mother, Cagney was so convincing that after the bloody finale Warners tacked on a pious title. It warned audiences that "The END of Tom Powers is the end of every hoodlum. 'The Public Enemy' is not a man, nor is it a character — it is a problem that sooner or later WE, the public, must solve."

In *Little Caesar,* as Bandello is gunned down, a phrase from his simple Catholic boyhood becomes an epitaph: "Mother of Mercy, is this the end of Rico?"

Warners knew a good thing when they saw it, and gangland dramas ripped from the headlines were a very good thing indeed. It didn't matter that Robinson was actually a cultivated gentleman who collected fine art and flinched so badly when he fired a gun that numerous retakes were required. He was the studio's prime wrongo, and Jack Warner saw no reason to accommodate anyone from the original cast of *The Petrified Forest* — except, of course, for the celebrated Leslie Howard.

Visibly upset at the Robinson disclosure, Humphrey cabled Howard, then vacationing in Scotland, with the bad news; Leslie wired back that he would handle things. Howard's agent was instructed to press the Bogart name, and when there was no response, the star made a personal appeal. As it happened, Howard found himself pushing on an open door. For just at that moment Robinson had gotten mad at Warners, and Warners had gotten fed up with Robinson, who wanted major money and equal billing with Howard. Jack Warner regarded his contract player as ungrateful, expensive, and too big for his pants. Whereas Bogart would surely come cheap, and would just as surely take whatever billing the studio dictated. In one of his I-made-you-and-I-can-break-you moments, Warner passed on Edward G. Robinson and sent Humphrey's agent a contract guaranteeing that his client would play Duke Mantee on-screen.

The contract wasn't as good as it sounded, but Humphrey signed it anyway. He would only be assured of three weeks' work before the camera; his salary was $750 per. He had been paid as much in 1930, during the first

Hollywood sojourn. Moreover, because he was more or less unknown to moviegoers, he would be billed below four members of the cast: Howard, of course, but also Genevieve Tobin, a seasoned character actress; Dick Foran, better known as the Singing Cowboy; and the rising young talent Bette Davis, who had completely eclipsed Humphrey when they worked together in *The Bad Sister.* Just the same, it was better than sitting around in New York, watching Mrs. Bogart get on in show business.

Humphrey made his three weeks count. The daily footage showed Jack Warner and director Archie Mayo that Bogart was something new on-screen. Robinson (born Edward Emanuel Goldenberg) and Muni were Jewish; Cagney was half Irish, and that half dominated his appearance and style. The appeal of these men was ethnic; they represented the human sorrow of every city — immigrants, or the children of immigrants, who had taken a wrong turn. In contrast to those stars, Humphrey was a WASP, but that actually helped him in *Petrified Forest.* He represented the notorious malefactors from the heart of the heart of the country: "Baby Face" Nelson, "Pretty Boy" Floyd, John Dillinger, Bonnie Parker and Clyde Barrow, all of whom had been dramatically and savagely hunted down and killed in 1934.

In the film version, Humphrey conveyed the same weary authority that had been so effective on Broadway. But the close-ups gave him something more. Duke Mantee seemed a guarded and intense man who was capable of larceny and murder, yet who had a speck of nobility buried deep within. Mantee's desperate persona came across so effectively because of the confluence of acting talent and canny direction, but it was given added impetus by Humphrey's situation. At the age of thirty-seven he sensed that *Petrified Forest* was his last chance for a career in movies. If he fell short, or if the film failed when it went into distribution, there would be no third opportunity. His unshaven face was a map of distress.

III

Mary Philips went out to California to see her husband for Christmas 1936. Proudly, Humphrey displayed his new Warners contract. It was good for $550 per week, and it would run for a guaranteed twenty-six weeks. There would be additional contract extensions and raises if things worked out. Humphrey felt certain that they would. Mary was unimpressed. She pointed out what Humphrey already knew. In the coming months he would be making *less* per week than he had when filming *Petrified Forest.* He pleaded with her to stay, help him build a solid career, be a homemaker, start a family. It would be a fine thing to raise kids in the California sun.

Mary wasn't interested. She had just landed the role of Cora, the steamy adulteress in *The Postman Always Rings Twice,* a theatrical adaptation of James M. Cain's best seller. It was a sensational part, her biggest so far. Why didn't Humphrey come east to be with *her* during rehearsals? Arguments ensued. He refused to be the tail on her kite; she refused to live in his shadow. And what kind of shadow was it anyway? He was a fifth-billing character actor; she was a leading lady. They parted on less than cordial terms.

As far as Humphrey's working life was concerned, Mary's instincts did not play her false. (Her feelings about the theater were a different matter; *Postman* ran for only seventy-six performances.) For by the time the Bogart contract took effect, Darryl F. Zanuck had left Warners to become the driving spirit of Twentieth Century Fox. His place was taken by Hal Wallis, a producer who believed, as the actors grumbled out of earshot, in getting every drop of milk from the cows. Under his aegis, low-budget "B" pictures were churned out on or ahead of schedule, to be double-billed with the million-dollar "A" films.

Humphrey nurtured plans to rise to the top of the bill, especially after the debut of *Petrified Forest* in New York. Ads for the film wove a garland of enthusiastic quotes. Both the *Post* and the *Tribune* called Humphrey's portrayal of Duke Mantee "brilliant"; the *American* labeled it "superb," and the *Times* topped off the raves by stating, "There should be a large measure of praise for Humphrey Bogart who can be a psychopathic gangster more like Dillinger than the outlaw himself." The movie turned a handsome profit everywhere it unreeled. Jack Warner was grateful; Hal Wallis was pleased. But that didn't mean they planned to elevate Humphrey; it only meant they would employ him full-time. He punched a clock like a factory employee — which, in effect, he was — appearing next in *Bullets or Ballots.* Edward G. Robinson, Joan Blondell, and Barton MacLane enjoyed the top spots. As Johnny Blake, an undercover cop, Robinson arouses the suspicion of Nick "Bugs" Fenner and the two die in a shoot-out. It was the first time Bogart and Robinson faced off. There would be many others.

After *Bullets* came *Two Against the World.* Humphrey did receive top billing for this media melodrama, but he felt no cause for rejoicing. It was a remake of the much-heralded 1931 film *Five Star Final,* starring Edward G. Robinson and Boris Karloff. The new version — an honest reporter fighting his bosses at a radio station this time, rather than a newspaper — had a slapdash air about it, and it was headed straight for the grind houses.

Humphrey got the message. He was going to be a journeyman out here, decently salaried but never a star. He stayed at the raffish Garden of Allah hotel, famous as a hangout for visiting New Yorkers like Robert Benchley and Dorothy Parker, as well as for its bacchanalias — "If a stark naked lady of acting fame," reported *The New Yorker,* "her head crowned by a chattering monkey, chose to open the door to Western Union, no one was abashed, least of all the lady and the monkey."

The actor drove to work in a dented old Chevrolet. When the weather turned windy, Humphrey put on a camel's hair coat frayed at the cuffs and collar. Criticized by publicists for his shabby outfits and beat-up jalopy, he countered, "I've seen too many guys come here, make one picture, and blow themselves to Cadillacs and big houses." They wound up wage slaves, forever in hock to the studio. That would not happen to him; he was putting all his extra cash in the F.Y. fund.

That fund grew in small increments as he went on to make *China Clipper,* an adventure film about an obsessed, heroic pilot modeled on Charles Lindbergh. Humphrey played the airborne sidekick. A brash but agreeable Pat O'Brien got all the attention and most of the good reviews. The *Times* was typical: "Mr. O'Brien has contributed a tense portrait of energy incarnate." As for Mr. Bogart, he "must be included on the credit side of an entirely creditable film ledger."

Next time out Humphrey played a beach-combing fugitive holed up in the South Seas. *Isle of Fury* was almost contemptuously hacked out and directed as if by machine. There was no way he could look anything but embarrassed, especially behind an unbecoming mustache, and in footage where he fought an ill-constructed octopus.

During this discouraging time, Humphrey ran into a singer-actress he had known slightly in New York. Mayo Methot, the daughter of a Portland, Oregon, newspaperwoman and a sea captain who plied the Orient, had been cast in amateur productions from the age of seven. She went to Broadway as a teenager, and spent most of the 1920s singing and dancing in musicals. But as the Depression took hold, the job market for chorines dried up. So, like many another performer, she came west to try her hand at movies. Mayo was just as comely out there as she had been back east — and just as wild and hard-drinking. At a Screen Actors Guild dinner Humphrey couldn't take his eyes off her. She was wearing a low-cut, flame-red dress; her eyes glittered and her smile ignited the room.

To Humphrey, Mayo seemed to be all the things Mary was not: she liked a good time, adored sailing, spoke her mind, and had an explosive sense of humor. He pursued her avidly, completely unaware that she had designs on him. In their profile of Humphrey Bogart, A. M. Sperber and Eric Lax quote the veteran actress Gloria Stuart. She knew Humphrey in the old days and recalled that Mayo "just went after Bogart and that was it. I think he found her amusing. She made him laugh a lot." At that particular time Bogart needed a laugh. Early in 1937, his little sister Kay had died of a ruptured appendix, worn and vulnerable at the age of thirty-three. Although the two were not close, he had kept track of her misadventures. In a melancholy recollection, Humphrey called her "a victim of the speakeasy era. She burned the candle at both ends, then decided to burn it in the middle." Kay's death, coupled with the sense that he was treading water in Hollywood, made Mayo seem all the more desirable, a woman who would mute his troubles and, perhaps, change his luck.

The trouble was that she was married. This led to scenes that could have come out of a Feydeau farce. On one occasion the lovers were at a dinner party at the home of Eric Hatch, scenarist of the hit comedy *My Man Godfrey*. The conversation was lively, the attendees witty. They included the gangling Russian character actor Mischa Auer and the former silent-movie star Louise Brooks. After supper the guests began to tango to recorded music when a call came in from Mayo's husband, restaurateur Percy T. Morgan Jr. He was on his way to pick up his wife and take her home. Humphrey made ready to sweep Mayo away. "But wait!" wrote Brooks in her memoir, *Lulu in Hollywood*. Mayo "had taken off her slippers to dance, and now one of them could not be found." Pandemonium reigned supreme.

Everyone was in on the clandestine romance; all in attendance began a frantic search — all, that is, except Louise. Humphrey furiously turned on her, demanding to know where she had hidden the slipper. Brooks was innocent, but "too stunned by this strange and violent Humphrey to speak." At the last instant, Auer stretched up to an oak beam. He was the only one tall enough to reach the place; obviously he had put the slipper there. The lovers exited into the night as Morgan insistently rang the front doorbell.

Not long after *Isle of Fury* wrapped, Mary crossed the country for a visit. Perhaps she had received word of the Methot-Bogart romance; perhaps she just missed her husband. In any case, she was less confrontational and insistent this time. Humphrey left his digs at the Garden of Allah, and he and Mary settled into a rented house. The surroundings made little difference; they still couldn't get along. While they were trying to decide whether their marriage was alive or dead, Mayo successfully sued Morgan for divorce, charging him with cruelty. Then she sat back, ready for Humphrey to fall into her lap. She did not have long to wait. Kenneth MacKenna had been in love with Mary for years. When it became obvious that Humphrey's heart was not in the reunion, Mary gave up on the dream of reconciliation, moved out, filed for divorce, and as soon as the papers were ratified final, became Mrs. MacKenna. Humphrey followed suit, marrying Mayo on August 20, 1938. He was about to be thirty-nine; she was thirty-five. It was the third marriage for both. At the wedding party, Mischa Auer stripped to the skin and did a Cossack dance. That evening, Mayo and Humphrey carried on the eccentricity: they had an argument that degenerated into a battle royal. Humphrey walked out and spent the rest of the night drinking with colleagues. Mayo slept in a friend's guest room.

They made up the next day, and all was smiles and kisses. Save for that outburst it seemed a perfect union. Mayo announced an eagerness to forsake her own career and attend to Humphrey's every need. He bought a house on Horn Street above the Sunset Strip, and filled it with attractive furniture, twenty-six finches and canaries, four dogs, and four cats. She went sailing with him on his newly purchased thirty-six-foot cruiser, cooked his dinners, kept his home spotless, played the genial hostess to his pals and their wives.

But the truth was that except for tobacco

she was his worst enemy. Mayo was jealous of every woman he talked to, and beside herself when he played love scenes. She and Humphrey had nightly arguments. Sometimes she would throw a bottle at his head, or slap him. He professed to admire her spirit, took to calling her "Sluggy," gave his boat and their Scottish terrier that name, and put a sign reading "Sluggy Hollow" on their front lawn. There were raucous scenes in restaurants and at parties, and rarely did Humphrey bother to ameliorate the situation by talking calmly to Mayo or taking her out of the room. She misbehaved in front of everyone; Humphrey goaded her on. Visiting the Bogarts one night, humorist James Thurber watched the hostilities and later sent Humphrey a sketch of the mêlée entitled "Jolly Times." Humphrey had it framed and hung over the mantelpiece. Columnists started referring to the couple as the Battling Bogarts. Humphrey enjoyed the label; he said it might be good for business. "I live dangerously," he declared in one interview. "I'm colorful. But Sluggy's crazy about me because she knows I'm tougher than Edward G. Robinson."

Mayo did have a soft side; she was very solicitous of Maud Bogart when Humphrey brought his mother out west. He set Maud up in a luxurious Sunset Boulevard apartment at the Chateau Marmont, a Hollywood landmark, where Mayo paid frequent visits, bringing flowers and food. People remembered the seventy-something lady from that period. One witness recalled that every day she would walk to Schwab's drugstore "as proud as Queen Mary out for an airing, still erect and wasp-waisted." Most of the patrons knew who she was; Maud Bogart "talked to everyone, made little purchases and then strolled grandly home again."

Mayo's tender feelings ended with her mother-in-law. When she dealt with Humphrey she was verbally abusive, and sometimes a lot worse than that. One night, for example, raving drunk, Mayo went after him with a knife. He avoided the first thrust, but when he headed for the door she stabbed him in the back. Humphrey slumped to the floor, unconscious. A doctor was hysterically summoned; he removed the knife and discovered that it had only penetrated about an inch. The back muscle was torn, but no other damage had been done. For five hundred dollars the physician agreed to stitch up the wound and keep his mouth shut.

Alternately distracted, appalled, and

amused, Humphrey kept working. From 1937 to 1940 he appeared in twenty-four films. Most of them were standard products of the Warners assembly line and looked it — although Humphrey found a moment of transcendence. In *The Great O'Malley* he was a memorable second banana to Pat O'Brien; rounding out a scene reminiscent of Warners' earlier film *I Am a Fugitive from a Chain Gang,* he played a down-at-the-heels war veteran, trying to peddle his military decorations. The pawnbroker dismisses him: they're worthless. With a combination of rage and pathos the onetime soldier replies, "The only things left to remind me that I was once a man, and you call them junk!"

Cast opposite Bette Davis once more, in the efficient and forgettable *Marked Woman,* Humphrey played a crusading district attorney. *Kid Galahad* found him in a struggle with Edward G. Robinson over a prizefighter whose future they both want to control. At the predictable bloody finale they gun each other down. In *San Quentin,* Humphrey is a convict in the high-security penitentiary. Informed that a yard captain (Pat O'Brien) is romancing his sister, he escapes and tries to slay the uniformed Romeo. Instead, he himself is fatally shot.

Stand-In was one of Humphrey's rare

ventures into comedy. As a boozy producer who produces schlock films like *Sex and Satan,* he mistreats employees and gives a hard time to the lead, Leslie Howard, who heads a revolution against the studio. Leslie and Humphrey would never make another film together. In *The Ultimate Bogart,* Ernest W. Cunningham notes that director Tay Garnett thought a change of pace might be beneficial for Humphrey. Things didn't work out as he expected. Viewing some daily footage, an assistant complained about Bogart's diction: "The son of a bitch lisps!"

There were odd B pictures like *Crime School,* in which Humphrey plays a decent man attempting to clean up a brutal reformatory. In *The Oklahoma Kid* he's a two-dimensional villain, outfitted entirely in black, tracked down and slain by an upright James Cagney. In *Black Legion,* an intelligent exposé of the Ku Klux Klan, he plays Frank Taylor, an ambitious worker who gets passed over for promotion. The man who gets the job has an Eastern European name, fueling Taylor's rage and resentment. He's ripe for a xenophobic message delivered via radio: "We the challengers have raised our rallying cry: 'America for Americans' . . . the real, one hundred percent Americans must stop and think. He who is not with us is against us." Taylor passes the word to his young son ("Listen to this guy — he's talking sense!"), blames the long lines of unemployed on "foreigners," and becomes a hooded and murderous fascist. Caught by police, he gets nailed with a life sentence. Critics were impressed: the film was compared favorably with Paul Muni's 1933 social-conscience shocker, *I Am a Fugitive from a Chain Gang.* The *Hollywood Reporter* predicted that *Legion* was "almost certain to make a top-flight character star out of Humphrey Bogart," and the *New York Post* raved, "No more B-pix for Bogart!"

The tabloid had a clouded crystal ball. Humphrey's next picture, a Bette Davis vehicle called *Dark Victory,* miscast him as a philosophical horse trainer with an Irish brogue. Oddly enough, the picture boosted his career. In the opinion of the *New York Post* reviewer, "After a while you stopped expecting Bogart to whip out a rod. You accepted him as a horse trainer. That's acting." Warners also liked what Humphrey did in *Victory* and offered him the lead opposite Davis in her next film, *The Old Maid,* a Civil War picture. But on the fourth day of shooting he was replaced by George Brent. According to Charles Higham, Davis's biographer, at a farewell scene in a railroad station, Humphrey was so hopeless, "so thin and pathetic in his uniform and so unromantic in his last wave goodbye, that Warner demanded that he be fired." Producer Hal Wallis was "forced to tell him that he was dismissed forthwith. He stalked off in a rage." For the next few years, when audiences spotted the name Humphrey Bogart in the credits they expected to see a gangster movie. Warner Bros. saw to it that they were not disappointed.

There were *Racket Busters,* with Humphrey as a powerful thug; *King of the Underworld,* with Humphrey in the title role; *Angels with Dirty Faces,* featuring Humphrey as a dishonest lawyer; *The Roaring Twenties,* with Humphrey as a scheming bootlegger; *You Can't Get Away with Murder,* in which he played a latter-day Fagin, introducing boys to a life of crime. The archetype casting became so obvious that in March 1939, the *New York Times* complained that such "valuable stock players" as Humphrey Bogart were "held not so much by five-year contracts, as by five-year sentences."

And yet in all this celluloid waste, two features glinted. Warners loaned Humphrey out to the Goldywn studio for one picture, *Dead End.* The studio negotiations clearly reveal the actor as indentured servant.

Humphrey's contract called for him to be paid $650 a week. Warners offered him to Goldwyn for $2,000 a week, with a guaranteed minimum of five weeks. Thus Humphrey would get $3,250 for his work, and Warners would grab $6,750 for doing nothing at all.

Sidney Kingsley's play had been adapted for the screen by Lillian Hellman. It boasted phosphorescent photography by Gregg Toland, later the cinematographer of *Citizen Kane;* and it was sharply directed by William Wyler. Even though Joel McCrae was the nominal star, Humphrey made the film his own. As Baby Face Martin, he was far from the standard lowlife of so many previous movies.

Kingsley was not known for his subtlety: in the roiled world of Depression New York, the privileged folks of *Dead End* live cheek by jowl with the poor. The contrasts are heavily stressed, particularly when two boyhood friends meet after a separation of decades. Dave Connell (McCrae) has become an architect who wants to redesign the slums. Baby Face has taken the low road, succumbing to the temptations of violence and dirty money. The movie launched the careers of half a dozen youths who went on to play virtually the same sassy punks in a series of low-budget features, variously billed as the Dead End Kids, the Little Tough Guys, the East Side Kids, and the Bowery Boys. But it was the adult confrontations that made the film a standout. When Martin returns to see his mother (played with stark authority by Marjorie Main), she speaks of the shame he has brought her and withers him with a glare. He finds no surcease when he tracks down his old girlfriend Francey (Claire Trevor). Now a prostitute, Francey echoes Mrs. Martin's contempt — except that she's dying of syphilis. The woman who calls herself a "broken-down hoor" barely has the strength to face him down. Francey's physical deterioration seems a direct parallel to his moral one; Martin escapes from her sickly stare, but he cannot run from himself and ends in the gutter, slain by Connell.

There is tragic poetry in these scenes, thanks to Humphrey's charismatic on-screen presence. He's gritty, ruined, dangerous, and wholly believable. Small wonder that the film was praised in America and that it did even better in Britain. Novelist Graham Greene, then a film critic for the *Spectator,* wrote, "This is the finest performance Bogart has ever given — the ruthless sentimentalist who had melodramatized himself from the start." Had there been any justice in Hollywood, *Dead End* would have been Humphrey's breakthrough.

But Warners had other plans. The studio's homecoming gift to Humphrey Bogart was a role as a wrestling promoter in *Swing Your Lady.* The raucous hillbilly comedy ran a mercifully brief seventy-nine minutes and expired at the box office. Humphrey did a little better in *They Drive by Night,* the story of two brothers in the trucking business. But the star of that film was George Raft, a journeyman ex-hoofer with a distinctly urban style. Ann Sheridan provided the glamour and Ida Lupino received an Academy Award nomination for her mad scene in a courtroom. Humphrey faded into the background as a pathetic loser whose arm is amputated in a truck accident.

There was one other distinguished Humphrey Bogart film in this period — and it was never planned to be a Bogart picture at all. Raft had been given a big buildup by the studio — so big that he had come to believe the hype manufactured by his press agent and the studio publicity department. In 1939 he sent a letter of complaint to Jack Warner, reminding the mogul of a promise: "I was afraid the studio would put me in parts that Humphrey Bogart should play and you told me that I would never have to play a Humphrey Bogart part." Jack Warner knew better than to force the issue. He sent the script of *High Sierra* to Paul Muni. The vain and much-lauded actor turned it down cold. He had no interest in playing Roy "Mad Dog" Earle. Or, for that matter, in appearing in *any* gangster film, even one removed from the usual urban background and placed in the bleak Sierra mountains. Biographies like the Academy Award–nominated *Story of Louis Pasteur* and *Life of Emile Zola* were more his style nowadays.

Humphrey took advantage of their disdain for *High Sierra*. As soon as he learned that Raft and Muni were out of the picture, he telegraphed Wallis: "Dear Hal: You once told me to let you know when I found a part I wanted." The part was Roy Earle. Wallis accommodated him.

IV

In many ways it was *High Sierra,* rather than *Petrified Forest,* that truly and finally turned things around. The screenplay was an adaptation of W. R. Burnett's elegiac crime novel. Burnett got credit as co-writer, but the sharpest work was done by John Huston, son of the veteran actor Walter Huston. At the age of thirty-four John had a series of successful collaborations behind him, including the scripts for *Jezebel* and *Sergeant York.* He had learned how to pare a book down to its essentials, retaining only the most vital, pivotal scenes and conflicts. In Huston's hands Earle became a symbol of 1920s excess, an Indiana farm boy (as was John Dillinger) who had turned bad during the Prohibition era. He had robbed, killed, gotten arrested, and gone to prison. Paroled, he returned to the gangster life only to find himself obsolete and unwanted, a man outside his time. The difference between this felon and the ones in standard celluloid melodramas was his deep feelings for rural America, for animals and damaged people. Huston's script offered a look at the protagonist's inner life, making Earle sympathetic without exonerating him.

Wallis had misgivings about *High Sierra;* a noble crook was not something he wished to endorse. Then Mark Hellinger took over the producer's chores. A dynamic New York journalist turned Hollywood producer, Hellinger had come up with the idea for *The Roaring Twenties,* one of the first gangster films. Back in Manhattan he had cultivated a great many racketeers, and liked to emulate their style. He wore flashy suits, blue shirts, and white ties even on the hottest Los Angeles days, and let everyone know that his big car was once owned by the murdered bootlegger Dutch Schultz. Hellinger was an old friend of Humphrey's from the speakeasy days. From a distance he had watched both phases of the Bogart film career, took delight in the complexities of Duke Mantee, but had no use for the slew of B movies that demanded so little of Humphrey's talent.

Hellinger talked up the feature, protecting Huston and director Raoul Walsh from front-office memos. He did what he could for Humphrey as well, but lost the battle to give him star billing. There were two reasons for the failure. Wallis pointed out that Bogart had been in too many second features, and would not be a box office draw; ergo, Humphrey's comely co-star, twenty-two-year-old Ida Lupino, deserved the top billing. But there was a hidden cause, left undiscussed. Martin Dies Jr., a Republican congressman from Texas, had chosen this moment to investigate the "subversive element" in Hollywood. Y. Frank Freeman, president of the Association of Motion Picture Producers, appeared at the congressman's hotel room along with select members of the press. There he stated that filmmakers would "not yield to anyone in their true Americanism." Meantime, in Philharmonic Hall, Dorothy Parker spoke to a group of self-styled "progressives." Addressing the congressman from afar, she shouted defiantly: "You're out here, Mr. Dies . . . because you've got to control this medium if you want to bring fascism to this country." Dies responded in the newspapers, claiming that he wanted nothing of the kind. All he wanted to do was conduct a few interviews, ask a few questions.

With the help of a local district attorney, Dies found just the man he needed to justify his probe. John L. Leech had been an executive secretary of the Communist Party in Los Angeles. His fellow members had expelled him in 1937 for unstable behavior, but this personal history was of no interest to Dies. He induced Leech to testify before a grand jury, telling the empaneled citizens what he had told the congressman: there were dangerous Communists in the film colony, and he was willing to name names. Franchot Tone, for example. And Fredric March. And Humphrey Bogart, who, Leech claimed, had been a member of a "subversive academy" and had attended a secret meeting at the Malibu home of Paramount production chief B. P. Schulberg. There, he and others had "studied the doctrines of

Karl Marx."

These men and others were duly summoned to testify on their own behalf. As they did, Leech was exposed as a charlatan by investigative reporters for the *Los Angeles Times;* according to their information, he had invented the allegations out of whole cloth. Vindicated, Humphrey defended himself in a brief, pugnacious statement.

"I have never contributed money to a political organization of any form. That includes Republican, Democratic, Hollywood Anti-Nazi League or the Communist Party. Furthermore, I have never attended the school mentioned nor do I know what school that may be.

"I dare the men who are attempting this investigation to call me to the stand. I want to face them myself and not by a proxy to whom I am only a name."

Dies granted a private hearing, where Humphrey again aired his resentment. He began by denying that he knew any card-carrying members of the Party, and finished by stating that it was "completely un-American" to allow Leech, a man accused of lying on more than one occasion, "to be allowed to testify before a grand jury without the accused being permitted to have an opportunity to answer those charges."

Without quite apologizing, Dies put out the word that Mr. Bogart and the others had been "very frank and submitted their books and records for our inspection." Said inspection "showed that they are not and never have been Communist sympathizers." Humphrey washed his hands of the whole business and went to work, convinced that he could handle these Washington headline hunters with his hands tied behind his back. But the damage had already been done. Too much bad attention had been directed at Humphrey Bogart. The studio felt that giving him top billing would only invite trouble.

With his marriage deteriorating and his career on hold, Humphrey took to drinking before noon, then griping about the script to anyone who would listen — principally the director. Raoul Walsh was his kind of guy: he had roped cattle in the West, acted onstage in New York, switched to celluloid, apprenticed himself to D. W. Griffith, who taught him how to make movies, played the young Pancho Villa in a biography of the Mexican general (Villa played himself in the later scenes), and mastered an astonishing variety of styles, from fantasy (*The Thief of Bagdad,* with Douglas Fairbanks Sr.) to swashbuckling adventure (*They Died with*

Their Boots On, with Errol Flynn) to crime epic (*White Heat,* with James Cagney). He had lost an eye making one film and wore a black eyepatch, making him the most recognizable nonactor in Hollywood. He was not about to be intimidated by Humphrey Bogart, but he was not about to bully him, either; Walsh was too shrewd for that.

"When Bogart had one too many," the director recalled, "he used to come in and complain about his lines. 'What a load of garbage, that script.' 'But you approved it,' I answered. 'I must have been drunk. You'll change that for me, won't you?' I changed a couple of lines and he was happy and we could start working again."

The producer, director, and screenwriter discussed tactics, each conversing privately with Humphrey, urging him to make Earle a credible, innately decent soul. Their strategy worked. "Bogart was a medium-sized man," Huston recalled, "not particularly impressive offscreen." But something happened when he came on as Roy Earle. "Those lights and shadows composed themselves into another, nobler personality: heroic." In *High Sierra* the camera had "a way of looking into a person and perceiving things the naked eye doesn't register."

Added to this was the influence of a writer

who had nothing to do with the script, but whose outlook and technique could be felt in every scene. "The world breaks everyone and afterward many are strong in the broken places," he had written. "But those that will not break it kills. It kills the very good and the very gentle and the very brave impartially. If you are none of these you can be sure it will kill you too but there will be no special hurry."

In an appraisal of Ernest Hemingway, critic Edmund Wilson pointed out that the author had "expressed with genius the terrors of modern man at the danger of losing control of his world." At the same time, Hemingway provided an antidote. Though his heroes are preoccupied, not to say obsessed, with physical contests, they're "almost always defeated physically, nervously, practically; their victories are moral ones." This approach was apparent in Burnett's imitative prose style, and in the "virile ugliness" of the main character. Huston amplified Hemingway's tough-minded masculine approach, and Walsh and Bogart took it from there.

For a gangster film, *High Sierra* has an unusually sensitive opening. After establishing shots of a foreboding prison, the parolee gets into a car. Rather than be driven directly to his destination, "Mad Dog" demands to be taken to a park, where he gets out and strolls along, carefully noticing the things that have been missing from his life for ten years: the sky, the grass, trees, birds. Only then can he continue the journey. Earle has been sprung from jail early, not for good behavior, but because a crime boss has suborned a corrupt prison official. He wants the experienced Earle to lead a million-dollar hotel heist. Roy follows instructions, taking a long, circuitous drive to a camp in the Sierra mountains. There he meets the men who will abet him in the robbery. Mendoza and Red (Cornel Wilde and Arthur Kennedy in early roles) seem reliable enough. A third man, Babe (Alan Curtis), has brought along a woman, Marie (Ida Lupino). Roy regards him as trouble and her as bad luck. But Marie is both tough and flirtatious; she persuades the feisty Mad Dog to keep her on.

During the weeks that Roy plans the robbery, a stray canine named Pard (actually Humphrey's own dog Zero) adopts him and Marie falls in love with him. But Roy has eyes for another, a sweet-faced, clubfooted young woman named Velma (Joan Leslie) he met on the drive to the hideout. One afternoon Roy gathers his remaining cash, drives down the mountain, and funds an expensive operation. When it cures Velma's limp, Roy asks the grateful girl for her hand. But a new Velma now emerges, conniving and self-involved. She spurns the offer; while she was recuperating she met a man her own age and they got engaged. Roy meets the unprepossessing and vulgar fiancé. With something more than jealousy, he loathes the man on sight. Bitter but resigned, in the manner of a Hemingway protagonist, Roy accepts the decision and hooks up with Marie. As it turns out, this lady has more dignity and class than Velma. But she *has* brought bad luck with her. In the midst of the robbery a security guard wanders in. Shots are fired. Red and Babe attempt to flee but crack up their car. The police close in on Mendoza. Terrified, he rats out his companions.

Roy puts Marie and Pard on a bus to Las Vegas, then lights out for the Sierras, hoping the cops will pass by. Not a chance. A dragnet has been set up, and Roy is soon tracked down by the police. On the bus, Marie hears a radio broadcast, outlining the situation. ("It is some five hours since Roy Earle took cover on the rock and there is no indication on his part to surrender.") She and Pard get off and reverse direction. Arriving at the foot of the mountain, she's spotted by a reporter. He spills her location to the police. They ask Marie to shout out to the fugitive, pleading with him to surrender before it's too late. She refuses and, just after sunrise, sharpshooters climb the mountain. As Pard barks below, Roy Earle emerges from his hideaway for the last time, aware that Marie is within earshot. As he calls out to her, a rifleman shoots him in the back. Pard licks his dead owner's hand. Marie weeps for a moment, then straightens up. Her lover has the one thing he wanted all along: freedom.

Theoretically this was just another violent and sentimental gangster movie, with the villain getting his just deserts at the end. As it turned out, though, *High Sierra* became an important piece of Hollywood history: it marked the sunset of the gangster genre. The film was released in 1941. World War II approached, and larger and more threatening villains than John Dillinger and Al Capone had risen to power overseas. But it had a professional significance as well. *High Sierra* marked the last time Humphrey Bogart failed to receive first billing. His performance was too impressive to ignore. Belmont Bogart had been wrong: it wasn't the sea that would be his son's Yale and Harvard, it was second-rate movies. Without being aware of it, Humphrey had been in training for the role of "Mad Dog" Earle, paying his dues, learning his lines, honing his skills, digging into his characters' psyches. All the years of B pictures, all the violent deaths he suffered in melodramatic parts, all the semiliterate scripts and fights with Warners, led up to this role, and he was more than equal to the challenge. As the ill-fated Earle, Humphrey could easily have overemphasized the character's hardboiled aspects, or his softheartedness. But he never asked for the viewers' sympathy. They knew he was a killer with a dark and brutal past — he was dubbed "Mad Dog" for a reason — but they liked him anyway. Partly, of course, it was because of his charitable gestures. But mostly it was because Humphrey brought a reality to a bad man capable of humane acts, a puzzling figure who, in other circumstances, might have been someone worth saving.

His body language, as well as his facial expressions, registers shock when reporters label him "Mad Dog." He never thinks of himself that way, and indeed regards the little mongrel as his only friend. He's kind to a taxi dancer who briefly becomes his lover, and goes out of his way to help a crippled girl — one of those deeds that do not go unpunished. For all his heists, the only thing Roy Earle has ever wanted is liberty. Sarcasm doesn't get him anywhere; neither does pity. His salvation comes only at the close, when on a lonely mountain peak he escapes his pursuers for good.

The film was a bona fide hit across the country with critics and moviegoers. Other studios asked to borrow Humphrey for their features. Fox and MGM guaranteed star billing. Universal even wanted him to co-star in *My Little Chickadee* alongside Mae West and W. C. Fields. Humphrey was in demand for radio dramas, product endorsements (shirts, chocolates, cigarettes), and personal appearances.

Nathaniel Benchley remembered one such appearance at a Broadway movie palace. Humphrey's act began right after one of his death scenes was shown on-screen. When the houselights were turned on, the audience saw him lying prone on the stage. He got up, remarked, "It's a hell of a way to make a living," wiped his hands on his trousers, and spoke a few prepared words. "It was the first time most people had seen the cheerful side of him, and the effect was startling. Hordes of people, the majority of them women, mobbed his dressing room door."

The success of *High Sierra* could well have meant disaster for Humphrey. For if this was to be the finale of a genre, where would he go? Just past his fortieth birthday, underweight and balding, he was not handsome, like Tyrone Power or Robert Taylor or Clark Gable or any of the other leading men of the early 1940s. Nor could he bring off sophisticated comedy in the manner of Cary Grant or William Powell. Nor could he be a folk hero along the lines of Jimmy Stewart and Gary Cooper. Nor could he sing or dance. With the demise of the gangster film, what parts were open to such an incomplete actor?

Humphrey's very next film indicated how dire his situation was. *The Wagons Roll at Night* cast him as Nick Coster, owner of a squalid traveling carnival. Eddie Albert plays Matt, a naïve lion tamer who makes a near-fatal mistake: he falls for the owner's overprotected sister Mary (Joan Leslie, in another virginal role). When the lions turn feral, Nick forces Matt to go in and calm the big cats. It amounts to murder, and when Mary sees what's happening she begs her brother to intervene. Guiltily, Nick enters the cage, rescues Matt, and gets clawed to death. This was the nadir of Humphrey's Warners period; it was as if the door had been opened and then, just as he was about to cross the threshold, slammed shut. And in addition to his fading marriage, he had a new sorrow: on November 22, 1940, Maud died after a long battle with cancer. Humphrey memorialized her with the line "She died as she had lived. With guts." But he also grumbled that "cruel as it may sound, Maud was not a woman one loved. For such was her drive, her singleness of purpose, that none of us could really get at her."

He and his mother had never been simpatico. Maud's only son had been harboring resentments from early childhood onward, and now they asserted themselves. She had been one of the most famous commercial illustrators of the early twentieth century, and a lifelong advocate of women's rights. Yet on her death certificate, Humphrey listed the deceased's occupation simply as "housewife." In their book, Maud's biographers wonder, "What was Humphrey Bogart's motive for this written 'slap in the face,' for even in her retirement Maud had still been painting?" No one could say for certain, least of all Humphrey himself.

His sullen mood was not improved by the reviews of *Wagons*. The *Times* assessment said it best: "Nothing at all can be said for the definitely unoriginal plot; Mr. Bogart is badly hampered in a ridiculously fustian villain role. Except for the lions and Mr. Albert, *The Wagons Roll at Night* is honkytonk." The *News* reported that showings at the Strand Theater had been greeted with catcalls and raspberries.

Warners was of no help at all. A picture called *Out of the Fog,* based on Irwin Shaw's play *The Gentle People,* was ready to go. It concerned the lives of simple folk, brutalized by a thief who squeezes them for money. Ida Lupino had already been cast as the female lead, and Humphrey saw himself playing opposite her as he had in *High Sierra*. He thought Lupino had liked working with him in that picture. He was wrong. She told Warners that she didn't want Bogart as her costar, and John Garfield got the role.

Then came *Manpower.* Warners assigned Humphrey to the picture, along with George Raft and Marlene Dietrich. Then Raft did a little backstairs politicking. Humphrey was removed from the cast. He asked around, then sent a carefully worded telegram to Hal Wallis informing him that he was EXTREMELY UPSET. It continued: I TRIED TO

126

GET GEORGE TO TELL ME THIS MORNING WHAT HE WAS ANGRY ABOUT BUT HE WOULDN'T TELL ME. I FEEL VERY HURT BY THIS BECAUSE IT'S THE SECOND TIME I HAVE BEEN KEPT OUT OF A GOOD PICTURE AND A GOOD PART BY AN ACTOR'S REFUSING TO WORK WITH ME.

Unresponsive, the studio gave the role to Edward G. Robinson, and as an added insult assigned Humphrey to play Cole Younger in a Western called *Bad Men of Missouri.* He took one look at the script and shot off a note to the casting department: "Are you kidding — this is certainly rubbing it in — since Lupino and Raft are casting pictures, maybe I can." Smoldering, he clambered aboard his yacht *Sluggy* and took her out to sea where he would be unreachable. Five days later, the studio placed him on suspension. Jack Warner was adamant — no salary, no side income from radio programs or personal appearances, no future movies until Bogart capitulated. The capable journeyman Dennis Morgan was cast as Cole Younger, and Humphrey went back to cruising the Pacific. If there was a way out of this impasse, no one could see it.

CHAPTER 3
INCORRODIBLE AS A ZINC BAR

I

At the time of Bogart's suspension, the United States was suffering from a kind of bipolar affliction. On one hand the nation struggled with the effects of the Crash. By the late 1930s unemployment approached 15 percent. Isolationist senators eyed the rise of Hitler and Mussolini in Europe, read of the collapse and surrender of France and the Nazi attack on Britain, and declared it was none of America's business. Washington, D.C., trumpeting its status as the nation's capital, was actually a southern tank town. It had fifteen thousand privies, numerous murders, unsafe streets. In 1939 the black opera diva Marian Anderson was barred from singing in Constitution Hall, and the first lady, Eleanor Roosevelt, had to make private arrangements so that Anderson's concert could take place on the steps of the Lincoln Memorial.

On the other hand, President Franklin Delano Roosevelt had firmly taken over the machinery of government and energized the labor force. He decided to run for an unprecedented third term and had little trouble defeating his Republican challenger, Wendell Willkie. Unions, ethnic groups, and the Solid South all got behind him. Over the protests of the America First Committee, including Charles Lindbergh and a group of midwestern senators, the Selective Service Act was passed. Lend-Lease aid to Britain and the Soviet Union began to flow, giving those beleaguered nations weapons for the war with Germany. U.S. factories began to retool for what was termed "defense purposes," and the gross national product jumped from $866.5 billion in 1939 to 941.2 a year later. Unemployment started to drop. The decrease would continue.

Even during the Depression's deepest troughs, people felt a great need to get away from their troubles for a few hours. The big studios had flourished in those worst of times. Now that the United States stood on the edge of global conflict, moviemakers were ready to prosper yet again. The problem was selecting the right material. It was a bit too early for international political satire (though Charlie Chaplin had mocked Hitler in *The Great Dictator* and Ernst Lubitsch had made a mockery of Nazism in *To Be or Not to Be*), and not quite time for full-out war pictures. A middle way had to be found.

In 1940 the big studio productions reflected this contradiction. Several chose to take a look at U.S. history in the rearview mirror (*Abe Lincoln in Illinois, Knute Rockne: All American, The Grapes of Wrath*). Others ignored current events in favor of screwball comedies (*My Favorite Wife, Great McGinty, His Girl Friday*). Still others concentrated on melodrama, aiming principally for a female audience (*Kitty Foyle; The Letter; All This, and Heaven Too*). As they prepared for 1941, none of the moguls was secure enough to say exactly what the American moviegoer was looking for. In such a climate Humphrey needed a miracle. He got two of them.

He was taken off suspension, thanks in part to some interference by the woman they called (behind her back) the Gay Illiterate. The subject of much loathing, fear, and genuflection, Louella Parsons had worked her way up from hack journalist in Chicago to failed scenarist to dictatorial

Hollywood gossip columnist, thanks to the backing of press lord William Randolph Hearst. She had taken a shine to Humphrey, and decided his dry, instantly recognizable voice would enliven her radio show, *Hollywood Hotel,* a program crammed with celebrities. But there was no way he could go on the air if he was suspended. Louella put some pressure on Warners, and since they had already hung Humphrey out to dry for two months, they relented and placed him back on the payroll.

Miracle two came from a familiar source. George Raft, ever fixated on George Raft, sent another of his cranky memos to Jack Warner, complaining about an upcoming film. "As you know," he wrote, "I strongly feel that *The Maltese Falcon,* which you want me to do, is not an important picture and, in this connection, I must remind you again, before I signed the new contract with you, you promised me that you would not require me to perform in anything but important pictures. . . ." Again Warner backed off, selecting a substitute who had just been chastened and who was unlikely to give the studio any more trouble. Besides, he was reminded, there was Humphrey's personal appearance in New York, during which hordes of people, the majority of them women, mobbed his dressing room door. . . .

Despite Raft's petulant tone, he had a valid argument. Dashiell Hammett's novella *The Maltese Falcon* had already been filmed twice, both times with Hammett as co-scenarist. In 1931 it went out under the original title, with Bebe Daniels as the villainess and Ricardo Cortez as Sam Spade, private eye. Five years later *Falcon* was remade as *Satan Met a Lady,* with Bette Davis as the bad girl and Warren William as an unsubtly lascivious gumshoe. Neither one thrived. The third version would be in the hands of a thirty-five-year-old screenwriter making his directorial debut. Raft didn't trust John Huston, and Huston didn't care much for Raft. "So I fell heir to Bogie," Huston remembered, "for which I was duly thankful."

The reunion of actor and director was social as well as professional. Both enjoyed knocking back a few drinks after work, and sometimes before it. Both considered themselves "men's men," tough-minded personalities who bucked authority, talked intelligently on a variety of subjects, worked professionally, and held their liquor. There was no sense of competition; they were anxious to get on with the show.

It took a while for matters to coalesce. Geraldine Fitzgerald was up for the part of the pathological liar Ruth Wonderly (a.k.a. Brigid O'Shaughnessy), but she had other commitments. This time it was Mary Astor's turn to be duly thankful. The actress had been in movies since the age of eighteen; she had played opposite Clark Gable in *Red Dust* and John Huston's father, Walter, in *Dodsworth.* In the Bette Davis vehicle *The Big Lie,* it was Astor who would get an Academy Award for her performance as an ambitious, egomaniacal concert pianist. She considered Huston's script for *Falcon* "a humdinger," and lobbied for the part of the manipulative leading lady. Perhaps the most persuasive argument for hiring Astor was not her screen credits but her steamy affair with George S. Kaufman. In 1936, her then husband had discovered Mary's diary, detailing romantic interludes with the playwright ("Ah desert night — with George's body plunging into mine, naked under the stars . . ."). The marriage ended in a well-publicized divorce, and the quotes, played up in the tabloids, lent the pale, rather delicate-looking actress an intriguing glamour.

Huston was familiar with Sydney Greenstreet's stage work: the stout actor had starred with Bob Hope in the Jerome Kern operetta *Roberta,* and toured with Alfred Lunt and Lynn Fontanne in the Robert Sherwood drama *There Shall Be No Night.* Huston saw him doing that play in Los Angeles and went backstage. The two struck up a friendship, and Greenstreet allowed himself to be persuaded to make his screen debut at the age of sixty-one. Casting for the other parts was a pleasure. Joel Cairo, the tightly closeted Levantine, would be played by Peter Lorre. At thirty-four, this sophisticated Hungarian refugee had already made nearly forty films, including *M;* Alfred Hitchcock's international classic about a child killer, *The Man Who Knew Too Much;* and eight features in the role of Mr. Moto, a wily Japanese detective. Ward Bond, the bluff, hearty veteran of Westerns and gang-ster movies, would play a police detective, as would the reliable Bart MacLane. The undersized homosexual gunsel, Wilmer Cook, would be impersonated by Elisha Cook Jr., the least social of the group, as befit Wilmer's alienated character. Elisha lived alone, way up in the Sierras, not un-like the fugitive Roy Earle, where he tied flies and fished for golden trout. He had no telephone; when studios wanted to reach him, they sent a man to his cabin.

What made this *Falcon* so different from its predecessors was not only the cast, but Huston's unfailing attention to detail. He noted that "the book was told entirely from the standpoint of Sam Spade, and so too is the picture, with Spade in every scene except the murder of his partner. The audience knows no more and no less than he does." Every bit of dialogue, much of it from the novella, was pared to the bone. During his youth Huston had taken classes at the Art Students League; he knew how to render the look and feel of a room. "I made a sketch of each set-up," he remarked in *An Open Book,* a memoir about his directorial debut. "If it was to be a pan or a dolly shot, I'd indicate it. I didn't ever want to be at a loss before the actors or the camera crew." He ran the sketches by his friend William Wyler, one of the premier Hollywood directors. Wyler was a Huston fan; he had brought him to Warners as a screenwriter. He offered a few suggestions, but by and large he liked what he saw. Just before the cameras began to grind, *Falcon* producer Henry Blanke whispered in John's ear, "Just remember that each scene, as you shoot it, is the most important scene in the picture." Huston considered his words "the best advice any young director could have."

As much as possible the movie was shot in sequence, giving the actors the opportunity to maintain a rare consistency and intensity. On most sets, at the end of the business day the cast members scatter, heading for their homes or their cronies. Not so on *Falcon.* "We were all having such a good time," Huston wrote in *An Open Book,* "that night after night after shooting, Bogie, Peter Lorre, Ward Bond, Mary Astor and I would go over to the Lakeside Club." They'd have a few drinks and a buffet supper, often staying on until midnight. Ordinarily this sort of behavior was frowned on by production executives, particularly at Warners, where not a moment was supposed to be squandered. But it was all right this time; *Falcon* was actually running ahead of schedule. The only downer came when Astor attempted to keep up with the wisecracks exploding around her. "The kidding was turned on me unmercifully," she remembered. "It was more than I could handle. Tears started popping and I whimpered, 'I just can't keep up with this!' " Humphrey wiped away her tears with his handkerchief and assured Astor that she was OK with the gang. She wasn't as quick as Lorre or Huston or himself, but so what? "You know it, and what the hell's wrong with that?" It was as close as he could come to an apology, she accepted it as such, and after that things were fine again.

The closeness grew over the weeks. Greenstreet and Lorre, raconteurs with scores of hilarious international anecdotes, broke up the crew between takes. The publicity department had tourists traipsing through the set until Humphrey and Mary conspired to put a stop to it. A group of priests heard her curse loudly; as a gaggle of middle-aged ladies passed by, Humphrey zipped up his fly and said, "See you later, Mary." The tours abruptly ceased, allowing all the cast members to concentrate, digging deep into their roles. Astor, for example, wanted to give Brigid an unstable persona bordering on hysteria. "So, I hyperventilated before going into most of the scenes. It gave me a heady feeling, of thinking at cross purposes." Lorre was appropriately underhanded and delicate. It was not his fault that the film's one weak scene, in which Humphrey is called upon to laugh at him, is artificial and unconvincing. That was a script and directorial failure — the only one in the entire film. Greenstreet was a revelation, a model of underhanded bonhomie. The forty-two-year-old Humphrey could be as hard-boiled as Baby Face or Mad Dog, but here the menace is accompanied by charm and a vital integrity. Sam Spade has little use for cops, or for the district attorney, but he stays on the right side of the law — although just barely. He has an easy way with women (including his partner's wife), but treats his secretary, Effie (Lee Patrick), with hands-off politesse. Wilmer is dealt with contemptuously, as if Humphrey were getting his own back after being forced to utter so many gangster clichés over the years. Holding a gun on Spade, Wilmer warns him: "Keep on ridin' me, they're gonna be pickin' iron out of your liver." Replies Sam: "The cheaper the crook, the gaudier the patter." Yet negotiating with Kasper Gutman, the Fat Man, Spade is respectful and courteous. When Gutman asks if he knows what the black bird is worth, Spade admits that he hasn't the slightest idea. The Fat Man smiles at his listener's ignorance. If he were to disclose the value, Spade would call him a liar. No, Spade disagrees, not even if he thought so.

Meta Wilde, Huston's assistant, described that first meeting of Spade and Gutman. Cinematographer Arthur Edeson followed Humphrey "down a long hallway, and finally into a living room; there the camera moved up and down in what is referred to as a bottom-up and boom-down shot, then panned from left to right and back to Bogart's face; the next pan shot was to Greenstreet's massive stomach from Bogart's point of view. The choreography of it was exacting and exciting. One miss and we had to begin all over again." But they didn't have to begin again. Everything went off without a hitch. After about seven minutes of continuous shooting, "Huston shouted 'CUT' and 'PRINT IT!,' a shout went up and crew members heartily congratulated Bogart, Greenstreet, and Edeson and his camera specialists."

Over the years, much has been made of *Lulu in Hollywood,* Louise Brooks's memoir of Los Angeles and New York, and of her shrewd analyses of fellow actors — including Humphrey Bogart. She could be piercingly accurate, but she could also be perversely mistaken, as she was in the case of *The Maltese Falcon.* Sam Spade, wrote Brooks, "was uncomplicated, but too much dialogue betrayed the fact that Humphrey's miserable theatrical training had left him permanently afraid of words. In short speeches he cleverly masked his fear with his tricks of mouth and voice. But when he was allotted part of the burden of exposition in this film, his eyes glazed and invisible comic strip balloons circled his dialogue."

Just the opposite is true. There was no other actor in the Warners studio, not James Cagney, Edward G. Robinson, or John Garfield, and certainly not George Raft, who could have so effectively brought off the finale, with its crowded words and thoughts. A frantic Spade learns that the statuette of the falcon was a counterfeit all along, that many people, including his partner, Miles Archer, have died for nothing. The Fat Man, Joel Cairo, and Wilmer have fled, leaving Spade holding the bag in the form of a leaden statuette. Suspected of murdering Archer, he confronts the woman who has his heart, but who has betrayed him and killed his associate. He decides to turn her in to the police. In shock, she begins to cry. For the next several minutes, Spade explains his fundamental principles. He didn't much like Miles Archer. But he can't stand by and let the woman who shot his partner get away with murder. It would be bad for him, bad for detectives everywhere.

Brigid protests that these are insufficient reasons to hand her to the police, especially if he loves her. Spade has a ready answer: if he lets her go, she'll have something on him,

140

something she can use as blackmail. And if that fails, she can always resort to the gun, just as she did with Archer. He lists the arguments in her favor, then those in his favor. He admits that love is powerful, that all of him wants to let her go regardless of consequences. But the sad fact is, she's counted on just that, as she has with countless others who enjoyed her sexual favors. Sam admits that he'll have some hard, sleepless nights after Brigid's been put in prison, but that he'll get over it, and get over her.

All this was said in well over a hundred words (and he had uttered another hundred in an earlier expository passage). Yet those words flew by, tautly and confidently delivered. Previous versions of the story played up Sam's wolfish tendencies, and the first filming sedulously copied Hammett's ending. Iva (Gladys George), Miles Archer's widow, is in the waiting room. "Send her in, darling," Sam tells Effie. That sequence would have ruined the moral tragedy of Huston's carefully made film. Yet he thought he had no alternative. He shot it as written, looked at what he had done, and hated it. After a discussion with Humphrey, the producer and the director made an epochal decision.

On July 19, 1941, unit manager Al Alleborn reported to the front office: "The picture is finished, but at Blanke's and Huston's request we eliminated the ending, as written in the script, which takes place on Stage Three in Spade's office." On July 30, Blanke followed up. The final scene would be "staged differently, as with their exit out of the room we will continue in the corridor to the elevator. Mary Astor and Lt. Dundy [Barton MacLane] will get into the elevator as Bogart and the other detectives come into the corridor and see Dundy and Astor descend in the elevator with last looks between Bogart and Astor played between them." What he didn't mention was the last exchange between Lieutenant Polhaus (Ward Bond) and Sam Spade. Curious, Polhaus wants to know what the black statuette is, and what it means. Says Spade, it's "the stuff that dreams are made of."

Humphrey himself had suggested the final line, with its Shakespearean echo of *The Tempest:* "We are such stuff / as dreams are made on; and our little life / Is rounded with a sleep."

The final sequence — the evidence turned over to the officials, exonerating Spade; Brigid arrested, Sam's grieving integrity; the romance, like the statue, suddenly bereft of meaning — was pure magic. It would become one of the most fondly remembered scenes of viewers worldwide.

Cinema critics and scholars realized what had happened. Casting against the part, Huston had created (and Warners had underwritten) a dark, fascinating leading man with intelligence, honor, and soul. It had not been planned, but it had not been an accident, either. This was the greatest opportunity of them all, and Humphrey was not about to blow it. As Mary Astor wrote in *A Life on Film,* Bogart's "technical skill was quite brilliant. He kept other actors on their toes because he *listened* to them, he watched, he *looked* at them. He was never 'upstage center' acting all by himself. He was there. With you." This was not the customary behavior of male stars. However gifted, most of them had eyes for Number One. Their standard was best articulated in six words by the great Chaplin himself. Asked by a second lead how he should play a scene, Charlie said: "Behind me, and to the left."

Other leading men at Warner Bros., as well as the other major studios, had experience in the theater. But few had appeared in as many Broadway plays as Humphrey, over a longer stretch of time. There are only two paths to top-of-the-marquee status in Hollywood: overnight success or a long, winding apprenticeship. At forty-one, Humphrey was far past wunderkind age. His ascent had been a lengthy slog through minor roles in plays until his success in *The Petrified Forest,* and two-dimensional villains and second leads in movies until his challenging roles in *High Sierra* and now in *The Maltese Falcon.* But these outstanding performances were not what they appeared to be: a matter of luck and timing. All along, he had been picking up technique, sometimes accidentally, often deliberately. Over the decades he had learned how to listen and look at his fellow players, how to appear natural in the most artificial of circumstances, how to *be* rather than to seem a character. In the process, he had turned himself into an authentic leading man.

The sudden change of villain into hero had happened before. In 1939 Basil Rathbone, a suave evildoer in picture after picture, from *David Copperfield* to *A Tale of Two Cities* to *Robin Hood,* had been cast as Sherlock Holmes and a new kind of sleuth was born. This Holmes was not warm or likeable; he was only brilliant, intuitive, and above all truthful. He was also irresistible — so irresistible that Rathbone would be remembered more for that role (in fourteen movies) than for any other performances in his career. Humphrey's story was not unlike Basil's, except that he wouldn't play Sam Spade anymore. But he *would* play the kind of character Spade represented, over and over again: wounded, cynical, romantic, and as incorrodible as a zinc bar.

In 1941–42, that on-screen presence was a man that Americans wanted — indeed, needed — to see. At the end of the year the Japanese attack on Pearl Harbor triggered the entry of the United States into World War II. In the beginning the Allied losses were horrific. Manila was captured by the Japanese. The siege of the Bataan peninsula began, with the eventual surrender of U.S. forces and the resultant Death March. Germany enjoyed quick, spectacular victories in the Crimea, the Ukraine, and the Western Desert of North Africa. As young American men went off to battle, perhaps to be maimed or to die in distant lands, their home country needed reassuring symbols to hold on to. Allied leaders like Roosevelt, Churchill, Stalin, and de Gaulle became icons, but that was not enough. Film stars were also transformed into figures who symbolized the American Way. The truculent James Cagney became George M. Cohan, the Yankee Doodle dandy. Tall-in-the-saddle Gary Cooper became the intrepid Sergeant York, sharpshooting loner of World War I. And the onetime crook Humphrey Bogart became the quintessential American male. The iniquitous could only push him so far. Once they crossed the line, he became an implacable foe — the story of the country itself, which had been slow to respond to the Axis of Germany, Italy, and Japan, but which now demanded nothing less than unconditional surrender.

At this moment in history, something about Humphrey caught on with the public: *"Those lights and shadows composed themselves into another, nobler personality: heroic."* He knew it, Huston knew it, audiences knew it, and, most important, the studio knew it. Humphrey had crystallized the image of masculinity precisely at this moment in American history, and Warners was going to make sure he had plenty of A pictures to star in from now on, and lots of room to grow. There would be wrangles with the front office in times to come — that was the kind of guy Humphrey was — but there would be no more bottom-of-the-bill movies for Bogart, no more *Wagons Roll at Night* or *Roaring Twenties.* Once more he had arrived. But this time it was for good.

In the 1920s Damon Runyon invented a literary scene. He called it Broadway, but it was a fantasyland quite unlike the real one, populated with gamblers and chiselers who spoke only in the present or future tense. Men had names like Harry the Horse and Izzy Cheesecake, referred to their girlfriends as dolls, and were as colorful and harmless as a bunch of toy balloons. ("Now most any doll will be very glad indeed to have Handsome Jack Madigan give her a tumble. . . .") By 1941 the conflict in Europe had at last caught the attention of filmmakers. Warners came up with an idea: without exactly making a war picture, they could produce a comedy with Runyonesque characters versus German spies. That way the studio could take advantage of American sentiments, and yet keep it light.

The old, feisty Humphrey would probably not have agreed to play the part of Gloves Donahue in *All Through the Night,* even though the studio provided top billing and allowed him to stretch by doing some light material. But it was the summer of 1941, and he was back in Jack Warner's good graces, and while good things were expected of *The Maltese Falcon* the reviews were not in yet. No one really knew which way the cat would jump. Humphrey began filming the comedy in mid-August, heading a cast that included the foreigners Conrad Veidt and Peter Lorre, as well as the rising comedians Phil Silvers and Jackie Gleason. Either Bogart or a Warners press agent took advantage of Gleason's bulk; Humphrey was reported to have said that Jackie looked like the man who had come to dinner — and eaten the guests.

He knew that *All Through the Night* was fluff, but a contract was a contract. Besides, the movie had a plucky cast. They enlivened the story, confected by humorists Leo Rosten (under the name Leonard Q. Ross) and Leonard Spigelgass, and had a lot of fun with the hoodlums versus Nazis plot. Humphrey, who saw plenty of vaudeville as a youth, was particularly taken by William Demarest. That vaudeville veteran was required to speak double-talk at a German rally in the final scenes. Humphrey could barely hold in the laughs as he picked up the cue: "How right you are, Herr Schultz, scradavan is definitely on the paratoot." The picture turned out well under Vincent Sherman's direction. Under other circumstances it might have had a chance, but the opening months of U.S. involvement in World War II rendered the film trivial if not downright offensive. Coy espionage agents were not going to play in an atmosphere of early defeats.

But *Falcon* was immune to the headlines. It was not about war. It was about greed and sex and integrity. And the notices were the stuff that dreams are made of. *Time* called the acting "practically perfect," with Humphrey "giving the performance of his career." The magazine also informed its readers of something that had gone unreported. "John Huston accepted only a slight assist from his father in his new venture: as an unlisted bit player, Huston Sr., sieved with bullet holes, appears long enough to deliver the falcon to Sam Spade, mumble a word or two, and fall dead." In the *New York Times,* Bosley Crowther wondered why Warner Bros. had been so "strangely bashful" about this wonderful film, and went on to praise the picture's "excellent revelation of character. Mr. Bogart is a shrewd, tough detective with a mind that cuts like a blade." The other reviews stayed on message.

The production cost $381,000 and was set to gross millions. An elated Hal Wallis sent off a letter to Jack Warner, vacationing in Hot Springs, Arkansas. According to some of the New York notices, wrote Wallis, *The Maltese Falcon* "came in 'under wraps' 'on rubber heels,' 'was a delightful surprise because unheralded' etc. etc." He pleaded for his boss to give the New York office "a slight goose" and make them get behind the movie. That Jack did, and Warners reaped millions more as the reputation of their "sleeper" grew over the next six decades.

Studio executives tossed around ideas for the next Bogart picture. What about the adventures of Sam Spade, Part 2, with the same splendid cast? The next day the front office came to its senses. By *Falcon*'s fade-out Brigid had already been "sent over," and the Fat Man and the other conspirators had been captured. Some other property would have to be used so that Bogart, Astor, Huston, et al. could be reunited while they were hot. Lorre was already working on another picture, but the director and three stars from *Falcon* were quickly signed to do *Across the Pacific.* Loudly ballyhooed, this Warner Bros. follow-up turned out to be a rather slapdash effort, quite unlike its predecessor. The war was on. John Huston, impatiently awaiting his commission, had much less at stake in this picture than in his debut film. It showed. Mary and Humphrey and Sydney got along well, but the plot was thin and burdened with propaganda. Even the love scenes felt spurious. Humphrey had never been very good at on-screen kissing; during a passionate two-shot with Astor she suddenly pulled away. As the cast looked on, she snapped, "Try not to knock my teeth out next time." Acknowledged Humphrey, "I don't like love scenes, maybe because I don't do them very well. It isn't possible to shoot a love scene without having a hairy-chested group of grips standing four feet away from you, chewing tobacco. I'll handle that in the privacy of my bedroom."

The feature was based on *Aloha Means Goodbye,* a popular international thriller centered on the Japanese plot to bomb Pearl Harbor. A year later, that scheme was old news; a rewrite focused on the Panama Canal and its vulnerability to bombers from Imperial Japan. Humphrey starred as a cashiered officer, sullen, disobedient, ready to sell out to any country that meets his price. Actually he is nothing of the kind; he's an undercover U.S. agent who has been put aboard the *Genoa Maru,* a cargo ship headed for the Canal Zone, in order to attract bidders and collect military intelligence. During the days at sea he meets Dr. Lorenz (Greenstreet), a great admirer of the Japanese ("An amazing little people"); Alberta Marlow (Astor), whose background remains a mystery; and a slew of suspicious Asians who smile insincerely, sneak around, and speak broken English. West Coast nisei (Japanese Americans) were being rounded up and sent to internment camps in 1942; Japanese behavior in *Across the Pacific* accorded with the racial stereotyping of the day. With Japanese actors out of favor, the film made do with Chinese performers like Victor Sen Yung and Lee Tung Foo — most viewers wouldn't be able to tell the difference anyway.

Though the picture was studio-bound, the set was placed on hydraulic lifts that made it shift to and fro like a ship at sea. The actors seemed on the edge of mal de mer all through the filming. Just before *Across the Pacific* wrapped, Huston received his commission as a lieutenant in the U.S. Army Signal Corps. Vincent Sherman was assigned to finish the film, and Huston, with nothing but mischief in mind, invented a story that he continued to tell for decades afterward. In the Huston version, the outgoing director arranged a climactic scene in which Humphrey was tied to a chair, surrounded by heavily armed Japanese soldiers. "There was no way in God's green world that Bogart could logically escape," maintained John. "I shot the scene, then called

Jack Warner and said, 'Jack, I'm on my way. I'm in the army. Bogie will know how to get out.' Bogie didn't know how to escape. Neither did Sherman. The entire scene had to be rewritten and shot so that Humphrey was guarded by only one soldier, whom, of course, he quickly overpowered." The reality was somewhat different: the final scenes were actually written two days before Huston donned his uniform.

Across the Pacific did well enough at the box office. The heat and cohesion of *Falcon* was missing, but Arthur Edeson's cinematography gave the film a documentary feel, and the anti-Japanese sentiment in the country did the rest. As usual, *Times* critic Bosley Crowther led the cheering: "Mr. Huston has given the Warners a delightfully fear-jerking picture. . . . Mr. Bogart is as tough and sharp a customer as ever faced the world with bitter eyes."

In Hollywood it is not enough to succeed; your colleague must have failed. So it was not without schadenfreude that Humphrey read his own good notices, and then heard about George Raft's grumbling reference to *Falcon:* "There but for the grace of me, go I." Raft was, in fact, on his way out; he would make one more film for Warner Bros. and then move on to diminished parts at other studios. Humphrey, on the basis of his newest triumphs, had just broken into the top rank of Warners stars, with a guaranteed salary of $2,750 a week. It was a strange time for him. An iconoclast since childhood, a rebel on the theatrical and sound stages, he was currently in favor with everyone important — and something of an icon in the making. Louis Sobol, a widely syndicated Broadway columnist, went so far as to call Bogart the "white-haired boy of Hollywood." On one hand, Humphrey cherished his reputation as a complicated and difficult man, ever ready to do battle with father-figure directors and studio chiefs. On the other hand, he had experienced more than his share of disappointments and setbacks; he had worked with great diligence to reach this new peak. Why not enjoy it to the full?

But somehow he couldn't. It was not in him to drive ahead without peeking in the rearview mirror. No one knew more about the hazards of show business than he did. No one was more aware of the way luck could change for an actor, up one day, down the next, like all those pathetic silent-movie guys who used to own the town, and now had a rented convertible and nothing in the bank. Even with all the adulation he could still wind up like Raft, making wrong choices, ceding good roles to some careerist with better luck and shrewder advisers. So he moved warily. Like a lot of writers and actors, he bore in mind "Provide, Provide," the Robert Frost poem published only seven years before:

No memory of having starred
Atones for later disregard
Or keeps the end from being hard.

III

While Humphrey was pondering his next step, an unproduced play, *Everybody Comes to Rick's,* came to the attention of Warner Bros. The co-author, Murray Burnett, had visited Vienna at the time of the *anschluss;* he saw the open hatred of Jews and the terror apparatus being put in place. Moving on to the south of France he watched desperate refugees attempting to flee the Hitler-backed Vichy regime. Just before returning to America he dropped into a nightclub in Juanles-Pins, where a black singer enthralled an audience with pop tunes. Burnett melded the scenes and, with his more experienced writing partner, Joan Alison, wrote a straight play about an expatriate American who owns a casino in

Casablanca, surrounded by Nazis and their French collaborators, as well as a swirl of refugees stranded in that still-neutral area. Irene Lee, head of the Warners story department, thought it might have a new life on film. To make sure, she asked one of her low-level readers, a thirty-five-year-old named Stephen Karnot, to appraise it. Karnot would leave the following October for a job in a defense plant — it was the patriotic thing to do, and besides, Warners was paying him all of $1.12 an hour. His judgment was remarkably prescient nonetheless: "Excellent melodrama. Colorful, timely background, tense mood, suspense, psychological and physical conflict, tight plotting, sophisticated hokum. A box office natural, for Bogart, or Cagney, or Raft, in one of the out-of-the-usual roles, and perhaps Mary Astor."

Warners bought the script and set about finding the right team to turn it into a movie. As Aljean Harmetz remarks in her luminous study, *Round Up the Usual Suspects,* "No one could have known that the central — though serial — collaboration [of screenwriters] would produce a script with more memorable lines than any other Hollywood film." Thus far, the screenplay *Everybody Comes to Rick's* had no new dialogue, just a working title. Warners called it *Casablanca*.

IV

Several teams had a try at adaptation and then withdrew. Nobody knew how to lick *Casablanca*'s central problem. The romantic duo, Rick Blaine and Lois Meredith, had been lovers before the war. She was married; he was a solitary adventurer. The Production Code, set up by producers in 1930 to avoid government censorship, specifically forbade mentions of sexual misconduct. Yet without that amorous experience back in Paris, why would Rick be so upset when she shows up at his nightclub?

The thirty-four-year-old Epstein twins were assigned to the film. Philip and Julius were New Yorkers who had prospered in Hollywood. Julius went there in 1935; Philip joined him in 1936. For a couple of years they worked independently, then joined forces in 1939, collaborating on a series of hits that included *The Strawberry Blonde, The Bride Came C.O.D.,* and *The Male Animal.* Thin, bald, fast-talking wise guys, they were good enough to get away with impudent remarks that would have finished other writers. When Jack Warner saw them com-

157

ing to work for the first time at 1:30 p.m., he bawled them out. "Railroad presidents get in at nine o'clock, bank presidents get in at nine o'clock, read your contract, you're coming in at nine o'clock." That afternoon they sent Jack a note: "Dear J.L., have the bank president finish the script."

Jack knew that they were industrious and that they were first-class. Aside from his customary eruptions he stayed out of their way. Hal Wallis would produce *Casablanca,* and that winter he began putting the pieces in place. Despite many rumors that George Raft, Ronald Reagan, and others were considered for the role of the owner of Rick's Café Américain, Wallis had Humphrey in mind from the start. He hired scenarist Howard Koch, who had written dialogue for the Bette Davis hit *The Letter,* and for the Gary Cooper vehicle *Sergeant York.* Koch would oversee the Epsteins' work, and they would then correct his corrections. Rarely did the trio write in the same room at the same time, but somehow the arrangement worked. Koch made no secret of his leftist views; the Epsteins were more interested in wit than in geopolitics. And yet when Koch wrote Rick's cantankerous line, "I don't buy or sell human beings," it was the Epsteins who made it immortal with the riposte: "That's too bad. That's Casablanca's leading commodity."

Wallis wanted Michael Curtiz to direct. The Hungarian was not a pleasant man; many actors hated him. Once Bette Davis established herself in the late 1930s, she refused to work for him. Fay Wray, the screaming blonde in *King Kong,* spoke of the way the director fired an extra in front of a crowd of onlookers. "He kept saying, 'Move to your right. More. More. Now you are out of the picture.' " But Curtiz had also made a series of major swashbucklers with Errol Flynn — *Captain Blood, The Charge of the Light Brigade, The Sea Hawk.* His brisk, animated style seemed right for a film with so many interior shots and, at least thus far, with so many holes in the plot. ("Who cares about character?" Curtiz once inquired. "I make it go so fast nobody notices.") And his mangling of the English language amused all but his worst foes. In his study, *Casablanca: As Time Goes By,* Frank Miller tells the story of Curtiz demanding "a poodle, a black poodle" for one scene. The prop man feared to question his boss, and set about finding the proper canine. Within an hour he presented a panting animal to Curtiz. "Very nice," he said, "but I want a poodle." When the "poor technician tried to

159

explain that's what he was holding, Curtiz exploded. 'I wanted a poodle in the street! A poodle of water! Not a goddamn dog!' "

In the play, the female lead is something of a wanton. That would never do. Her virtue could be restored by some crafty writing, but what were *two* Americans, Rick and Lois, doing in Casablanca in the first place? Wallis mentioned the problem to Casey Robinson, a scenarist and friend. Robinson asked why the lady had to be American. Why not make her a foreigner? It would add to the exotic nature of the movie. Films like the romantic tragedy *Intermezzo* showed that the camera loved the twenty-six-year-old Ingrid Bergman, and the horror film *Dr. Jekyll and Mr. Hyde* demonstrated that she was more than just a pretty face. Lately, though, she had been out of the business, living with her husband in Rochester, New York, where he was studying to be a neurosurgeon. She felt out of things, ignored and melancholy. She wrote to her friend, dialogue coach Ruth Roberts, "Having a home, husband and child, ought to be enough for any woman's life. I mean, that's what we are meant for, isn't it? But still I think every day is a lost day. As if only half of me is alive. The other half is pressed down in a bag and suffocated." When the script ar-

160

rived she said yes without bothering to question any of the story details. The part and the name would be changed, that was the important thing; Lois Meredith was now Ilsa Lund.

En route to May 1942, when *Casablanca* went into production, other members of the cast were signed. Peter Lorre and Sydney Greenstreet came aboard; Lorre would be Ugarte, an underhanded dealer in passages of safe conduct; Greenstreet, Signor Ferrari, owner of a rival nightclub. Leonid Kinskey would play Sascha, a bartender; S. Z. Sakall, Carl, a waiter; Marcel Dalio, a croupier. Claude Rains would be Renault, the corrupt Vichy captain always looking out for Number One; Conrad Veidt, a German movie star forced to flee the Nazis because he had a Jewish wife, but whose piercing glare would condemn him to play Nazis in film after film, would be the imperious Major Strasser.

The third element of the love triangle that haunts *Casablanca* is Victor Laszlo, leader of the anti-Nazi underground. Warners considered a long roster of actors, found them all unsatisfactory, and hired thirty-four-year-old Paul Henreid at the last minute. A tall, distinguished Viennese with stage experience in Europe, Henreid had actually fled the Nazis in 1935, working in Britain before trying his luck in Hollywood. His breakthrough came with *Now, Voyager,* in which he co-starred with Bette Davis. She plays an overweight, dowdy spinster, completely dominated by her mother. On a cruise, the ugly duckling meets the unhappily married Henreid, and under his ministrations turns into an enchanting and self-assured swan. The film had two indelible moments. In one, Henreid puts two cigarettes in his lips, lights them both, and hands one to Davis. That was to become one of the most imitated (and parodied) gestures of the 1940s. But the film's last line was what made it a classic weeper. No longer lovers, just friends, they look up at the night sky. He asks if she's happy. "Oh," she murmurs, "don't let's ask for the moon . . . we have the stars."

Henreid not only had the stars, he *was* a star. He told Harmetz that he had been destitute in four countries and now, overnight, he was rich. "I had been paid by Warner Bros. $32,000 for *Now, Voyager.* A fortune. A bloody fortune." Anxious to keep playing a hot hand, he accepted the role of Laszlo, hoping to parlay it into bigger parts in better pictures. When he signed on, he knew only the barest plot outline because the script was undergoing intense revisions: on the run from fascist enemies, Laszlo and his young wife, Ilsa, are marooned in Casablanca. The only person who can save them is Rick, the man whom she deserted in Paris. How it all turned out was a mystery to Henreid — and to everyone else, including the writers.

If chemistry is a vital part of filmmaking, particularly when a love story lies at the center of the narrative, *Casablanca* got off to an unpromising start. Off-screen, Humphrey had his hands full with Mayo; he wanted no part of a romance, even a platonic one, with his co-star. Nor was Ingrid attracted to either of her leading men. Paul Henreid bored her, and Humphrey Bogart seemed so distant it was hard to think of him as a lover. "I kissed him, but I never knew him," was the way she put it. She also repelled the advances of Curtiz, a notorious womanizer.

On the second level, much the same applied. Claude Rains had come a long way from his Cockney origins; he carried himself like an officer — he had been a lieutenant in World War I — and made no attempt to hide his distaste for Southern California. Not that he wanted to return to his native England. He and his fourth wife owned a

380-acre farm in Pennsylvania, and between takes he read agricultural brochures. Rains respected Humphrey and spent some time in conversation with him. But he had no real interest in cultivating friendships, only vegetables. Sydney Greenstreet was a merry soul, but he was on the set for very few scenes and never appeared with Lorre, with whom he had been so effective in *The Maltese Falcon*. As for Lorre, the little man with large, expressive eyes possessed extraordinary skills, accompanied by a quirky temperament. In the role of Ugarte, the black marketer who dealt in souls, he almost stole the film; as his admiring biographer Stephen D. Youngkin observes, in *Casablanca* Peter "captured the camera and gleaned a virtuoso performance from leftovers." He did it with nervous gestures and a mobile forehead, and by chain-smoking cigarettes as he appraised the world with a wary, feline gaze. This was not Sam Spade versus Joel Cairo. As an actor, Humphrey was continually outpointed by the devious Peter. All he could do was rely on dialogue to strengthen his position. "You despise me, don't you?" asks Ugarte. "Well," Rick responds, "if I gave you any thought, I probably would."

As able as Lorre was, he had no idea what

Casablanca would mean to him profession-ally. Since he got only a few weeks' work before his character was knocked off by the Germans, he regarded the role of Ugarte as just another job — worth doing, but not worth exalting. He clowned around the set, taking a mischievous joy in hiding an eye-dropper full of water and releasing a single bead on Curtiz's cigarette when the direc-tor looked the other way. Otherwise he could be abstracted and asocial. Only a few people knew the reason why. In earlier years he had suffered from acute gallbladder problems. Morphine was prescribed, and in a situation eerily similar to Belmont Bo-gart's, he'd gotten hooked.

Whatever their strengths or shortcomings, Lorre, Bergman, Henreid, Rains, Green-street, Veidt, Kinskey, Dalio, Sakall, and almost all the others shared one characteris-tic, and it gave *Casablanca* an authenticity and texture no scriptwriter could have provided. They all had European or English accents. They knew the mind-set of the refugees; they *were* those refugees — except that they happened to be the fortunate ones who ended up in the movie business. Rick was supposed to be American and sound American. So was the club's African Ameri-can piano player, Sam (Dooley Wilson). But among the other key players only the heavy-weight doorman Dan Seymour and seventeen-year-old Joy Page (not coincidentally Jack Warner's stepdaughter) were born in the United States, and both were encouraged to speak with foreign intonations. Page played a young Bulgarian whose husband (Helmut Dantine, another Viennese refugee) keeps losing at roulette. Her virtue is at stake; they need money to purchase a contraband visa. Captain Renault might help — if she trades her body for his good-will.

Rick's interventions save her, even as he maintains, "I stick my neck out for nobody." Koch and the Epsteins understood that Rick had to show the public a Sam Spade–like façade: hard-nosed, indifferent to women, and resistant to authority. They also knew that the attitude had to be a carapace. It was meant to cover the psychic injuries of a decent man trying to forget the past. And so, in a scene between Captain Renault and Rick, the café owner's credentials pass in review. As it develops, Rick not only aided the troops fighting Mussolini's Italian troops in Africa, he also showed up in the losing cause against Francisco Franco, the fascist leader whose soldiers won the Spanish Civil War. "I happen to be familiar with your record," states Renault. He points out that in 1935, Rick ran guns to Ethiopia. The following year he fought in Spain on the Loyalist side. Cornered by facts, Rick retreats to his customary cynicism: he was amply compensated on both occasions.

Hints and innuendos haunt the script. The days when Ilsa and Rick carried on in Paris could not be made explicit in 1942. Flashbacks show the young widow, whose husband has recently perished. She drives through the city with her new amour, Ilsa radiant, Rick lighthearted. They toast each other with champagne, and Bogart utters yet another immortal line: "Here's looking at you, kid." Plans to go away together are enthusiastically made — but she never shows up at the railroad station. Sam brings a message. Her "Dear Richard" is fraught with pain and mystery: "I cannot go with you or ever see you again. You must not ask why." Humphrey was formidably equipped to play this kind of scene; and his agonized response needed no lines of dialogue to put it across. Rick and Sam go off to North Africa, leaving Ilsa forever. Or so they think, until one evening, "of all the gin joints in all the towns in all the world" she walks into Rick's Café Américain with Victor Laszlo, the husband she thought she had lost. The recriminations begin.

Save for the exotic locale and wartime circumstances, this was the classic woman-forced-to-choose-between-two-men situation. Moviegoers had seen it a hundred times. If *Casablanca* was different it was because three elements separated the film from all the previous romances.

First, *Casablanca* was laced with compelling subplots. There were contretemps between the refugees; Ugarte holding letters of transit guaranteeing safe passages out of Casablanca for four people, hiding them with Rick before being slain; Rick's ex-lover Yvonne (Madeleine Lebeau, and Mrs. Marcel Dalio in real life) dating German officers; Nazis singing the German national anthem, drowned out by French patriots singing "La Marseillaise"; members of the Third Reich closing in on the French underground; Rick's place closed down by Captain Renault on order from his German masters because Laszlo has awakened the patriotism of the clientele.

The second element was the dialogue. At this point in history, almost every line had significance. The smallest parts gave actors a chance to glow, if only for a moment. An elderly couple pathetically attempt to learn English so that they can get on in an unattainable America. The man asks his wife, "*Liebchen,* sweetnessheart, what watch?" She consults her timepiece. "Ten watch." Carl diplomatically assures them that they'll get on in the New World.

An imperious patron wants Rick to join his table. After all, he boasts, he once ran the second-largest banking house in Amsterdam. Carl is unimpressed. The banker who ran the *largest* house in Amsterdam is now Rick's pastry chef. Carl displays a cynical realism no matter who he addresses. Ordered to give the best table to Major Strasser, for example, he informs Captain Renault that he has already done so; the major is a German and would have grabbed it anyway.

The principals have the most memorable exchanges, phrases that have entered the world's lexicon of favorite movie quotes. Major Strasser tells Captain Renault to close Rick's café. On what grounds? Rick demands. Renault gets on his high horse: he is "shocked, shocked" to find that illegal betting is taking place on these very grounds. Whereupon a croupier hands the captain a sheaf of francs — his winnings from the night before.

Captain Renault admonishes Rick not to be so offhanded with a beautiful French *femme du monde:* women should not be thrown away like that; one day they may be scarce.

Almost all the classic quotes are uttered or prompted by Rick, and Humphrey gave them a unique tempo and authority. Asked how he has ended up in Casablanca, he explains that he came for the waters. Renault points out that they're in the desert. Rick drily replies that he was "misinformed."

Rick mentions the invasion of Paris, when he and Ilsa watch the invading soldiers from an apartment window. The Germans wore gray, Rick reminds Ilsa; she wore blue.

Rick's selfless gift — Ugarte's passages of safety turned over to Laszlo and the beloved Ilsa — is expressed in tight-lipped remarks to the beautiful lady. He's never been good at striking a noble pose. The facts are simple and stark: the problems of three people don't amount to much when the world is aflame. Ilsa's too young to understand what he's doing, but someday it'll all be clear to her. He wipes away her tears with the now-familiar salute: "Now, now, here's looking at you, kid."

The final lines are, of course, legend, but they did not come easily. Script revisions had been handed to the actors on an almost daily basis. Everyone was edgy, particularly Bergman. The most ungainly expository dialogue was assigned to her: "Oh, Victor, please don't go to the underground meeting tonight." So was the most cloying romantic line: "Was that cannon fire, or is it my heart pounding?" Moreover, as the last weeks approached, *Casablanca* still had no ending. "Every day we were shooting off the cuff," Ingrid was to remember, "and we were trying to make some sense of it. No one knew where the picture was going and no one knew how it was going to end, which didn't help any of us with our characterizations. And all the time I wanted to know who I was supposed to be in love with, Paul Henreid or Humphrey Bogart." Beseeching Curtiz, she was told, "We don't know yet — just play it, well . . . in between." That did little to calm her mind. "I didn't dare to look at Humphrey Bogart with love because then I had to look at Paul Henreid with something that was not love." Her situation was unwittingly stated in an exchange between Ilsa and Rick, when she tries to explain where she's been since they parted in Paris.

She hesitates, scarcely knowing how to begin the autobiography and unsure of its finale. Rick tells Ilsa to say whatever's on her mind; perhaps an ending will come to her as she goes along.

Once the triangle was worked out, there remained the problem of locale. Curtiz, the Epsteins, and Koch knew very well that Casablanca is an arid region with an absence of heavy mists. They also knew that when a movie is subject to budget constraints and a firm deadline, the first casualty is truth. The atmosphere was made murky so that a jerry-built wooden simulacrum of a plane — the aircraft that would spirit the Lazlos away — could be indistinctly revealed in the background. Even then, the set was so shallow that airport mechanics had to be played by midgets to trick the eye and add perspective, thanks yet again to the camerawork of Arthur Edeson. On orders from Wallis, Edeson had supplied the "real blacks and whites, with the walls and backgrounds in shadow and dim, sketchy lighting."

Every other aspect of the film inexplicably fell into place. Even the most negative Hollywood personalities helped, no matter how inadvertently, to improve the film. Joseph Breen, head of the Motion Picture Producers and Distributors Association, was well-known for his censorious view of risqué material. He read a pivotal scene in which Ilsa confronts Rick with a pistol, demanding the letters of transit. Breen put his order in the form of a suggestion: "The present material seems to contain a suggestion of a sex affair which would be unacceptable if it came through in the finished picture. We believe this could possibly be corrected by replacing the fadeout with a dissolve, and shooting the succeeding scene without any sign of a bed or couch, or anything whatever suggestive of a sex affair." His wishes were carried out, and the dissolve not only sped up the narrative, it made the confrontation *more* suggestive rather than less.

Max Steiner was brought in to write the stirring music for *Casablanca,* and he didn't think much of the song "As Time Goes By." Classically trained under Gustav Mahler, he felt, not unreasonably, that its composer-lyricist, Herman Hupfeld, was a hack who specialized in novelty numbers like "When Yuba Plays the Rhumba on the Tuba." Besides, "As Time Goes By" was already eleven years old, having been featured in an insignificant Broadway show called *Everybody's Welcome.* Rudy Vallee's recording had enjoyed a brief vogue and then disappeared from stores. But the melody and rhymes had not disappeared from the memory of Murray Burnett, who heard them as a college student and quoted Hupfeld's lyrics in *Everybody Comes to Rick's*. Much had been changed since then, yet somehow the song remained, and Dooley Wilson gave it elegance and style. Steiner argued for reshooting the scenes with "As Time Goes By," getting rid of the thing for good. But by this time Ingrid Bergman had been cast in *For Whom the Bell Tolls*, and her hair had been cropped for the role of the innocent Spanish girl Maria. There was nothing Steiner could do except use his considerable expertise. With canny orchestrations, he turned the tune into an integral part of the drama. It had a sad and haunting eroticism, but the words

It's still the same old story
A fight for love and glory

also gave it a wartime significance. Using the melody underneath the last farewell, Steiner provided an operatic tone to Humphrey's sacrificial speech, and suddenly the problems of three people in *Casablanca* didn't seem so little after all.

In the years to follow, a great deal was written about the fortunate accidents that made the film jell. All sort of arguments ensued: Was *Casablanca* the ultimate refutation of the auteur theory — that movies are the quintessence of the director's personality and aesthetic? Or was it merely an exception to the rule? Was the script the work of a committee, rather than the two men who got the credit? Did Warner Bros. get lucky with this one, or was Jack Warner just pretending to be indifferent, pulling the strings all along?

But when it came time to discuss the acting, there was no dispute at all. No one would ever refer to *Casablanca* as an Ingrid Bergman picture or a Paul Henreid picture, or for that matter a Michael Curtiz picture. It was, and would remain, a Humphrey Bogart movie because he was the one who furnished the work with a moral center. There was no other player who could have so credibly inhabited the role of Rick Blaine, expatriate, misanthrope, habitual drinker, and, ultimately, the most self-sacrificing, most romantic Hollywood hero of the war years. To watch him in this extraordinary feature was not only to see a character rise to the occasion. It was to see a performer mature, to become the kind of man American males yearned to be. When Humphrey Bogart started filming *Casablanca* on May 25, 1942, he was a star without stature;

when he finished, on August 1, he was the most important American film actor of his time and place.

V

All through 1942, war news meant bad news: General Rommel's Afrika Korps penetrated deep into Egypt, threatening Cairo, Alexandria, and, most vitally, the Suez Canal. German U-boats sank some nine hundred Allied vessels, severely weakening the supply line to Britain. Singapore, Burma, and the Philippines fell to the Japanese. And then, on November 8, a tidal change began as Allied forces invaded North Africa. A week later Casablanca was theirs. The exotic city made headlines all over the world; the biggest public relations break in cinema history had fallen into Jack Warner's lap. His New York office jumped at the opportunity with all the wrong ideas. They suggested tacking on a hearty new ending for *Casablanca:* how about U.S. soldiers crushing the Nazi occupiers? Humphrey Bogart was still on hand for retakes; there was talk of flying Claude Rains from his Pennsylvania farm. Jack mulled it over, then sent a wire: "It's such a great picture as it is, would be a misrepresentation if we were to come in now with a small scene about American troops landing etcetera . . . the longer we wait to release it the less important the title will be." At this time, an unlikely fan climbed into Humphrey's corner. Hedda Hopper, one of the most feared journalists in town, had begun as a film actress. After more than a hundred movies, she failed to become a star, quit the silent screen, and became a gossip columnist. She grew famous for her flamboyant hats, her feud with archrival columnist Louella Parsons, her right-wing politics, and her vindictive personality. Zasu Pitts compared her to a ferret, and Joan Fontaine once sent Hopper a live skunk. The note read: "I stink and so do you." Yet for some reason Hedda had taken a shine to Humphrey, overlooking his liberal views, pushing his career, and writing kind words about him. After viewing *Casablanca* she asked him how he felt about being on the level after all those years of crime. " 'It's all right with me, Hedda,' " he said. " 'I take 'em as they come. I just work here, you know.' Then I asked him if he'd ever turned down a part because it was too small or for any other reason.

" 'Somebody once asked my pal [character actor] George Tobias that same question,' said Bogie, 'and George said, "There are no

small parts, there are only small actors."
Well, that goes for me, too.' "

There was some public relations swagger
to that statement, but not much. Humphrey
enjoyed the status and the money that came
with stardom. But he also admired the tradi-
tions of the West End, where British actors
had no compunction about taking small
parts as well as major roles. He thought it a
pity that American leading men were forced
to turn down pictures with lower budgets
or shorter speeches or less notable co-stars
than their previous movies.

At the same time, he did nothing to
discourage the Warners publicity department from burnishing his hard-boiled image. Humphrey was amused rather than appalled by *American* magazine's transparently
bogus profile "Hollywood's Trigger Man."
It included a letter, allegedly sent from a
man behind bars. " 'Dear Humph,' penned
an anxious inmate of a Southern prison
recently; 'I have a little problem. Next
month I'm walking the last mile to the hot
seat. You've been there so many times
yourself. I wonder if you'd write me a word-
picture of what it's like?' "

Such items were meant to help the Bogart
cause, but the real buzz began when *Casablanca* debuted on Thanksgiving Day 1942.

Most of the reviews glowed with praise, though several had acerbic things to say; *Time* observed that Humphrey looked like Buster Keaton playing Paul Gauguin. Not that the negatives mattered, because yet another public relations bonanza lay straight ahead. From January 14 to January 24, 1943, a secret meeting took place between President Franklin D. Roosevelt and British prime minister Winston Churchill. It was held in Casablanca. No sitting president had ever been to Africa, nor had any American chief executive left the country during a time of war. This was a historic event, deliberately kept from the press until both leaders had safely returned home. The following week *Casablanca* went on national release, accompanied by headlines like BULLETS, MYSTERY, SECRECY, AND CENSORSHIP PLAGUED REPORTERS OF CASABLANCA CONFERENCE. *Film Daily* excitedly predicted that "this Warner picture should have the impact of a bombshell on film audiences of the country." The trade paper was correct; the news items were invaluable. Made at a cost of $1,309,000, the movie grossed almost three times that amount in its initial run, riding the waves of national optimism about the war. Earlier in the year, defeat was in the air. By the first months of 1943, battles had gone to the Allies in North Africa, Stalingrad, Guadalcanal. It was, in Churchill's words, perhaps not the beginning of the end, but the end of the beginning. Now, Rick Blaine was not just the fulcrum of a melodramatic movie. He was a symbol of the nation itself, at first wary and isolationist, then changing incrementally until he headed in the opposite direction. At the finale Rick Blaine had turned into a warrior. That was the way moviegoers, especially male moviegoers, saw themselves in 1943. That year they did the most unlikely, and unrepeatable thing in the history of American cinema. They made *Casablanca* a smash, which was not unexpected. But they also made the middle-aged, creased, scarred, lisping Humphrey Bogart into a superstar. No one expected that. Not even Humphrey Bogart. Especially not Humphrey Bogart.

CHAPTER 4
BOGART CAN BE TOUGH
WITHOUT A GUN

I

MGM star Clark Gable volunteered for military service; so did Twentieth Century Fox's leading man Tyrone Power, Columbia's James Stewart, and many other prominent actors. It would not do to have Warner Bros. looked upon as the slacker studio. In the early 1940s masculinity was defined by the appearances of men in uniform. Those who couldn't make the grade were defined as lacking in virility or, worse, in patriotism. And so its current mainstays, swashbuckler Errol Flynn (4-F because of a heart irregularity) and leathery Humphrey Bogart (overage) were assigned to war pictures that dealt with heroism under fire. In the process, they gave masculinity a face, and the screenwriters furnished it with a narrative. Flynn outdid himself in films like *Desperate Journey,* in which the hero outwits the German army — "The iron fist has a glass jaw!"

— steals a bomber, and safely lands in England. No time to rest, though; his exit line is "Now to Australia, and a crack at those Japs!"

Action in the North Atlantic, Humphrey's newest picture, had fewer comic-book episodes. But the star had to wrestle with a plodding script by John Howard Lawson, punched up with additional dialogue by W. R. Burnett. In the end, the film essentially relied on Bogart as the resolute, sacrificial male of the war years. A real soldier or sailor, enlisted man or officer, did his griping and then got on with the job. If he got wounded, if he died, he did so not for some patriotism with a capital *P,* but because he didn't want to let the team down, whether that team was a squad of GIs or a boatload of matériel. Humphrey perfectly embodied this weary but intrepid fighting spirit.

The movie was about the Murmansk run, a strategy that sent Allied convoys up the dangerous coast of Norway, bringing armaments to the Soviet Union. Lawson belonged to a Hollywood cell of the Communist Party and liked to address his fellow members on the value of propaganda. *Esquire*'s film critic had been a member of the Hollywood Anti-Nazi League; he remembered the Party line as articulated by Lawson: "As a writer try to get five minutes of the Communist doctrine . . . in every script you write. If you can, make the message come from the mouth of Gary Cooper or some other important star who is unaware of what he is saying; by the time it is discovered he is in New York and a great deal of expense will be involved to bring him back and reshoot the scene." Lawson showed the way with *Action in the North Atlantic.*

The first part fulfilled the promise of its title, with vivid battle scenes and colorful personalities. The *North Star,* one of the convoy's largest ships, is torpedoed by a Nazi submarine. The by-the-book captain (Raymond Massey), his easygoing first officer (Humphrey), and a cross-section-of-America crew — O'Hara, Pulaski, and Abrams (Alan Hale, Dane Clark, and Sam Levene) — survive by clinging to a lifeboat and navigating through heavy seas. Rescued by the navy, they spend a brief holiday stateside, where Humphrey falls in love with a nightclub singer (Julie Bishop) and impulsively marries her before shipping out for another run to the USSR.

The second part also featured explosions and shoot-outs with the enemy. Some of them were so graphic that stunt men were brought in to do the long-distance sequences of fire and explosions at sea. As they watched from the sidelines, Massey needled his colleague: "My double is braver than yours." Humphrey rose to the bait: "He is like hell. My double is the bravest double there is." The verbal war escalated until both actors decided to outperform each other by doing their own stunts. They got too near the heat: the Massey trousers caught fire, and the Bogart eyebrows were badly singed. "The horrified reaction we got from the director and producer made it worthwhile," Massey impishly recalled. "If Humphrey had gotten hurt it would have cost Warners millions."

It was at the end that agitprop made a cameo appearance. With the captain severely wounded, the first officer takes charge, outwitting the maneuvers of a German submarine. Fighter planes appear overhead. Are they German? No, says a crewman, as he spots the red star on a fuselage: "They're ours all right! Russian planes off the starboard quarter!" As the Americans safely dock in Murmansk, grateful Soviet troops warmly embrace their allies. They don't speak English, but Alan Hale has picked up a little Russian. He explains, "Tovarich? That means friend!" Harmless enough, but untrue; in fact there had been no contact between the Allied sailors and the Soviets, except for a few carefully managed photo opportunities for propaganda purposes.

None of this mattered much in 1943; after all, the USSR was a key U.S. ally in the fight against Nazi Germany. In the same year, *Life* magazine's Russian issue described the Soviets as "one hell of a people" and Stalin's secret police, the NKVD, as merely "a national police similar to the FBI," whose job was "tracking traitors." And Warners proudly produced *Mission to Moscow*. Like the naïve book on which it was based, the film treated the Soviet invasion of Finland and Poland as "self-defense," explained Stalin's lethal purge trials as an attempt to get rid of Trotskyite fifth columnists, and romanticized the commissars as benign leaders of a happy and well-fed populace. In *Time,* James Agee said the movie was "almost describable as the first Soviet production to come from a major American studio . . . a great, glad, two-million-dollar bowl of canned borscht."

It would all matter very much in a few years, though, and even now a New Jersey congressman named J. Parnell Thomas was making plans to investigate Hollywood's leftist writers and directors. During a 1938 investigation of the Federal Theater Project, the rising Republican star had made his position clear: "Practically every play presented under the auspices of the Project is sheer propaganda for Communism or the New Deal" — two groups he found virtually synonymous. Worse, in Thomas's opinion, was the leftist dogma of too many Hollywood films. He would be quiet during the war, but his time was coming. Those on his wrong side would pay a price for their political views, and Humphrey Bogart would be swept along with them.

II

After *Action,* Humphrey went on loan to Columbia for *Sahara,* another war film written by Lawson. This one was derived from a 1937 Russian film, *The Thirteen,* about intrepid Red Army soldiers hounded across the Gobi Desert by Royalist White Army troops. Lawson turned it into a tale of an American tank crew in Libya pursued by ruthless Germans (played, for the most part, by members of the U.S. Army's Fourth Armored Division, deployed to the Mojave Desert for a month). Substituting for the Sahara was an arid region in California just north of the Mexican border. It was familiar turf to filmmakers; some twenty-two years before, Rudolph Valentino had crossed the same sands to woo an English maiden in *The Sheik*. The cast of *Sahara* stopped at a tourist hotel in the small town of Brawley, where there was nothing for most of them to do at night but imbibe adult beverages. Mayo Methot stayed with Humphrey, so in his case quarreling was added to drinking; the Battling Bogarts were at it again.

During the day Humphrey was Sergeant Joe Gunn, tank commander. The sarge is in charge of a one-world crew, including a Sudanese NCO (Rex Ingram), an Italian prisoner of war (J. Carroll Naish), a downed enemy pilot (Kurt Krueger), and several Americans (Bruce Bennett, Dan Duryea, Lloyd Bridges). For Duryea, the role was a rare break from his long list of villains. *Sahara,* he recalled, was "a picture which practically nobody remembers my being in; one of the few pictures I didn't play a heel and maybe for that reason."

But people remembered Humphrey in that picture. If he was too old for the role of a wartime noncom, no one noticed it. Asked where he hails from, Sergeant Gunn replies, "No place, just the army," and no one doubted it. When he outwitted the thirst-crazed Germans, after taking some severe losses, the victory rang true. Still, off-screen, the time was far from happy. Humphrey's relationship with fellow actors was convivial enough; in retrospect Kurt Krueger said he "couldn't have been more outgoing." The German refugee also recalled one of the few pleasant conversations with Mayo ever recorded. One morning the two shared a ride from the hotel to the location. Mayo cradled a thermos in her lap, and Krueger asked her why she was bringing coffee when there was always a pot brewing on the set. She responded with a loud peal of laughter. "Coffee? Hell no! Bogie needs his ice-cold Martinis."

Because *Sahara* was an all-male film, Mayo had no reason to be jealous of Humphrey's current project. She was argumentative by nature, however, and held her alcohol badly. Night after night she lit into Humphrey, sometimes for no reason at all; he seemed to set her off merely by being present. Many evenings, those on the same floor of the hotel heard the sound of broken glass and the crash of furniture. Humphrey's disposition was not sweetened by a break in filming, when he was assigned to appear in Warners' narcissistic, studio-plugging *Thank Your Lucky Stars.* The documentary was shot in Burbank, and the time away from the desert should have provided some surcease from the heat, and from Mayo's tantrums. But while the movie appeared to acknowledge Humphrey's star status, it actually served to humiliate him. He and S. Z. Sakall, the jowly waiter in *Casablanca,* perform a skit in which he snarls: "I'm talking to you, Fatso," but shrinks from a fight when Sakall calls him a chiseler and shoves him away. An onlooker comments, "Let the old man bulldoze you, eh?" Humphrey grumbles, "Yes, that ain't like me. Gee, I hope none of my movie fans hear about this." The sound track plays the Disney song "Who's Afraid of the Big Bad Wolf?" as Humphrey turns up his collar and slinks off. In his study of New York leading men, *City Boys,* historian Robert Sklar rightly concludes that "Warner Bros. wanted a Bogart who could be bulldozed."

Back on the set, Humphrey tried hard to maintain professional standards, but on certain mornings he was manifestly hungover and unprepared. On those occasions he would pick a fight with *Sahara* director Zoltan Korda, complaining about the dialogue he was required to speak. After the filming was done Korda, who liked to maintain cordial relationships with his cast, complained about Humphrey's behavior to Bruce Bennett. "Don't you realize what was going on?" Bennett inquired. "He was learning his *lines*."

Some of his best lines from that time were unscripted and unfilmed. Mayo had no problems with the *Sahara* personnel, but thought Humphrey might be seeing someone when he wasn't on the set. She decided to hire a private eye. That worthy shadowed her husband for several days — apparently with the ineptitude of a Wilmer Cook. Humphrey spotted the shamus early on, guessed that he worked for the biggest detective agency in Los Angeles, called the office, and left a message: "Hello, this is Humphrey Bogart. You got a man on my tail. Would you check with him and find out where I am?"

When the Bogarts returned to Hollywood, Humphrey hosted a dinner for the film's military adviser, Colonel Reinicke, and his wife, as well as for several other officers and their wives. It took place at a Hollywood restaurant, and all went well over cocktails. As the meal progressed, though, Mayo got redder and redder. Without any warning she turned on her husband: "Goddam 4-F shirking bastard!" Humphrey tried to quiet her. "Don't tell me to shut up, you neutral 4-F creep!" she yelled, and ran off. Embarrassed but game, Humphrey invited the guests back to his house for a nightcap. As they entered he advised them, "Mayo is here somewhere. If you say anything about her make it complimentary. She'll come out in due time." The Marines followed orders, loudly overpraising her beauty and her wardrobe, and raving about the house. Sure enough, Mayo emerged — from behind a couch, mad drunk, grumbling and cursing until the uncomfortable guests excused themselves and headed back to base.

If *Sahara* had showcased the gritty and honorable Bogart, Warners had something else in mind for his return, assigning him the lead in *Pentacle,* eventually retitled *Conflict.* It was the story of a murder, but the central topic — the matrimonial hell at the movie's center — hit too close to home. Humphrey wanted no part of it or in it. He planned to go straight into *Passage to Marseilles,* a war movie that would reunite him with the vital center of *Casablanca,* Michael Curtiz, Sydney Greenstreet, Peter Lorre, Claude Rains, and Helmut Dantine. The news went around Warners in an hour: Humphrey refused to appear in *Conflict.* Jack Warner was in no mood to argue; he had made Bogart, and by God he could break him. He roared, he pressured, he cajoled; one telegram read DEAR HUM-

191

PHREY, YOU MUST REMEMBER THIS; AM DEPENDING ON YOU AS THE REGULAR GUY YOU ARE. Nothing worked. Humphrey remained adamant: "I'm sorry, Jack," he told his boss, "I just can't do it." Humphrey's agent, Sam Jaffe, intervened, begging him to do just this one picture as a personal favor. The answer was no. He remained inflexible, and might well have gone on suspension or lost the starring role in *Passage to Marseilles* to Jean Gabin. Warner was planning to carry out one threat or the other. But on June 3, 1943, just as he was about to take action, the *New York Times* carried a tragic announcement: NAZIS HIT AIRLINE; LESLIE HOWARD AMONG 17 MISSING.

The British actor had been on a goodwill tour of Portugal and Spain, sent there by his government in hopes of persuading English-speaking citizens of the neutral nations to aid Britain in its hour of need. Perhaps he had also been gathering intelligence; 10 Downing Street had no comment. It was Howard's misfortune to catch a flight on the *Ibis,* an unarmed BOAC carrier, on the very day that Winston Churchill was also returning to London. German spies learned of the prime minister's journey, but didn't know which plane he had boarded. A Luftwaffe squadron was taking no chances. Two hundred miles off the coast of Spain, the German planes shot down the undefended *Ibis* in cold blood. Speculation about the passengers' last few seconds was Topic A the next day. The *New York Times* confirmed the rumors: "It was believed in London that the Nazi raiders had attacked on the outside chance that the Prime Minister might be among the passengers."

The fatal case of mistaken identity sent chills through the country and traumatized Hollywood. The stuff of spy pictures turned out to be all too real. Humphrey hadn't been in touch with Howard for quite a while; both actors were burdened by crammed schedules. Yet the man who had been responsible for his first big break was never far from Humphrey's mind and the loss was irreparable. The starch went out of him. Demoralized and melancholy, he let Warner know that he would do *Conflict* after all. What the hell; life was too short to make a federal case out of a lousy movie.

III

Humphrey and Mayo made a point of telling everyone on the set of *Conflict* that they had just passed their fifth wedding anniversary. The Bogarts showed Alexis Smith,

Sydney Greenstreet, and other cast members the anniversary presents they had given each other: a hand-carved chess set and monogrammed board for Humphrey, gold earrings for Mayo. The celebration was for display purposes only; there had been no lull in the Bogarts' conjugal war.

Humphrey had quietly begun to seek the company of other women, including his ex-wife Helen Menken and his personal hairdresser, a spirited little brunette named Verita Thompson. In her memoir, *Bogie and Me,* Thompson writes of their lengthy affair. Her marriage was also unhappy, but Thompson's husband was conveniently away in the service, and they would meet at her place in Burbank. "Often he'd spend the night," she recalled, "usually leaving for the studio at around five in the morning." Those were the occasions when Mayo "had driven him from the house with a barrage of bottles, dishes, pots and pans, and drunken screams." Clearly Mayo had descended from alcoholism and neuroses into full-time instability. Humphrey had seen mental illness up close, in his mother's long-ago summer outbursts and in his sister's unshakeable postpartum depression. It reminded him of bad times, and he backed away. Rationalizing his conduct, he told a friend, "My wife is an actress. She's a clever actress. It just so happens she's not working right now. When an actress isn't working she's got to have scenes to play. And I've got to give her cues." Mayo may have been beyond ordinary therapy by this time; in any case she never received the psychiatric counsel she needed and the marriage rapidly headed for its final, fatal crash.

Meantime, there was one last war movie to be made. If ever there was proof of Thomas Wolfe's warning that you can't go home again, it was *Passage to Marseille.* The film was based on the novel *Men Without Country* by Charles Nordoff and James Norman Hall, best-selling authors of *Mutiny on the Bounty.* Encouraged by the Warners front office, screenwriters Casey Robinson and Jack Moffitt attempted to produce a Gallic version of Rick Blaine. In *Passage,* Humphrey plays Jean Matrac, a French newspaper editor framed for a murder he didn't commit. Railroaded to Devil's Island, he shares a room with other prisoners, among them Lorre and Dantine. Each man has a tale to tell, and so begins the ungainly narrative, with flashbacks, flashbacks within flashbacks, and flashbacks within *those* flashbacks. Though Matrac is initially as cynical as Rick Blaine, he evolves into a patriot, challenges a Nazi sympathizer (Greenstreet), makes his escape, and joins the Free French air force. Warner Bros. had always been known for violent, over-the-top scenes; toward the end, Matrac has an under-the-bottom confrontation. He trains his machine gun on a group of German airmen, just as they wave their hands in a gesture of surrender. He pulls the trigger and kills every one of them. This was more than propaganda; it was a war crime, and the footage was excised when *Passage* was shown in European movie houses. Moreover, in *Casablanca* the audience never knows what's going to happen to Rick; in *Passage,* they see Jean die in a bombing raid. What had begun as a terse, intriguing drama got weighed down with backstories, moral compromises, and an end that might have come from a World Federalist pamphlet. A letter from the deceased Jean Matrac begins: "My dear son, today you are five years old and your father has never seen you. But some day, in a better world, he will." The missive goes on to envision a future "where youth may love without fear, and where parents may grow old with their children, and where men will be worthy of each other's faith."

Somehow Humphrey got through this

weighty, studio-bound film. There were times when he reeked of liquor early in the morning, but he never called in sick and frequently managed to give a good performance on the very first take. About the only joy he had while filming was conspiring with his drinking buddy Peter Lorre. As Curtiz prepared a scene, Humphrey would launch into a long and pointless story. The director paid him no mind and called for action. Dissatisfied with the result, he would have to reshoot. At this point, Peter would tell his own long, unfunny joke. Again Curtiz would film, and again the scene would turn out badly. It took him, said Peter, "about two days to find out that whenever he laughed he got the scene in one take and whenever he didn't laugh he didn't get a take. Two mornings later, Bogie and I, two staggering little figures, arrived on the big set. Mike saw us a block away and he started laughing like crazy in advance."

By the time *Passage* was finished, late in 1943, the tide of battle had turned and the Allies were on their way to the victory that Roosevelt and Churchill had planned for the previous year. Rommel's troops were in retreat, Italy had surrendered, the Allies had bombed Hamburg and the Ploesti oil fields in Romania. The invasion of France could not be far off. Warners delayed the release of the film, hoping that American troops would occupy Marseilles en route to the liberation of Paris — thereby giving the studio a repeat of the public relations coup they had enjoyed with *Casablanca*. With Humphrey's next picture still in preparation, the Bogarts signed up for an eleven-week USO tour of North Africa and Italy. Accompanied only by Don Cummings, a freelance actor with time on his hands, and Ralph Hark, an accordion player, the self-designated "Filthy Four" had no set act; they made it up as they went along. Humphrey played the tough guy for battle-weary GIs, quoting passages from his early films. Accompanied by Hark, the soldiers sang choruses of "As Time Goes By" and Mayo reprised "Without a Song," a number she had sung in a 1929 Broadway musical, as well as a few tunes from the current hit parade.

When they were not performing, Mayo and Humphrey visited hospitals, attempting to buck up the severely wounded. Perhaps the most difficult moment came when Humphrey stopped by the bed of a triple amputee. As a nurse took down his words, the young soldier dictated a letter to his fiancée. He wondered aloud whether he should tell her he had lost both legs and an arm. Humphrey broke in: "It's not going to make any difference to her," he said with the assurance of an actor playing a key scene. "She loves you, and the only thing that matters is that you come home." He moved on before the kid could see the tears brimming in his eyes.

The Battling Bogarts behaved themselves until they arrived in Naples. After one performance, some enlisted men in the audience presented the entertainers with souvenir guns. Humphrey and Mayo thanked them, hoisted a few glasses, and went to their suite on the top floor of a building reserved for high-ranking officers. Both the weapons and the Bogarts were loaded, and as soon as they entered, Humphrey and Mayo began to shoot bullets into the ceiling. The crashes of plaster were almost as loud as the shots. Alarmed, a group of senior officers rushed to the room and confiscated the weapons then and there.

"Name, rank, and serial number," demanded a red-faced colonel.

"Got no name, rank, and serial number," Humphrey snarled. "And go to hell!"

Hauled before a group of senior officials the next day, Humphrey was compelled to apologize for his behavior and remarks.

"I didn't mean to insult the uniform," he told the offended colonel. "I just meant to insult you."

It was definitely time to return to the business of making movies.

The Bogarts landed in New York, where they intended to hang out for a couple of weeks. Humphrey wanted to revisit scenes of his boyhood, catch a few shows, maybe party with a few old friends. Jack Warner was having none of it. He wanted his star back out west, and he wanted him now. Once again, Humphrey capitulated. He and Mayo caught the 20th Century Limited, switched to the Santa Fe Chief in Chicago, and showed up in Los Angeles two days later. Reporters awaited. Mayo spoke in glowing terms about the GIs, and Humphrey said there were no heroes out there, just good men doing dirty jobs under harsh conditions. Then he went off to face Jack Warner.

It could have been worse. The boss was full of equanimity now that his champion was back in the stable. For the first time, Humphrey had been nominated for an Academy Award, cited as Best Actor for his work in *Casablanca*. Moreover, a poll of theater owners had just placed him among the top box office stars. His new picture would be *To Have and Have Not,* based on Ernest Hemingway's novel and with a script by the novelist William Faulkner, then drinking hard and down on his luck, and Jules Furthman, who had received an Academy Award nomination for his adaptation of *Mutiny on the Bounty.* Howard Hawks would direct. A veteran of World War I, former tennis champion and racing car driver, Hawks was another "man's man." Humphrey had an idea they would get along. He also liked the roster of character actors who would join him, including Walter Brennan, Hoagy Carmichael, and Marcel Dalio and Dan Seymour, who had been with him in *Casablanca.* But when he was told about the female lead he expressed discomfort. Her name was Lauren Bacall and she was nineteen years old. Humphrey was forty-four. What was Hawks thinking of? How would a cradle robber look on the big screen?

IV

She was a Brooklynite, born Betty Joan Ann Perske, the only daughter of William and Natalie Perske. The marriage was troubled, and by Betty's sixth birthday her parents had separated. William's visits were intermittent, and finally ceased altogether. After the divorce Natalie took the surname Bacal, a shortened version of her maiden name, Weinstein-Bacal — "wineglass" in German. The child also assumed the name. With no money coming in from William, Natalie went back to work as a secretary. But this presented a new problem. Betty was a bright, spunky girl, and needed someone to look after her until her mother came home. No one Natalie interviewed seemed dependable enough. With financial aid from two brothers, both attorneys, the divorcée sent Betty to Highland Manor, a private grade school in Tarrytown, New York, about an hour from the city.

When Betty graduated, she moved in with her maternal grandmother and entered Julia Richman, a high school on the East Side of Manhattan. She was restive and unhappy there — but she was a good test taker, and highly motivated. The sixteen-year-old had also developed into something of a beauty; after graduation she decided to seek a career on the stage. Her uncles paid for a year's tuition at the American Academy of Dramatic Arts, where Betty impressed the faculty and her fellow students, among them another Jewish actor who would soon change his name from Issur Danielovich to Kirk Douglas. Betty was invited back for a second year, but by then the money had run out, and in 1941 no scholarships were provided for women. Disappointed but unbowed, she tried her hand at modeling. After hearing "Bacal" repeatedly pronounced as if it rhymed with "cackle," she added another "l" and became Bacall. The new spelling seemed to bring her luck and a lot of new assignments. But wearing designer clothes did not accord with Betty's ambitious career plans. She abandoned the runway and took a salary cut to become a Broadway theater usher. It only paid eight dollars a week, but allowed her to see shows and performers for free, and pick up some new acting techniques along the way.

George Jean Nathan, a drama reviewer with a sharp eye for feminine pulchritude, mentioned her in his *Esquire* column as "the prettiest usher" in town. The praise was welcome, but Nathan never mentioned Betty's name because he never bothered to speak to her. Critics would not see the Bacall name in print until her walk-on in *Johnny 2 X 4,* a Broadway play that closed after sixty-five performances. She went to a lot of open calls over the next two months, received no offers, and went back to modeling. Diana Vreeland, the fashion editor for *Harper's Bazaar,* liked Betty Bacall's affect, used her to showcase new dresses and suits, and put her on the magazine's cover in January 1943. The model was posed before a Red Cross office wearing a blue suit and knitted cap, her eyes defiantly staring at the camera. The photo caught the attention of Nancy "Slim" Hawks, the wife of Howard Hawks. In her autobiography, Slim records her first impressions of the *Harper's* photo: Bacall "was certainly my taste in beauty — scrubbed clean, healthy, shining and golden and there was definitely a bit of the panther about her."

Other studios made inquiries, as they often did when a model struck their fancy, but the only serious offer came from Howard Hawks. He paid for Betty's fare west and covered her hotel bills while she prepared for her screen test. Hawks liked what he saw; he was less pleased with what he heard. Betty's voice tended to go up in pitch when she was excited, and Hawks wanted an actress with a strong, unshakeable tone. To achieve the desired effect, Betty recited page after page of Lloyd C. Douglas's biblical epic, *The Robe,* reading it aloud in a low-pitched voice. At about the same time a young actress with more experience was attempting to correct her own tendency to speak in a high register. Riding along with her boyfriend, Desi Arnaz, Lucille Ball suddenly began to scream. Alarmed, he asked what was wrong. Nothing, she assured him. She had been instructed to lower her voice an octave or two, and Katharine Hepburn said that screaming was the best way. "Okay," responded Desi. "You scream and I'll drive." Contraltos were all the rage that season.

While Betty was acquiring a sultry voice, Slim Hawks advised her on clothing and shoes and general demeanor. Howard also changed her first name — there were enough Bettys in movies: Betty Grable, Betty Hutton, Bette Davis. Lauren had something intriguing to it, something sexy. Lauren tripped off the tongue; Lauren Bacall would stand out on marquees. When both the Hawkses were satisfied with their new protégée, Howard took Lauren to the set of *Passage to Marseilles* and introduced her to Humphrey. The meeting was pleasant but perfunctory. Contrary to legend, no steamy looks were exchanged, no suggestive remarks made. Nor did anything occur when the two ran into each other outside Howard Hawks's office. Humphrey smiled, mentioned *To Have and Have Not,* and predicted reassuringly, "We're going to have a lot of fun together." And they went their separate ways.

The screenplay of *To Have and Have Not* emerged from a dare. Hawks knew Ernest Hemingway well enough to go fishing with him in 1939. The author grumbled about film adaptations of his work, and his guest responded by calling him "a damn fool." Hawks reminded Hemingway that Hollywood movie money was just as green as New York publisher royalties. "If I make three dollars in a picture, you get one of them. I can make a picture out of your worst story." Hemingway was curious: "What's my worst story?" "That Goddamned piece of junk called *To Have and Have Not*." In a way, Hawks was right. Published in 1936, Hemingway's first novel since *A Farewell to Arms* was actually two short stories and a novella with the same characters. It featured some classic passages, but was dragged down by a self-conscious tone of social significance. For the first and last time, a Hemingway work reflected a literary fashion. In the view of those on the left, writers like Thornton Wilder were useless to the cause. In Clifford Odets's opinion, Wilder wrote "chambermaid literature." Odets amplified his position in the leftist *New Masses:* "Send us a giant who can shame our writers to their task of civilizing America. Send a soldier who has studied history. Send a strong poet who loves the masses and their future. . . . Send a Man." Hemingway attempted to be that Man in *To Have and Have Not,* and learned from the hostile criticism and slumping sales that he had failed.

"You can't make anything out of that," he told Hawks. "Yes, I can," the director insisted. "You've got the character of Harry Morgan; I think I can give you the wife. All you have to do is make a story about how they met."

Four years later it was Hawks, along with Furthman and Faulkner, who made the story, reworking plot and locale until the original was virtually unrecognizable. The central character remained Harry Morgan, skipper of a boat running between Key West and Cuba during the Great Depression. In the book, Morgan tries to make an honest living, supporting his wife and three daughters by taking sportsmen out for deep-sea fishing. But when one of them cheats him out of a large fee, he turns to the dangerous work of shipping contraband. First he runs illegal rum between Cuba and the States, and loses an arm during a shoot-out with

U.S. government agents. Then he runs Cuban revolutionaries, and dies in the process.

It would not do for a film star to lose either a limb or his life, and besides, Cuba was deemed irrelevant during World War II. The mise-en-scène was relocated to French Martinique, and the time changed from the mid-1930s to the beginning of the war. Morgan is single, and his alcoholic pal Eddie (Walter Brennan) — a serious character in the book — is played for laughs ("Ever been stung by a dead bee?").

Filming began on February 29, 1944. Mayo stopped by to check out her husband's new co-star. If she saw something special, she didn't say anything audible. After all, Lauren Bacall was only nineteen years old. Mayo was amused to see the kid's self-assurance vanish when the cameras rolled. Lauren held a cigarette in her right hand and said her first line, "Anybody got a match?" On the first two takes her hand shook so discernibly the film was useless. Encouraged by the director, she took a couple of deep breaths, said the line in a husky, commanding tone, kept her head low, and peered up at Humphrey with a heated come-hither look. Hawks thought the stare wasn't much in person, but it seemed to work on camera. Whether it would hold up throughout the movie was another matter entirely. He hoped for the best.

Two nights later, Humphrey and Mayo attended the Academy Awards ceremonies at Grauman's Chinese Theatre. For the price of ten dollars, anyone could buy a ticket at the box office. Formerly, the Oscars had been given out at a special dinner closed to the public. In 1944 Hollywood, however, democracy reigned supreme.

For *Casablanca* fans, and of course for Warner Bros., the evening had its disappointments. In the category of Best Actor, Humphrey lost to Paul Lukas, the lead in *Watch on the Rhine*. Ingrid Bergman had been nominated not as Ilsa but as Maria, the Spanish partisan in *For Whom the Bell Tolls,* and she lost to Jennifer Jones, centerpiece of the pious *Song of Bernadette.* Ingrid appeared in the nominated documentary *Swedes in America.* That didn't win either; the U.S. Navy film *December 7th* took first place. In the category of Supporting Actor, Claude Rains lost to Charles Coburn, featured in the comedy *The More the Merrier.* Arthur Miller's black-and-white cinematography for *Song of Bernadette* was judged superior to Arthur Edelson's for

Casablanca, and Max Steiner's score for the same film gave way to Alfred Newman's for *Bernadette.*

Yet all was not lost. When the Academy got around to recognizing scenarios, Julius J. Epstein, Philip G. Epstein, and Howard Koch received a statuette for Best Screenplay. The Epsteins were in New York working on a stage play; Koch accepted the award, graciously thanking all concerned. Better still, Michael Curtiz took Best Director. According to Koch, the Hungarian arrived onstage breathless and unprepared. Throughout the years, Curtiz told the audience, he was "always a bridesmaid, never a mother." At last he had his reward. And best of all, in the Best Picture category *Casablanca* beat out some formidable competition: the adaptation of *For Whom the Bell Tolls;* a fantasy-comedy, *Heaven Can Wait;* a biography, *Madame Curie;* a Western, *The Ox-Bow Incident;* a religious allegory, *The Song of Bernadette;* and three World War II–themed films, *In Which We Serve, The Human Comedy,* and *The More the Merrier.*

A bit of one-upmanship then occurred. Jack Warner leapt to his feet and grabbed the statuette before Hal Wallis could get to the stage. The livid producer could only return to his seat and fume while Warner traded lines with the master of ceremonies, radio comedian Jack Benny. A few minutes later Wallis received a different kind of recognition when he went onstage to accept the Irving Thalberg Award, given for a commendable body of work. But it did not assuage his wounded feelings. Their relationship had never been comfortable; *Casablanca* provided them with a casus belli. The two men never worked together again.

VI

The liaison began before anyone noticed — including the principals. Lauren had written to her mother about Humphrey; her name in the movie was Slim, and Humphrey's was Steve. The two would "kid around — he's always gagging — trying to break me up and is very, very fond of me." Fond was all he was, until about three weeks into filming. As work ended, Humphrey stopped by her dressing room. He was standing behind her, Lauren recalled in her memoir, *By Myself,* joking as usual. Suddenly he leaned over, put his hand under her chin, and kissed her. "It was impulsive — he was a bit shy — no lunging wolf tactics." Humphrey took a worn book of matches out of his pocket and asked her to write her phone number on the back. She did, even though she knew that her co-star was married to a notorious drinker and fighter, "a tough lady who would hit you with an ashtray, lamp, anything, as soon as not."

They began to see each other, tentatively getting closer. "I was an innocent sexually," Lauren confessed, and Humphrey "began awakening feelings that were new to me." Hollywood is a small town, and a movie set is a village where no secret can be kept for long. Even though Humphrey and Lauren tried to be discreet, their body language and the way they delivered their dialogue gave the whole show away. Hawks used it to great effect, building up Lauren's part, and giving her the best lines in the film: "You know you don't have to act with me, Steve. You don't have to say anything, and you don't have to do anything. Not a thing. Oh, maybe just whistle. You know how to whistle, don't you, Steve? You just put your lips together — and *blow.*"

Nevertheless, the director disapproved of the affair and let Lauren know it. When he brought Betty Bacall to Hollywood, he scolded her, "I thought, 'This girl is really something.' Then you started fooling around with Bogart. For one thing, it means nothing to him — this sort of thing happens all the time, he's not serious about you." When the picture wrapped, he warned, Humphrey would forget all about her. If she continued to see him, Hawks said he would wash his hands of Lauren and sell her contract to Monogram, then considered the cheapest B-picture studio in town. She dissolved in tears and promised not to get involved with Bogart away from the sound stage. At the same time, and for the same reasons, Humphrey started to hit the bottle harder than usual. At a party he was introduced to a fighter for the Free French underground, in town to raise money for his cause. The visitor recognized the movie star and issued a challenge: "Do something tough."

"You got the wrong guy," Humphrey informed him.

"I can eat glass," the Frenchman persisted. He proceeded to crunch a champagne glass with his teeth. Humphrey applauded.

"I can also eat razor blades." He produced some and put them in his mouth. "If you can't do that, let's mix some drinks."

That was more like it. They made a potion of brandy, crème de menthe, Scotch, gin, bourbon, vermouth, and champagne. Humphrey matched him drink for drink.

The challenger pressed on. "I still don't think you're tough. You can't eat glass."

"Oh, I can so," Humphrey insisted. He took a cocktail glass and chewed the top and worked his way down to the stem. Blood gushed from his mouth.

"I guess you are all right," the Frenchman conceded. "We are both very tough guys. Let us go now and insult women together."

It was only a question of days before Humphrey cracked wide open. One afternoon unit manager Eric Stacy was compelled to file a disturbing report. The actor had failed to show up at the appointed time of 8:30 a.m. When Stacy went to the Bogart home he encountered an extremely hostile Mayo. Humphrey materialized, whereupon "the atmosphere became extremely strained. I felt that my presence there would serve no useful purpose since Bogart himself kept asking, 'Are we holding a wake?'

"I really do not feel that Bogart's condition can be straightened out overnight since he has been drinking for approximately three weeks and it is not only the liquor, but also the mental turmoil regarding his domestic life that is entering into this situation. . . ."

On an extended visit, Natalie Bacal learned of her daughter's new crush. She,

214

too, raised hell, and not only because Humphrey was married and twenty-five years Lauren's senior. Natalie thought the young woman was acting like a starry-eyed love slave. One rainy night Humphrey called and asked Lauren to meet him. She dressed immediately. "You can't jump every time he calls," Natalie warned. "He'll have no respect for you. Let him know that you won't meet him any hour of the day or night. He's taking advantage of you — it's ridiculous."

There was no way Lauren could honor her pledge to Hawks or obey her mother. She was far beyond smitten. So was Humphrey. The couple would take great pains to stay away from each other when the filming was done for the day, drive off in separate cars, and then, when they were away from prying eyes, park on a secluded street. He would come to her car and they would sit in the front seat, holding hands like a couple of schoolkids. On other occasions they were overheated and intimate, sometimes even during breaks on the set, closing the door of a dressing room and emerging half an hour later, disheveled but radiant.

There was a strong oedipal component to Lauren's affection. "I wanted to give Bogie so much that he hadn't had," she acknowledged, "all the love that had been stored inside of me, all my life for an invisible father, for a man. I could finally think of allowing it to pour over *this* man and fill his life with laughter, warmth, joy — things he hadn't had for such a long time, if ever."

Those sentiments jibed with the longings of many American women. Their husbands and boyfriends were overseas, and they looked for the certainty and authority of their elders. In 1944, the most prominent men in military and political roles were father figures or even grandfather figures. In 1944, Admiral Ernest King, commander in chief of the U.S. Navy Fleet, was sixty-six. General Douglas MacArthur, supreme commander of the Southwest Pacific Area, was sixty-four. So was General George C. Marshall, army chief of staff. General George S. Patton, Third Army commander, was fifty-nine, as was Admiral Chester Nimitz, commander in chief of the Pacific Fleet. President Roosevelt, gearing up for his fourth national campaign, was sixty-two. Americans — particularly American women — needed to believe in these gray-haired leaders. So, in fact, did Humphrey. He endorsed FDR yet again, this time over the protests of Republicans who showered him with letters. The most aggressive were anonymous: "You cheap sissy — portrayer of gangster parts, have the asinine impudence to attempt to tell your superiors how to vote. You of the celluloid, stay in your film field." "You contaminate the air of free America." "Keep your personal opinions under your hat. You'll stay in pictures longer and lose fewer fans." When the *Hollywood Reporter* advised actors to stay out of political discussions, Humphrey sat down at his typewriter, set his opinions down, and arranged to have them printed in the *Saturday Evening Post*.

"I Stuck My Neck Out" made no attempt to be conciliatory. "When the 'treat 'em nice so long as they stay in their sound stage cages and perform entertaining tricks but rap their noses when they come out of them' school of thought finds a champion in a Hollywood motion picture trade paper, I think it is time for one of the 'menagerie' to speak up." Humphrey urged actors to express themselves on any subject — with a great emphasis on politics. He thought it wrong "to be threatened with boycott of our screen performances because we spoke out for Franklin Roosevelt or Tom Dewey any more than we think it is right for German composers and painters to have their works destroyed because they don't believe in Hitler's Nazi philosophy." Personally, he concluded, "I'm going to keep right on sticking my neck out, without worrying about its possible effect upon my career. I love doing it. You meet so many interesting people that way."

Humphrey would have reason to regret that article in a few years. Right now, though, his moral indignation went down well. At forty-four he had found himself newly popular, along with the forty-four-year-old Spencer Tracy and the forty-seven-year-old Walter Pidgeon. Even the thirty-seven-year-old John Wayne had begun to play tough, paternal roles, usually of a grizzled soldier grown old before his time, leading baby-faced GIs into battle.

One day this new generation of actors would redefine the male image, though no one predicted it at the time. As Jeanine Basinger notes in *The Star Machine,* "The effect of World War II on shaping the 'new hero' as a 'sensitive' male has never been fully explored." In later years credit was given to the Actors Studio for producing a new kind of leading man — Montgomery Clift, James Dean, Marlon Brando, et al. "Who remembers that the type was already in place, thanks to World War II having brought us Van Johnson, Marshall Thompson, Dane Clark, Lon McCallister, Robert Walker?" For when the men went to war, the boys began to take over. They needed girls next door to romance, and younger sidekick actors to hang out with and younger parents to have raised them. "Once the 'boy star' emerged," concludes Basinger, "he would not go away."

For the time being, however, the Bogart generation was still in control. Under those conditions, the romance of a young woman in the last of her teenage years and a thrice-married man with thinning hair was not as unseemly as it might have been in another era. And besides, the couple was truly in love. The variance in age, and even the fact that he had a wife, made no difference. Lauren came from a broken home and believed marriage was a legal thing that rarely made it past the five-year mark anyway. She just wanted to be with Humphrey and he wanted to be with her. The two kept dodging bullets, slipping away from the press, setting up a tryst at Peter Lorre's ranch, trying to evade the questions of Hawks and other colleagues. Mayo, eternally suspicious of her husband's co-stars, kept trying to find out Humphrey's whereabouts when he was away from home. But she was getting more and more sodden with liquor, and had trouble thinking it all through. She did make one nasty call, tracking him down at Warners one afternoon. "Hello, lover boy. How're you doing with your daughter? She's half your age, you know."

At the same time, she must have been aware that she was the prime cause of their deteriorating marriage. For Mayo vowed to make a prodigious effort to clean up her act, to quit drinking and change her bristling, hostile behavior. During an interview with a *Life* reporter she went so far as to link arms with Humphrey, projecting sobriety and brightness. "In five years," she predicted saucily, the Bogarts were "going to retire and become beachcombers. That is, if he can keep his hair and teeth that long." Humphrey stayed true to his code. He wanted to believe his wife and felt that he owed her this one last chance. Bacall was to remember, "He told me, 'I had to go back. I wouldn't throw a dog out in the street in her condition. I have to give her every chance.' So he went back, and I cried. What else was there to do?"

In October, *To Have and Have Not* opened to rave reviews. Lauren's long hair and up-from-under gaze was labeled "the Look" and ignited a fashion trend. The film itself was compared favorably to *Casablanca.*

Humphrey assumed the status of Warners' biggest box office draw, and the young woman who played opposite him vaulted into national celebrity. Not since Greta Garbo's 1939 performance as a no-nonsense Bolshevik in *Ninotchka* had audiences seen so strong a female performer. Throughout the film Lauren had given as good as she got, standing up to Captain Morgan and even singing in her own, true husky voice, accompanied by Hoagy Carmichael. Steam seemed to form on the windows whenever she made an entrance, prompting the *New York Times* to comment: "Hers is mainly a job of radiating as much sex as the law will allow." It was a heady time, with praise coming in from both coasts. The only discouraging words were uttered by playwright Moss Hart. When he met Lauren during a publicity tour in New York, he offered his congratulations — and then warned, "You realize, of course, from here on you have nowhere to go but down." She laughed his words away. In the next few weeks she would have reason to recall them.

As the raves continued, the affair ebbed. Humphrey's timing could not have been worse: he and Lauren were about to co-star in a new movie, *The Big Sleep,* an adaptation of the Raymond Chandler mystery.

This, too, would be directed by Howard Hawks, the disapproving critic of the Bogart-Bacall romance. Acutely miserable as filming began, Lauren pretended to be nothing more than a friend to the love of her life; for his part, Humphrey kept an emotional distance. The deep freeze lasted only a month.

For, given a final opportunity to turn her life around and save her marriage, Mayo had violently backslid. She hit the bottle hard and began a new series of irrational harangues and arguments. Humphrey could stand no more: he left home, took a room in a Beverly Hills hotel, and made an official statement to the press. This was a trial separation; it had nothing to do with "another woman." Immediately afterward, reporters went to the other half of the Battling Bogarts for her view of the separation. She said she loved Humphrey and would attempt to get back in his good graces. She would go to rehab; that would demonstrate her goodwill. So she did, and the Bogarts tried yet another reconciliation. Three days later Mayo started drinking again. She heard Humphrey on the phone with Lauren and grabbed the receiver: "Listen, you Jewish bitch — who's going to wash his socks? Are *you?* Are *you* going to take care of him?" After that incident, Lauren's mother told her she was throwing her life away, friends told her she was making a tragic mistake, and Howard Hawks told her she was a damn fool. "Bogart likes his life," the director insisted. "He likes the drinking and he likes his wife — you're throwing away a whole career because of something that's just not going to happen." To distract Lauren, he and Slim tried to fix her up with a widower, an actor whose wife had perished in a wartime plane crash. He came to call in a captain's uniform, handsome, compelling, dimpled, the cynosure of a million women. Lauren found him dull and unappealing. Even now she was too far gone on Humphrey to look at another man, even if that man was Clark Gable.

Hawks resented her attitude, and disliked Humphrey's inability to make up his mind. But he was too much of a pro to let it destroy the picture. On the contrary; when he saw sparks continue to fly between the leading man and leading lady on-screen, he diminished the roles of the other young women in *The Big Sleep* and built up Lauren's part. Originally, Raymond Chandler expressed great happiness when Humphrey was chosen to play Philip Marlowe. "Bogart can be tough without a gun," he wrote his

British publisher. "Also he has a sense of humor that contains the grating undertone of contempt. [Alan] Ladd is hard, bitter and occasionally charming, but he is after all a small boy's idea of a tough guy. Bogart is the genuine article." The novelist was less satisfied when Martha Vickers, who played Lauren's nymphomaniac sister, turned out to be "so good she shattered Miss Bacall completely. So they cut the picture in such a way that all her best scenes were left out except one." And he was unhappier still when Hawks shoehorned in some new double-entendre dialogue that was not in the book. The heiress Vivian Rutledge (Lauren) spars with Philip Marlowe, private eye, in a conversation about playing the horses when Vivian speaks of watching a stallion to see whether he likes to be a front-runner or come from behind. She figures Marlowe is the kind who gets out in front, opens up a lead, then takes it easy in the backstretch before coming home.

On the detective's part, he believes she has a touch of class, but he isn't certain how far she can go.

That, Vivian informs him, depends on who's in the saddle.

Hawks and his writers were still heating up the script when Chandler saw an early print. He was not asked to view later versions. *The Big Sleep* no longer belonged to him and he knew it. Warners had taken over. The novelist shrugged it off; no one had a better sense of place, but plotting was not his long suit. When screenwriters Jules Furthman and William Faulkner phoned to ask who had killed one of the victims, Chandler read over his work — and couldn't give an answer. He consoled himself with the hope that with all the confusion, "If Hawks got his way, the picture will be the best of its kind." Hawks did get his way, and while he was about it, made Humphrey into a Philip Marlowe no other actor has ever approached — even though there have been many who tried. These included Robert Mitchum and James Garner, who more closely resembled the novelist's description of Marlowe; Robert Montgomery and Dick Powell, who brought some comedy to the detective's backchat, but who could not furnish him with a soul; and George Montgomery and Elliot Gould, who, in Chandler's phrase, were as sophisticated as a French count in a high school play.

Only Humphrey gave his Marlowe the essential tone of film noir. He seemed born to play this part, with a face as stark and angular as the cinematography. His lean

225

physique suggested self-denial, as if any indulgences — other than booze, of course — were not to be admitted. His voice was terse but oddly musical, so that in one scene he could convey amusement and a rude wit, and in another he could be romantic and sexually suggestive, and in yet another he could be so unyielding and masculine that even big-league gangsters gave him a wide berth. Perhaps the best example of Marlowe's dangerous quality came when women were out of the picture. Marlowe and Eddie Mars, a smooth, callous mob figure, face off when the sleuth wants to know how come Mars has the key to a house.

MARS: Is it any of your business?
MARLOWE: I could make it my business.
MARS: I could make your business mine.
MARLOWE: Oh, you wouldn't like it. The pay's too small.

The end of the filming coincided with the conclusion of the Bogart marriage. This time there was no going back. Humphrey tried to handle Mayo with kindness and assurance, impressing on her the fact that their marriage simply didn't work anymore, that it was his fault as well as hers, that he wasn't angry with her, and that he would make a generous financial settlement. He left the house, moved to the Garden of Allah, but continued to call her, offering advice and consolation. To his astonishment, Mayo agreed to go to Reno for a quickie divorce. She had battled all the phantom competition like a tigress, observed Humphrey's friend Nathaniel Benchley. "Now that the real thing had arrived it was almost as though she sensed the futility of trying to fight any longer." A few rough moments remained; then it was over. The divorce took place on May 10, 1945.

The world war and the domestic one were winding down at the same time and optimism was abroad in the land. The novelist Louis Bromfield had struck up a friendship with Humphrey during one of his frequent visits to Hollywood, and when the romance with Bacall went public he offered the couple refuge two thousand miles from California. Twelve days after his divorce from Mayo became final, Humphrey and Lauren boarded the Super Chief in Pasadena and journeyed to Lucas, Ohio. From there they were conveyed to Bromfield's Malabar Farm, where a judge quietly married them in the great hallway of the main house. The *Los Angeles Times* reported that "Miss Bacall was dressed in a light pink, two-piece dress with brown accessories and wore a bracelet on each arm. Bogart, clad in a gray suit, maroon tie, and sporting a white carnation in his lapel, appeared more at ease than the bride." Perhaps, but Bacall remembered that her new husband gave the lie to his tough-guy image by crying throughout the ceremony.

Several days later the Bogarts returned to California. They settled into a furnished house in Beverly Hills, along with a cook and handyman-gardener. In time, a butler was added. Humphrey had grown up with servants, but having a retinue was heady stuff for Lauren; until the marriage, the only live-in help she knew were her mother and grandmother. Even the news that Warners was going to hold up the release of *The Big Sleep* couldn't bother her now. Besides, the studio had its own good reasons: its backlog of war movies had to go first, before the country wearied of battle scenes and grim heroics. So, after a few days' rest, Mr. and Mrs. Bogart philosophically went forth to work on their respective films. Humphrey would star in *Dead Reckoning* with the blond Bad Girl Lizabeth Scott; Lauren was the female lead in *Confidential Agent* opposite the romantic Frenchman Charles Boyer — born, incidentally, the same year as her husband. All seemed well. But the new Mrs. B. was a congenital worrier. Would there be room for a star like Humphrey when all the young, good-looking actors returned from service and wanted back into films? Would his "experienced face" be desirable in the postwar period? Or would her husband become a back number like George Raft and so many other onetime stars? And what of her own career? How would Lauren Bacall do when she wasn't acting with Humphrey Bogart? At such times, the flippant words of Moss Hart came back to haunt her. In the months ahead she was to note ruefully, "He turned out to be a prophet."

CHAPTER 5
MAY YOU NEVER DIE TILL I
KILL YOU

I

When the war ended, Humphrey sold *Sluggy* and acquired a new boat: a fifty-four-foot yawl called *Santana,* the name of the yacht in *Key Largo.* He also bought a luxurious new home at 2707 Benedict Canyon Road in Beverly Hills. (Both were previously owned by onetime stars, the vessel by Dick Powell, the house by Hedy Lamarr.) These purchases were eminently affordable, as was the Bogarts' domestic staff, as were new furnishings and a long, top-of-the-line mink coat for Betty, aka "Baby" (Humphrey refused to address his wife by her professional name, and she addressed him as "Bogie"). A new Warner Bros. contract guaranteed the studio's prize possession, Humphrey DeForest Bogart, one studio project per year at a fee of $200,000, plus director and script approval, plus permission to do one film per year for another studio. These terms were valid for the next fifteen years, come what may. The portents were all good: in 1946 alone he earned $467,000, making him the highest-paid actor in the world. He felt relaxed enough to look back on his career with the tone of an elder statesman: "I believe if I had not been given the movie role of Duke Mantee, in *The Petrified Forest,* I'd now be out of films altogether. Duke was my first heavy role, and I like heavies, having no desire to be sympathetic or romantic. Roles like those Van Johnson gets would give me the screaming meemies." Besides, he added, most of the time Mantee had to be menacing while sitting down. "I had had so many violently active stage parts that the chair felt fine. Putting across a characterization without benefit of the usual movement and gestures that help hold an audience's attention is a special kind of problem."

Humphrey's friends kidded him: now he wouldn't have to worry about money until he was sixty-one, by which time he'd be getting ready for Social Security. With a mock growl, Humphrey reminded them that he had worked goddamn hard for that loose change. At the age of forty-seven he had already appeared in nineteen plays and fifty-three films. Name another actor who could say as much. And, he added with a wink, he was just getting started.

His young wife really *was* just getting started, and she quickly took a nosedive. *Confidential Agent,* an adaptation of Graham Greene's Spanish Civil War espionage novel, was Lauren Bacall's third film and her first disaster. The director, Herman Shumlin, had enjoyed a string of Broadway successes (*The Children's Hour, Grand Hotel, The Little Foxes*). But his cinema experience consisted of one previous film, *Watch on the Rhine* — essentially a photographed play. In the role of a world-weary foreign operative, Boyer needed no guidance from Shumlin. Nor did the great character actors Peter Lorre, George Colouris, and Katina Paxinou, and they got none. The director neglected his leading lady as well, and this proved to be a crucial error. Early in November 1946, critics announced to the world that Lauren was an overrated talent, and so she appeared to audiences as well. In the first place, she was playing Rose Cullen, a young British heiress, and she couldn't manage any intonation east of Manhattan. In the second place, she had no idea how to move. Slinking was all very well for Vivian; it was inappropriate for Rose, and the smoldering, sultry stare that wowed Bogart in *The Big Sleep* made her laughable when played against Boyer's Luis Denard. Audiences stayed away. The twenty-year-old was devastated by the failure; in time she acknowledged that "to cast me as an aristocratic English girl was more than a stretch. It was dementia. . . . I just didn't know enough, hadn't a clue as to how to be British, and Shumlin never gave me a clue. So I remained my awkward, inexperienced, miscast self."

Humphrey did what he could to comfort Lauren during the painful setback to her career. They went sailing, had friends to their new house, savored their marriage. He still imbibed, but not nearly so much as before, when he had used alcohol as a psychological painkiller — particularly during the final years with Mayo. Now he could joke about booze; asked whether he had ever quit drinking, he answered blithely, "Yes, and it was the most miserable afternoon of my life." Again, the attitude of Ernest Hemingway hovered in the background: "Modern life is often a mechanical oppression and liquor is the only mechanical relief."

Of greater medical concern, although no one knew it at the moment, was Humphrey's addiction to tobacco. Toward the end of his life, when revival movie houses began to offer Bogart festivals, audiences remarked that they were watching the star kill himself with inhalations. But nearly everyone smoked in films of the 1930s and '40s; cigarette cases were constantly being filled and refilled, ashtrays emptied and re-emptied. Indeed, through the years, cigarettes had become a vital Bogartian prop. Producer Rob Long recalls that once, when a great deal of exposition had to be spoken in a concluding scene, Humphrey protested that the only way the monologue would work is "if two camels were in the background, fucking." The director had a better idea. The scene would be filmed as written — with one addendum. Humphrey would unwrap a pack of Chesterfields, remove one cigarette, tap it to pack down the tobacco, speaking all the while, ignite the cigarette with a match, toss it aside, add some more lines, take a large drag, exhale, and finish the speech, the words mingling with the smoke. "Cut. Print. Instant drama."

Humphrey and his prop became insepa-rable. In *Ashes to Ashes,* a scrupulous nuts-and-bolts history of the tobacco business in America, Richard Kluger devotes a long passage to Humphrey Bogart. Cinema's existential antihero of the 1940s, writes Kluger, was a man whose "every considered drag and expelled puff of smoke seemed to represent a mocking laugh of bitter defiance." Humphrey wielded his Chesterfield cigarette (a product he was paid to endorse) the way a duelist or gunslinger would flash his weapon. "But instead of slaying his tormentor, he was more likely to resolve matters ambiguously by deftly discarding his still burning butt in a low, flat trajectory that ended in life's gutter."

Humphrey was hardly alone in his habit. Classic fiction has numerous references to tobacco. The fallen Anna Karenina becomes a smoker. Another sinner, Madame Bovary, flaunts her new vice. "Her looks grew bolder, her speech more free; she even committed the impropriety of walking out with Monsieur Rodolphe, a cigarette in her mouth." Erich Maria Remarque's 1929 novel *All Quiet on the Western Front* speaks of the linkage between soldiers and nicotine: "Over our heads a cloud of smoke spreads out. What would a soldier be without tobacco?" (Exactly eight decades later, the Pentagon asked the same question. In the war zones of 2009, declared the secretary of defense, soldiers could smoke as much as they wanted.)

Later in the century popular songs celebrated smoking — Bing Crosby's "Two

Cigarettes in the Dark," Hoagy Carmichael's "Two Sleepy People" ("Here we are, out of cigarettes"), Holt Marvell's "These Foolish Things" ("A cigarette that bears a lipstick's traces"), and many more. Beyond the romance, there was a connection between tobacco and masculinity that had begun early in the century and carried on for decades. When the United States entered World War I, General John J. Pershing stated that tobacco was every bit as vital to the fighting man as victuals. During World War II the common expression of enlisted men on a break was "Smoke 'em if you got 'em." The Western leaders all smoked: Franklin Delano Roosevelt inhaled through an elegant cigarette holder; Winston Churchill chomped on cigars; Joseph Stalin puffed a pipe. Humphrey was right in line with them and much appreciated for his addiction. After all, Adolf Hitler was the one who didn't use tobacco or eat meat.

II

Two Bogart films made in 1945 were released in 1946. *Conflict,* which Humphrey had tried so hard to avoid, portrayed him as a psychopathic killer who murders his wife in order to marry her sister. He and Alexis Smith seemed to be reading from different scripts, and save for the adroit Sydney Greenstreet as a psychiatrist who inveigles the murderer into confessing his crime, it was a waste of time and talent. The picture proved to be a downer in every sense of the word; Humphrey looked depressed throughout, the lines delivered mechanically rather than provocatively, as the part required. It did very little business, and Warner Bros. executives wondered whether some of the Bogart magic had worn off. *The Big Sleep* reassured them. It was *Conflict*'s diametrical opposite, diverting, confusing, full of smart Raymond Chandler backchat and loaded with the Bogart-Bacall magic first glimpsed in *To Have and Have Not*. Lauren was once again the sexually charged, husky-voiced seductress. The effect was powerful enough to make her performance in *Confidential Agent* seem no more than a trivial error. As for Humphrey, he was both heartened and embarrassed by the film's enthusiastic reception in the papers and at the box office. He relished the praise of his fellow actors, journalists, and audiences. What made him uncomfortable were the trappings of celebrity. He was, for example, asked to leave the imprints of his hands and shoes on the Hollywood Walk of Fame in front of Grauman's Chinese Theatre. Though he protested privately, he knew that it would be impossible to boycott the ceremony; this was the way Hollywood staged its fondest tribute. His only comment was a dedication to the theater owner. He wrote in cement with one finger: "Sid — May You Never Die Till I Kill You."

Two other films followed, neither with any distinction. In *Dead Reckoning,* Humphrey played a veteran investigating the disappearance of an army buddy. The lethal temptress was Lizabeth Scott, whose brilliant blond hair and husky voice could not compensate for a lack of range; the villains, Morris Carnovsky and Marvin Miller, were more vaudevillian than cinematic. It was pathetically clear that the studios — in this case Columbia — were searching for another *Maltese Falcon,* even lifting lines from it almost verbatim ("A guy's pal was killed, he ought to do something about it"). Critics on both sides of the Atlantic panned the movie. Obviously Humphrey had outgrown his days as an out-and-out villain. He needed to show some redeeming quality, no matter how deeply buried. How he would do that remained a mystery to him as well as to the studio.

The Two Mrs. Carrolls was Humphrey's next film. It did nothing to ease his bewil-

238

derment. He was cast against type as a struggling painter — and homicidal lunatic. Having murdered one wife (Alexis Smith), he weds another (Barbara Stanwyck) and then plans to do away with her. The film was not successful with the public or the critics; some comments were harsher than any Humphrey had seen since his early days on Broadway ("He is equally unconvincing as artist, madman and murderer").

The survivor of so many bad films needed to reclaim the high ground. With an old New York friend, Humphrey established a new company, Mark Hellinger Productions. At first glance, the two ex–New Yorkers seemed polar opposites: Mark's parents were Orthodox Jews, Humphrey's were indifferent WASPs. Mark was from the outer borough of Queens. Humphrey was from high-toned Manhattan. In fact the partners had a great deal in common. Mark's father, Paul, was a prosperous real estate lawyer who wanted his son to follow in his profession. Early on, Belmont Bogart hoped his only son would also be a doctor. Both boys flouted family tradition. Mark was kicked out of public high school for being a student agitator; Humphrey, as we have seen, was ejected from prep school. So the Hellinger-Bogart union actually made sense, and began with enormous energy and optimism.

Hellinger had just produced a huge hit, *The Killers,* starring Burt Lancaster and introducing Ava Gardner, adapted from the famous Hemingway story. He and Humphrey thought they could do more pictures based on other tales by the same author. These had been written by a great talent, and no filmmaker had touched them. *The Killers* had demonstrated that good work could also be good box office. As 1947 began, Hemingway, Hellinger, and Bogart looked to be an ideal trio. And Humphrey had a good feeling about two of his own upcoming films, *Dark Passage* and *The Treasure of the Sierra Madre.* The former co-starred Humphrey and Lauren in their first feature since the marriage. Humphrey didn't lobby for Lauren; she got the part on her own merits. He was delighted with that news, and with the fact that he would appear in part of the film heavily bandaged from plastic surgery. "I can just hear Jack Warner scream," he chuckled. "He's paying me all this money to make the picture and nobody will even see me until it's a third over."

The year before, Robert Montgomery had done *The Lady in the Lake,* a Philip Marlowe mystery told with a "subjective camera technique" — all the action is seen from the star's point of view. The first half of *Dark Passage* borrowed this method, and used it with greater finesse. Vincent Parry (Humphrey) is an innocent man, framed for killing his wife. He escapes from San Quentin, hell-bent on finding the real assassin. To keep from being spotted in San Francisco, he undergoes major plastic surgery. All during these sequences the viewer perceives the world through his eyes. Only when the bandages come off does the camera become omniscient. Assisting Parry in his quest is Irene Jansen (Lauren), a rich artist whose own father was once wrongly accused of a crime. The story was somewhat murky, and Agnes Moorehead offered a caricature of wickedness, Cruella De Vil before her time. But the director, Delmer Daves, co-scenarist of *The Petrified Forest,* maintained a high regard for Humphrey's skills and knew about his marital history. He put them both on display. An exchange with a stranger contained just the right autobiographical tone:

PARRY: I'm hiding.
STRANGER: From what?
PARRY: My wife, my friends, my family, everybody.

STRANGER: Come on now, it can't be as bad as all that.

PARRY: Well, I'll tell you what you do. You go up there and spend seven years with my wife, and then if you're still in your right mind, come back down here and tell me about it.

Daves also used Lauren well, encouraging her to radiate domestic warmth, rather than the steam heat she had generated in the earlier films. With all the effort, though, *Dark Passage* was still a production-line film noir with no particular distinction; Warners knew the movie would need a lot of advertising and publicity to put it across.

The studio regarded *The Treasure of the Sierra Madre* as even less promising. John Huston had been enthralled by B. Traven's 1927 novella for years, but no production house shared his interest. It was not hard to see why. The tale was a downer: a group of adventurers climb a mountain in search of gold, promising to share and share alike. But when they strike the mother lode one of them becomes consumed by greed and suspicion, kills another, and in turn is cut to pieces by strangers even more avaricious than he is. In the end, the gold dust is carried away by the wind, going back to the

Sierra Madre from which it came.

The escapade takes place entirely in Mexico. To achieve any kind of authenticity the movie would have to be done on location, with all the concomitant expenses. And to further increase the odds against a box office success, it was a story without a significant female role. Only a man with Huston's powers of persuasion could have worn down the Warners executives. (It didn't hurt that he had induced Humphrey Bogart to play the unstable gold hunter Fred C. Dobbs — and John's father, Walter Huston, to be Howard, the foxy old prospector.)

Luck went John's way with the rest of the cast. Ronald Reagan was scheduled to play Bob Curtin, the third of the gold hunters. But when he and his agent played hard to get, Huston bypassed him for the underrated character actor Tim Holt. Zachary Scott, a fine performer but all wrong for the part of bounty hunter James Cody, was replaced by the versatile Bruce Bennett. The Mexican bandit Gold Hat was played by Alfonso Bedoya, who offered a disturbing blend of humor and malevolence ("I don't have to show you any stinkin' badges"). In the spring of 1947 they were all working away in Tampico. Lauren was on the set most of the time; she compared Walter and John to "a couple of kids together — they made each other laugh, they enjoyed and understood each other's wickedness." *Père et fils* had a chaffing, amiable relationship; they even smoked grass together. Walter enjoyed the experience; his son got sick.

Humphrey had no use for drugs. Not for any moral reasons; he just preferred good old-fashioned alcohol. According to Huston biographer Lawrence Grobel, Bogart felt that "Dos Equis" — the name of Mexico's leading beer — were the only Spanish words he needed to know. On the set, though, he came prepared to play the most difficult role of his career.

During the early search for nuggets, Dobbs is a boon companion and a likeable, if eccentric, adventurer. But when the trio finds success, he begins to exhibit signs of gold fever. Moment by moment, turn by turn, he makes a precipitous descent. It begins with a slight mistrust of his fellow miners, then slides downhill from angry suspicion to outright and mortal paranoia. With the exception of Gold Hat no one in the script is more repugnant. Humphrey had taken the part to prove something to himself as well as to the industry and the public who now saw him as a luminary rather than an actor. No one disputed that Humphrey Bogart knew his craft; the question was whether he had lost track of the art. *Treasure* gave him a chance to redeem himself. Thus it was with considerable joy that he told the *New York Post* film critic, "Wait till you see me in my next picture. I play the worst shit you ever saw."

Humphrey knew that motiveless malignity would not be enough to make Dobbs stand out. He needed memorable dialogue, and the script and direction were John Huston's best since *The Maltese Falcon.* To give the movie an extra spin, John made his acting debut in a cameo role. He plays a wealthy, white-suited tourist who initially feels sorry for the panhandling Dobbs, and then can't wait to get rid of him. "This is the very last you get from me," he declares, parceling out pesos for the second time. "From now on, you have to make your way through life without my assistance." (This was John's in-joke: having written the script for *High Sierra* and directed *Falcon* and *Across the Pacific,* he was now handing Humphrey yet another pivotal role.)

As Dobbs and Curtin make their way up the high, arid Sierra Madre, they grow weary and frustrated. Not Howard. The grizzled guide is decades older than his companions, but as Dobbs remarks, he's "part goat." The two men announce they're ready to quit: Why not admit it? All along, this exploit has been an exercise in self-delusion. Howard cackles, "Well, tell my old grandmother! I got two very elegant bed-fellers who kick at the first drop of rain and hide in the closet when the thunder rumbles. My, my, my, what great prospectors!"

Dobbs picks up a rock and threatens to knock him galley-west. Curtin gets in the way: "Can't you see the old man's nuts?" Howard responds with more laughter. "Nuts? Nuts am I? You're so dumb you don't even see the riches you're treadin' on with your own feet. Ah, haa, haa." To underline his opinion of the tenderfeet, he dances a derisive little jig over the gold dust. The camera closes in on Walter as he pockets the scene, and, in effect, the picture. John later said Walter's dance reminded him of the best moments of Chaplin, Jack Dempsey in his prime, and the bullfighter Manolete. When the director shouted "Cut!" Humphrey could only shake his head in wonder. "One Huston is bad enough, but two are murder."

Seen in retrospect, *The Treasure of the Sierra Madre* is indeed a love letter from a brilliant son to a gifted father. But it's something more: a portrait of rapacity, irony, and tragedy. The film's centerpiece is undoubtedly Walter Huston. And yet, faced with the old man's big moments and canny scene stealing, Humphrey delivers the more powerful performance, a detailed representation of a hustler who strikes it rich and gets ruined by his unchecked desire for more. There is no vanity in his work, no attempt to soften Dobbs's mean aspirations or vicious conduct. Indeed, after he murders Curtin, a stream-of-consciousness episode underlines the moral breakdown:

DOBBS: (*Vainly searching for the corpse*) Curtin! Curtin! Curtin! Where are you? Curtin! I gotta get a hold of myself. Mustn't lose my head. There's one thing certain; he ain't here. I got it! The tiger. Yeah, yeah, that's it. The tiger must have dragged him off to his lair, that's what. Yeah, pretty soon not even the bones will be left to tell the story. Done as if by order.

Long after the film ends, notes historian Ted Sennett, the audience recalls Dobbs and Curtin shaking hands as they form a partnership, with Howard watching them with the sharp, amused eyes of experience;

247

Curtin and Dobbs sitting in the darkness, guarding their hoard of nuggets and fighting sleep; the cat-and-mouse play of the bandits with Dobbs before they slay him with machetes: "The beaming smile of Gold Hat somehow expresses a primitive, terrifying evil."

At the start, Jack Warner had not been high on John Huston's latest project. When he saw the edited version he did an enthusiastic U-turn, cabling the studio's New York sales manager: THIS IS DEFINITELY THE GREATEST MOTION PICTURE WE HAVE EVER MADE. A few seasons back, he went on, THIS ONE PICTURE WOULD VIRTUALLY PUT OVER A WHOLE SEASON. Unfortunately for him and many others in Hollywood, this was not a few seasons back. This was the fall of 1947, and unforeseen historical forces were at work.

Warner, like most studio moguls, considered himself and his town to be outside of politics. There had been the nonsense with Martin Dies seven years ago, but that investigation had dried up and blown away. Now a new one had begun, run by some motormouthed New Jersey congressman named J. Parnell Thomas. It would be more of the same, Humphrey confided to a friend, a lot of noise and then a turn-tail retreat by the House Un-American Activities Committee (HUAC). If the gasbags in Washington ever investigate Hollywood, they'll find a spectrum of political opinions not very different from those in St. Louis or Indianapolis. Take Louis Bromfield for example. He's a conservative Republican. John Howard Lawson is a lefty. So they sign petitions. So they put their name on letterheads. So what? It's the credits on celluloid that count, not the names on paper.

But this was not wartime America, and J. Parnell Thomas was not Martin Dies. The Soviet Union was no longer an ally. As the postwar euphoria melted away, the USSR stood revealed as an implacable and ruthless enemy, hell-bent on acquiring the atomic bomb and threatening the very existence of the United States. America was gripped by the arms race and the nuclear jitters. Albert Einstein had spoken on the radio, warning that annihilation beckoned. The unelected president, Harry Truman, having replaced the fallen and beloved FDR, faced a hostile Republican Congress. As the Soviet Union advanced in Eastern Europe, Greece, and Turkey, senators and congressmen painted the administration as soft on Communism abroad and domestically. The chief executive responded with the Truman Doctrine, providing aid and money to needy nations overseas in order to confront and halt the progress of Communism. At home, he instituted a federal loyalty oath.

HUAC's ambitious new chairman seized the moment. Born John Feeney, he had taken his mother's maiden name upon his father's death (speaking of himself in the third person, he informed a judge that "your petitioner . . . believes he can get recognition and business under the name of Thomas that he could not get under the name of Feeney"). En route to the House of Representatives, Thomas also changed his religion from Roman Catholic to Baptist. He had advanced as planned, selling investment securities for a living while he made his presence felt in local politics. Thomas escalated quickly from mayor of Allendale, New Jersey, to state legislator, to congressman. He had been on HUAC since its inception in 1938; the seniority system gave him the chair early in 1947. At fifty-seven, the bald, assertive official had the full attention of the press, something he had craved for decades. One of his first public statements had to do with Hollywood: "Hundreds of very prominent film capital people have been named as Communists to us."

This was nonsense and he knew it. There was no solid evidence that more than a score of people in the film capital were Party members, and none of them held influential positions. Yet all Thomas had to do in 1947 was imply that it was otherwise and the West Coast cringed. He flew out to Hollywood in May to provoke headlines and interrogate witnesses. At his side was Robert Stripling, HUAC's chief investigator. In a suite at the Biltmore Hotel they conducted what were alleged to be private interviews, but after each session word was leaked to reporters. Thomas informed them, for example, that the Screen Writers Guild was "lousy with Communists." Among all the people he interviewed, he found only fourteen to be "friendly." One, Robert Taylor, testified that MGM wouldn't allow him to enlist in the navy until he finished *Song of Russia.* Representative Thomas had seen the film; he called it "Communist propaganda that favored its ideologies, its institutions and its way of life over the same things in America." Leila Rogers, better known as Ginger Rogers's mother than as an acting teacher, informed Stripling that her daughter would not say a line in *Tender Comrade* because of its Red tint: "Share and share alike — that's democracy."

Satisfied with the evidence he had uncovered, Thomas used the committee's subpoena power, summoning a lineup of "subversive" directors and screenwriters. They would be compelled to testify at a public hearing in the nation's capital. Nineteen of them consulted their lawyers and decided to fight back. The truth was that most of them had been Communists at one time or another; a few still retained their Party cards. In other cases involving the suspicion of Communism, witnesses invoked the Fifth Amendment, refusing to testify because the law protected them from self-incrimination. Here they planned to invoke the First Amendment, guaranteeing the right of free speech. Bearing in mind Thomas's label of the friendly fourteen, the *Hollywood Reporter* came up with a name for the resisters: they were the "Unfriendly Nineteen." It took less than a day for the waggish Billy Wilder to state that "only two of them have talent. The rest are just unfriendly."

Despite the wisecracks and nose thumbing, nearly every actor, director, and producer felt threatened by this federal intrusion. If Hollywood could be trampled underfoot by HUAC witch-hunters, what American institution was safe? Among intellectuals and artists, whenever a menace arises there is always one predictable response: a committee is formed. This one was born at the house of Lenore and Ira Gershwin. In *City of Nets,* historian Otto Friedrich quotes an attendee: "You could not get into the place. The excitement was intense. The town was full of enthusiasm because they all felt they were going to win. Every star was there."

Rita Hayworth volunteered to serve on the team, now calling itself the Committee for the First Amendment. So did Myrna Loy, Groucho Marx, Gene Kelly, Paulette Goddard, and many others. By far the biggest name on the list was Humphrey Bogart. As the pressure increased, the Unfriendly Nineteen pleaded with friends and coworkers for a public show of support. Another meeting was called, this time at the home of director William Wyler. "I was up in arms — fervent," recalled Lauren. "I said to Bogie, 'We must go.' He felt strongly about it, too." John Huston chartered a plane from his friend Howard Hughes, then president of Trans World Airlines. The passenger list included the Bogarts, Gene Kelly, John Garfield, Danny Kaye, Paul Henreid, and John Huston and his wife, actress Evelyn Keyes. On the way to Washington, the plane set down in several cities, and at each stop the group was met with sympathetic reporters. Invigorated, the travelers went on to the HUAC hearings, confident that they were riding the tide of history.

The show folk had reckoned without Thomas's gift for stage-managing. As they watched from a back row, the chairman summoned John Howard Lawson. He was the most self-righteous and dogmatic of the nineteen, and the least likely to attract independents to his cause. Lawson portrayed himself as the victim of rogue fascists, men who had seized control of the American government. In his view HUAC was conducting "an illegal and indecent trial of American citizens, whom the Committee has selected to be publicly pilloried and smeared. I am not here to defend myself, or to answer the agglomeration of falsehoods that has been heaped upon me." He refused to state whether or not he was a member of the Screen Writers Guild, even though it was on the public record. And of course he refused to state whether he was now, or ever had been, a member of the Communist Party, even though Thomas knew from back channels (including an FBI agent who had infiltrated the Hollywood cell) that he was. So, in fact, were many of the nineteen, including Dalton Trumbo. The next day that scenarist refused to answer questions about his Communist affiliations with one syllable because "very many questions can only be answered yes or no by a moron or a slave." He, too, launched into a speech about the rights of labor and accused the chairman of trying to equate membership in a trade union with membership in the Party. Thomas shouted, "Excuse the witness!" As security guards closed in, Trumbo countered, "This is the beginning of the American concentration camp!" Writer Albert Maltz joined the attack, addressing Stripling as "Mr. Quisling," a reference to the Norwegian leader Vidkun Quisling, who had collaborated with the Nazis.

Reading from a script by screenwriter Jerome Lawrence, Humphrey went on the radio to decry what had just occurred. "We saw the gavel of the committee chairman cutting off the words of free Americans. *The sound of that gavel, Mr. Thomas, rings across America!* Because every time your gavel struck, Mr. Thomas, it hit the First Amendment of the Constitution of the United States."

Thomas ignored the objections of Humphrey and the rest of the First Amendment Committee. Scenes like the ones played by

Lawson, Maltz, and Trumbo were exactly what HUAC had hoped for. The unfriendly witnesses said they would expose Thomas as a loud and pompous opportunist; instead they descended to his level, grandstanding, playing to the galleries, yapping away with red faces and outlandish forecasts. By the time Thomas closed the hearings, ten of the nineteen had been cited for contempt of court. In the process, the accused lost their most important sympathizers.

Huston was to condemn the mini-drama as "a sorry performance. You felt your skin crawl and your stomach turn. Before this spectacle, the attitude of the press had been extremely sympathetic. Now it changed." The director was not alone. As the hearings went on, Humphrey and a number of other movie people withdrew, buying one-way tickets back to Hollywood and washing their hands of the whole First Amendment business. But the press kept the story alive, running features and pictures, asking provocative questions. Hearst columnist George Sokolsky cornered the Bogarts and demanded to know why they had joined this pinko campaign in the first place. According to Lauren, Sokolsky suggested that her husband "issue a statement saying that he was not a Communist and had no sympathy for Communists, and denouncing the un-friendly witnesses. This he refused to do."

But Humphrey did go out of his way to dissociate himself from what the papers called "the Hollywood Ten." First he gave an interview to the press. In it, as Paul Hen-reid said resentfully, "he attempted to retract what he had said and done. 'I didn't know the people I was with were fellow travelers,' he told the reporters. I felt Bo-gart's statement was a form of betrayal, and it was the end of our friendship." Actually the betrayal was a two-way street. More than half of the hostile witnesses had lied to their own lawyers about their Communist past or present, and presented themselves to the Committee for the First Amendment as innocent victims framed by the govern-ment. Humphrey had this in mind when he attended a follow-up meeting, again at the Gershwins' house. Writer-director Abraham Polonsky, who would be blacklisted for seventeen years after refusing to testify before HUAC, remembered that "Bogart was furious. He was shouting at Danny Kaye, 'You fuckers sold me out' and he left." Alistair Cooke, then a correspondent for the *Guardian,* remarked afterward that "Bo-gart was aghast to discover" how many of the protesters "were down-the-line Communists coolly exploiting the protection of the First and Fifth Amendments to the Constitution. He had thought they were just freewheeling anarchists, like himself." Yet he could not bear to go over to the other side. With considerable rue, he predicted that HUAC would "nail anyone who ever scratched his ass during the National Anthem."

It was not a time Humphrey cared to remember in later years, but he was not alone in scurrying for cover. Eric Johnston, head of the Motion Picture Producers Association, originally spoke out against sensational testimony about Hollywood — "Scare-head stuff which is grossly unfair to a great American industry." As the pressure was raised, he backtracked, encouraging the committee to go about its business, because "an exposed Communist is an unarmed Communist." But, he pleaded, "don't put any American who isn't a Communist in a concentration camp of suspicion." Johnston then went about building just such a camp, working on a policy that would result in an industry-wide blacklist, not only of present and former Party members, but of those who appeared to have leftist sympathies that could range from out-and-out Stalinism to endorsing a group advocating the racial integration of major league baseball.

The "morals clause" was made a part of standard contracts during the 1930s. Its aim was to protect studios from being embarrassed by an employee's sexual misbehavior. (Fatty Arbuckle's rape charge and Charlie Chaplin's seduction of teenaged girls were examples that caused moguls many a sleepless night.) Thereafter, scandals were kept to a minimum because workers, from makeup artists to superstars, knew they could be summarily fired for misconduct. But now the clause was employed in a way the lawyers had not anticipated. A handful of executives took exception to this new policy, among them Sam Goldwyn, Dore Schary, and Walter Wanger; the other producers outvoted them. An official statement was handed to journalists: "We will not knowingly employ a Communist or a member of any party or group which advocates the overthrow of the government of the United States. . . . We are frank to recognize that such a policy involves dangers and risks. There is the danger of hurting innocent people. There is the risk of creating an atmosphere of fear. We will guard against this danger, this risk, this fear."

Immediately afterward came a ratcheting up of that danger, that risk, that fear. A blacklist spread across the industry. Motion picture directors, actors, even technicians, found themselves out of work because of current or bygone political activities. The only way for the listees to become rehabilitated was to furnish HUAC with names of similarly stigmatized friends, or to play the naïf before committee members. Humphrey was one of many who attempted to turn things around. The former screenwriter Dore Schary was called upon to explain the new studio policy. "We do not ask you to condone this," he said with a show of melancholy. Journalist Murray Kempton remarked that on the way out, Schary paused to put his hand on Dalton Trumbo's shoulder and commiserate for a moment. "A little later Trumbo went to prison and Dore Schary went to Metro-Goldwyn-Mayer as executive producer." John Garfield would arrange to place an article in the *Saturday Evening Post* entitled "I Was a Sucker for a Left Hook," only to die of heart failure before the piece could run. Eventually Edward G. Robinson would confess that "the Reds made a sucker out of me," and director Elia Kazan would run a full-page ad in the *New York Times* rationalizing the act of naming names.

During this tense period some directors

fled to Europe, where they found intermittent work. Some of the more skilled screenwriters fled to Mexico and submitted their scripts under pseudonyms. Actors were less fortunate; they could not perform under other faces. A few of them went east, where the Broadway and off-Broadway theaters maintained a stubborn resistance to political pressure. In their Bogart biography, A. M. Sperber and Eric Lax report that Helen Hayes urged Humphrey to return to New York rather than capitulate to the current Hollywood conditions. " 'My God,' he told her. 'I wouldn't do that!' He had been away too long; the confidence was gone."

He was in his late forties, balding, with a young wife and a career that was marking time. Doctors advised Humphrey that if he wanted children he would need to take hormone shots. These caused more of his hair to fall out, and his temper to be less than equable. *Dark Passage* was released in late 1947, at exactly the wrong time. The box office results were disappointing, and the studio blamed it on the political climate. New York *Daily News* columnist Ed Sullivan urged Humphrey to do some damage control. "I know you're OK," he pointed out. "So do your close friends. But the public is beginning to think you're a Red! Get that through your skull, Bogie."

Two instances of rehabilitation happened without any effort on Bogie's part. The *New York Times Sunday Magazine* ran an article headlined CAVALCADE OF HOLLYWOOD HEROES. Frank S. Nugent, a former *Times* movie reviewer, examined the trends in leading men from the silent days to the present. At first there was the "shy, bucolic, gangling youth, who never set foot in the house without kissing his mother, patting the dog and running his finger through the icing on the homemade cake on the kitchen table." He was followed, in time, by the man's man, who "cut a fumbling figure in the front parlor and was no match romantically for the mustached city slicker." Then came World War I, when "virility gained a bit of dash. Our hero learned to use the proper forks, smoke cigarettes and even wear a dinner jacket. His romantic image was improving." In the sound era the sophisticated bon vivant and the Latin Lover took over for a while, but they were not built for durability. In the 1930s they were supplanted by something unprecedented: the attractive but unyielding Tough Guy. "Nonchalance was his forte. He won and lost fortunes — or a month's pay — with a laugh. He worked hard, but not for mere gain and certainly not to make any down payments on any vine-covered cottage. He had nothing against dames as such. It was what they represented that annoyed him." And twenty years later, he was still in command. Nugent chose as his archetype the Philip Marlowe of *The Big Sleep*. In that character Humphrey was a neat composite of all that had gone before. "He is the Tough Guy (without his joy in living), the Great Lover (except that he usually is preoccupied and suffering from lack of sleep), the Sophisticate (but post-depression and enjoying a hangover) and the Dashing virile type (slowed down to a purposeful walk)."

And in the fall, *Good Housekeeping* ran "The Woman Who Dreamed About Humphrey Bogart," a short story by Mignon McLaughlin. In it, a childless couple, married for twelve years, begin to drift apart. Warren finds himself infatuated with a young redhead — though in the unspoken code of "shelter book" fiction he does nothing but flirt a little and squire her to a dance. Hilda finds her own lover in a reverie, dreaming of Bogart on a regular basis. In the end, Warren confesses his infatuation and promises never to see the redhead again. Hilda responds by silently swearing off Humphrey. She sees him in a final dream. The two are together at a nightclub, Humphrey in a dinner jacket, Hilda in a gold lamé gown. "Then, after they had been seated, they saw Warren, with That Girl." With Humphrey's patented combination of nobility and violence, he walks over to Warren and smacks him around as the girl melts away. "Then Humphrey Bogart turned away disdainfully, brushing his hands, and went back to Hilda. His eyes softened at sight of her; his mouth shaped a wry smile; his touch on her arm, as they swept out of the night club, was inexpressibly tender.

"Hilda, asleep in her husband's arms, sighed a little sigh.

"THE END."

The good news was that Humphrey's romantic status had remained undisturbed by the ideological wars in Washington, New York, and Hollywood. The bad news was that Ed Sullivan had read the entrails correctly: Humphrey couldn't afford to stay on the sidelines much longer. Under pressure, Warners arranged for *Photoplay* magazine to publish "I'm No Communist" over the Bogart byline. Until that dramatic flight to Washington, the piece testified, his political activity had consisted of endorsements for

FDR. This year, because of his objections to HUAC's ham-handed investigations of Hollywood, he was a Marxist in the eyes of the conservative press. "The *New York Times,* the *Herald Tribune* and other reputable publications editorially had questioned the House Committee on Un-American Activities, warning that it was infringing on free speech. When a group of us Hollywood actors and actresses said the same thing, the roof fell in on us. In some fashion, I took the brunt of the attack. Suddenly, the plane that had flown us East became 'Bogart's plane,' carrying 'Bogart's group.' For once, top billing became embarrassing." He went on to describe his trip to Washington as "ill-advised," and himself as a dupe and a "foolish and impetuous American." The moral of the story, he noted with asperity, could be seen in a gift presented to him when he got back to Hollywood. "Some friends sent me a mounted fish and underneath it was written: 'If I hadn't opened my big mouth, I wouldn't be here.'"

III

Writer and, later, director Richard Brooks maintained that Humphrey's renunciation of the First Amendment committee signaled an end "to the illusions of life, that everything is going to be fine, that there's going to be a happy ending. Bogie was never the same again." This smacks of the kind of romantic wish-dream that stayed with the Old Left for decades, crystallized in a film called *The Front.* Woody Allen, an apolitical schlemiel who lets blacklisted writers put his name on their scripts, is hauled before HUAC. Defiantly, he responds: "Fellas, I don't recognize the right of this committee to ask me these kinds of questions. And furthermore, you can go fuck yourselves." The frame freezes as the voice of Frank Sinatra is heard singing, "Fairy tales can come true . . ."

For two divergent groups of filmmakers, the period of the blacklist would redefine the notion of masculinity. Opponents of the new studio policy considered themselves loners standing against the violators of civil liberty (i.e., HUAC). Those who furnished the committee with names portrayed themselves as guardians of freedom, fighting thugs (i.e., Communists) who sought the violent overthrow of the U.S. government.

In his drama *The Crucible,* Arthur Miller would view the superstitious witch hunts of seventeenth-century Salem, Massachusetts, as a metaphor for the anti-Communist hysteria sweeping America in his own time.

The playwright's spokesman, upright farmer John Proctor, is willing to recite his own sins, but "I cannot judge another. I have no tongue for it." He is hanged for his principled silence.

Screenwriter Budd Schulberg and director Elia Kazan gave names to HUAC. In *On the Waterfront* they would make their hero, Terry Malloy, a failed boxer turned hired goon for a corrupt union chief. An investigating body is met with a code of silence. Only when Terry's brother is annihilated by racketeers does the thug spill what he knows to the investigators, and is nearly beaten to death for his action. Given the right occasion, the audience is meant to conclude, informing may be the only way to strike back at criminals.

Which was the true male, then? Was it the rigid Proctor, as originally played by Arthur Kennedy on Broadway? Or the informer Terry Malloy, as portrayed by Marlon Brando? It was a matter of great importance to those affected, but it was not the only way to take the measure of a man, and many refused to be defined in such narrow terms. Humphrey Bogart was one of them. As the decade wound down, he continued to present his own brand of masculinity, which had nothing to do with polemics.

For despite the dire pronouncements about the Bogart soul, Humphrey was not ruined personally or professionally by his choices. Though he remained a liberal in private life, he felt a justifiable anger about the way his name and reputation had been used. To be sure, if Humphrey and the other First Amendment committee members, *and* the studio heads, *and* the principal Wall Street investors in those studios had stood together in opposition to the so-called Inquisition in Eden, there might have been a chance to save the industry from the predators. That coalition never developed, however, and it is folly to assume that Humphrey Bogart should have sacrificed his reputation, standing mutely and obediently by as the Nineteen manipulated him for their own purposes.

In any case, the clash of committees was only one event that made Humphrey Bogart Topic B in Hollywood that year. On December 21, 1947, Mark Hellinger suffered his final heart attack. Hellinger had been a hard-driving, self-indulgent cardiac case for years, but friends thought of him as always dying, never dead. Now, at the age of forty-four, he drew his last breaths in Cedars of Lebanon hospital in West Hollywood. Born a Jew, he had never embraced any religion. Nevertheless, his funeral was staged — and that is the apposite word — at All Saints Episcopal Church in Beverly Hills. *Tout* Hollywood was there, actors, producers, reporters, all milling about, trying to avoid a glimpse of the gray-faced corpse in the satin-lined coffin. A Catholic priest gave a eulogy and made the sign of the cross. It was all too much for Humphrey. The Irish had it right, he told Lauren. They had a wake and celebrated life. When he went, he wanted to be cremated. "My friends can raise a glass and tell stories about me if they like. No mourning — don't believe in it."

David O. Selznick waited a decent interval, then canceled the agreement to produce film adaptations done by the Bogart-Hellinger company. Hellinger was no more, and he was the producing end of the team. No use pretending Humphrey could go it alone. Jack Warner expressed grief at the outcome; privately he was delighted. Bogart was back in the fold, working with Lauren in *Key Largo*. He was a Warner Bros. employee again, very high priced, granted, but an employee nonetheless. The situation did not bode well. Humphrey had matured in many ways, but when it came time to confront father figures, particularly ones who liked to exert their authority at every turn, he could become as insubordinate as a schoolboy. He and Warner regarded each other warily, like two boxers in the early rounds, as the film got under way.

Maxwell Anderson's overcooked drama had opened on Broadway in 1939. Richard Brooks and John Huston did the film adaptation, with Huston directing with his customary mix of intensity on the sound stage and chaffing humor off-screen. He liked to ride Humphrey between takes, always being careful not to push him too far. When the *New Yorker* reporter Lillian Ross visited the set, she sat with the Bogarts, Huston, and Edward G. Robinson, the film's snarling heavy. Huston told Ross that "Bogie has succeeded in not being a politician." Why? Because "he owns a fifty-four-foot yawl. When you own a fifty-four-foot yawl, you've got to provide for her upkeep." In a snarl that recalled *Little Caesar,* Edward G. Robinson spoke of his hero, Franklin D. Roosevelt: "The great chief died and everyone's guts died with him." Lauren was worried: "The *Daily Worker* runs Bogie's picture and right away he's a dangerous Communist. What will happen if the American Legion and the Legion of Decency boycott all his pictures?" Humphrey played it cool. "It's just that my picture in the *Daily Worker* offends me, baby." Robinson grunted. Huston had heard about a congressman who objected to a line in *Sierra Madre:* "An ounce of gold, mister, is worth what it is because of the human labor that went into the findin' and the gettin' of it." Maybe it was the word "labor" that bothered the representative. John changed the subject: "Let's eat."

Profound differences separated the theatrical version and the cinema adaptation made nine years later. Anderson had written the dialogue in free verse, as if to give his gangster melodrama a Shakespearean tone. The film actors spoke unadorned hostile American. The play concerned the moral battle between two disparate figures. Frank McCloud is a burned-out veteran of the Spanish Civil War, stopping at a hotel to visit its owner, the father of a buddy killed in battle. Johnny Rocco, a crime czar grown old and bitter, is stuck in the same place when a hurricane batters the Florida coast.

In the film, McCloud is a World War II veteran of the Italian campaign, weak in spirit and lacking all conviction — a distant relative of Alan Squier in *The Petrified Forest.* Rocco, far removed from the Roaring Twenties, seems more of a dinosaur than an aging kingpin — a heavyweight Duke Mantee, also surrounded by armed and dangerous henchmen. Not that he needs them: the man who runs the hotel is confined to a wheelchair, and the women are terrified. As for McCloud, he offers even less of a challenge:

MCCLOUD: I had hopes once, but I gave them up.

ROCCO: Hopes for what?

MCCLOUD: A world in which there's no place for Johnny Rocco.

ROCCO: *(Handing him a pistol)* OK, soldier. Here's your chance. . . . You can make your hopes come true. But you gotta die for it.
(Pointing his own sidearm at McCloud) See where I'm aiming? At your belly. Go ahead, shoot. . . . Show them how you're not afraid to die.

MCCLOUD: *(Giving up)* One Rocco more or less isn't worth dying for.

Alan Squier found salvation in withdrawal and self-sacrifice — an honorable stance to take between the wars. Twelve years later, that position was untenable. Frank McCloud could only show a momentary cowardice. In the end he would recover his manhood and morality by confronting Johnny Rocco at sea.

Working under the restraints of a limited budget and a short schedule, Huston completed the movie in seventy-eight days, an extraordinarily brief time for an A picture. To accomplish this feat, he had the down-at-heels hotel constructed on the Warners lot. Exterior shots of the storm were taken from stock footage used in *Night unto Night,* a Warner Bros. melodrama starring Ronald Reagan. Huston also benefited from a happy cast. Besides the Bogarts and Robinson, he had such experienced pros as Lionel Barrymore, Thomas Gomez, and Claire Trevor. Humphrey and Edward G. liked each other and took pleasure in their role reversals. In his early Hollywood years, the younger man was regularly gunned down by his elder. At the finale of *Key Largo,* Rocco is killed by McCloud, who regains the courage he thought had been lost forever. Robinson had no objection; he relished the role and made the most of it. In Huston's opinion, *Key Largo* was "best remembered by most people for the introductory scene, with Eddie in the bathtub, cigar in mouth. He looked like a crustacean with its shell off." Before filming began, Robinson and his agent complained about his reduced status. When he wrote his autobiography, though, Robinson steered away from any hints of acrimony. "Why not second billing?" he asked rhetorically. "At fifty-three I was lucky to get any billing at all."

Claire Trevor took a pay cut to play Gaye Dawn, Rocco's alcoholic mistress, a part that was not in the original play. It was obvious to her, as it was to Huston, that the role would showcase her ability to make a hooker into a sympathetic victim. The weary, humiliated Gaye will do anything for a shot of whiskey. Rocco makes her sing "Moanin' Low" before the group of appalled and helpless onlookers. The woman has no talent, but she plunges ahead anyway, her voice filled with tears. "I was after John all the time to rehearse this song," Trevor remembered, "and he would always say, 'Plenty of time.' " One day, after they came back from lunch, the director suddenly announced that she was on. Furious but ever professional, Trevor performed on cue, warbling in and out of key, pathetically vulnerable, psychologically isolated. Huston "knew what he was doing," she acknowledged. "I was embarrassed. I was *supposed* to be embarrassed. I thought that day would never end. That was torture. But that's what got the effect." Spontaneous applause greeted her effort. Out of earshot Harry Lewis, playing one of Rocco's henchmen, whispered to Gomez, his fellow hoodlum. "She's going to win the Academy Award for that song alone," he predicted — correctly, as it turned out. Humphrey was appreciative, but quiet. Sad women always got him down. His mother and both sisters had been afflicted with depression, and Mayo was a classic case of emotional despair. When Trevor sang in a pathetic, uncertain voice, she had to have reminded Humphrey of the days when he and Mayo went on the USO tour of Italy. Mayo warbled World War II favorites for the GIs in the same sort of quavering tone.

But he wasn't one to wallow. By the time *Key Largo* wrapped, Humphrey was in a celebratory mood. *The Treasure of the Sierra Madre* had received universal raves. *Variety* admired the picture's "compelling honesty" and predicted that the "distinguished work will take its place in the repertory of Hollywood's great and enduring achievements." In the *New York Times,* Bosley Crowther had nothing but admiration for *Treasure*'s steel-springed outdoor drama, and singled out the man who played Fred C. Dobbs for special commendation: "Mr. Bogart's performance in this film is perhaps the best

and most substantial that he has ever done."
The most extravagant praise came from
James Agee, then writing for two magazines.
In the *Nation* he called *Treasure* "one of the
most visually alive and beautiful movies I
have ever seen." In *Time,* which then had no
bylines, he wrote that the film was "one of
the best things Hollywood has done since it
learned to talk. . . . Humphrey Bogart cannot completely eliminate the existence of
Humphrey Bogart — but he makes a noble
effort to lose himself and does far and away
the best work of his career."

Key Largo opened in midsummer to generally appreciative reviews, although none to
match the reception of the previous Bogart-
Huston film. It was, after all, only a Warner
Bros. gangster movie outfitted with modern,
portentous dialogue and experienced professionals. Bogart and Robinson had been
doing this sort of material for so long that
the movie sometimes seemed like Old-
Timers Day for big-league crooks. Trevor
and Gomez went along for the ride, and
John Huston made sure they all gave a lot
better than they got from the shooting
script.

Nevertheless, *Key Largo* did better at the
box office than *The Treasure of the Sierra
Madre,* possibly because its leads were more

celebrated, and because Maxwell Anderson was something of a brand name. *Treasure*'s cast had only one authentic star, and the book's author, B. Traven, was a recluse whose personality and work were unknown to the general public. None of this seemed to matter to Humphrey. He had it both ways now, on top artistically *and* commercially. More good news came his way late in the year when Lauren informed him that he was going to be a father. At least *she* thought it was good news. Humphrey was not so sure. Yes, he had wanted a baby; why else had he taken those hormone shots? And yet, when he thought about it, what kind of life would the Bogarts have now? A child would surely come between them. Besides, at the age of forty-nine how would he relate to a newborn? He hardly knew how to talk to kids of any age. A story made the rounds, and one friend swore it was true: Humphrey had been told to speak to his godson about religion. The boy was thirteen and it was time to confront the relationship of God and man. He took the teenager to a restaurant, ordered a drink, and began. "Listen," Humphrey instructed. "There are twelve commandments."

Henry Luce had proclaimed the twentieth "the American Century," and his magazine, *Fortune,* euphorically offered exhibit A: 1947 had enjoyed "the greatest productive record in the peacetime history of this or any other nation." The ascent continued in 1948. Unemployment had just fallen below 4 percent. General Motors, Chrysler, and Ford were all prospering in this sunny economic climate, as were the steel, oil, and home-building industries. Americans seemed to prosper in every field, just as Luce foresaw. The Olympics were held in 1948, the first since Berlin hosted the "Hitler Olympics" of 1936. American athletes, especially Bob Mathias, Harrison Dillard, and Melvin Patton, dominated the track and field events and took home thirty-eight medals. At Mount Palomar, California, the world's largest telescope probed the skies. Chuck Yeager broke the sound barrier. New medicines, such as cortisone, aureomycin, and other wonder drugs, were being developed in U.S. laboratories.

But one sector ran counter to the national trends: moviemaking. To Wall Street's dismay, Hollywood found itself in a vast and deepening depression: film attendance was down by 25 percent. Only two years before, some eighty million people had gone to the movies *every week.* But that was before the advent of affordable television. Now one out of eight American families owned a set and their numbers grew by the week. No need for viewers to go out; entertainment and sports came to them. Current events, formerly the exclusive province of theatrically released newsreels, became available in the living room. (For the convenience of the networks, the Democrat and Republican conventions would both be held in Philadelphia.) And TV had not dealt the only body blow to the film business. The HUAC investigations and the resultant blacklist did considerable damage to the image of Hollywood as a "dream factory." At the year's end came the knockout punch, otherwise known as the Paramount decision. For years the Justice Department had accused the studios of monopolistic practices, and for years Hollywood's expensive lawyers had fended off the prosecutors. In 1948 the government finally triumphed in its battle against "vertical integration." In essence, this meant that the major studios could no longer control every aspect of the film industry from the actors to the composers all the way down to the technicians, and all the way out to the movie houses, which were owned and/or operated by the studios. Something had to give. "It is clear," wrote Justice William O. Douglas, that the big studios were guilty of a conspiracy and that "the conspiracy was exclusionary, i.e., that it was designed to strengthen their hold on the exhibition field." To break up the monopoly, the studios would have to relinquish their interests in about fourteen hundred movie theaters. The older moguls thought this decision was nothing to trouble their heads about. Once their more literate sycophants pointed the way, they found comfort in the words of Nietzsche: "That which does not destroy me makes me stronger." They told themselves that the latest emergency was like the hysteria once prompted by the arrival of sound, and the censorious production code, and the periodic money shortages. It would fade away like all the others. The realists knew better. This was the true fade to black. Justice Douglas had sounded the death knell of the studio system. Hollywood's Golden Era was done.

Because the production chiefs were so drastically weakened, actors with clout found themselves in a position to bargain. Humphrey, quick to see what was happening around him, acquired a new business associate. Robert Lord, a screenwriter turned producer, used his address at Columbia for the new company, Santana Productions. It was named after Humphrey's boat, and at the moment had only a little more capital than a new yacht would have cost. It hardly mattered; Bogart and Lord struck a fresh deal with Harry Cohn, the Columbia chief. Humphrey would star in Santana's first movie, *Knock on Any Door,* adapted from Willard Motley's book. Motley, a black novelist who had been raised among poor whites, knew more about slum folk than he knew about writing. His works were filled with finger-pointing platitudes, and his biggest best seller conveyed messages as terse as bumper stickers. Poverty creates criminals. Society is at fault. We are all murderers for looking the other way.

The focal point of *Knock on Any Door* is Nick Romano, a slum kid accused of murder. At the time Marlon Brando, a champion of underdogs everywhere, was rumored to be interested in playing the defendant. In fact, the sensational twenty-four-year-old star of *A Streetcar Named Desire* would hardly have been enticed by a courtroom melodrama, but the buzz didn't hurt. The new team of Bogart and Lord looked the field over, and gave the role to a handsome, dark-haired newcomer. Next, they needed a director. Insiders were talking up *They Live by Night,* Nicholas Ray's Depression-era film of a young couple on the run. Humphrey had to find out whether the advance word was RKO hype or the real thing. He got hold of a print and screened it at the house. Several days later Ray was signed to direct Santana's first feature, starring Humphrey Bogart and introducing John Derek. "Play the role as tough as you can — see, kid?" Humphrey advised the newcomer. "Look what happened to Gable, Tracy, Cagney, Robinson, Raft, Ladd and myself. We all got our start in crime."

As all this transpired, the Bogarts became parents. Lauren gave birth to a six-pound, six-ounce boy on January 6, 1949. In Cedars of Lebanon Hospital the infant was called Steve, in honor of the character in *To Have and Have Not.* The birth certificate was more formal; it read Stephen Humphrey Bogart, a name that would haunt the boy for decades. Friends of the family sent gifts and cards, none more heartening than one from the president. While he was campaigning, Harry Truman had been introduced to the Bogarts at a Democratic Party fund-raiser. Lauren was visibly pregnant, and Truman bet twenty dollars that the child would be a boy. Humphrey insisted that it would be a girl. After Steve's birth Humphrey mailed a check to 1600 Pennsylvania Ave. A thank-you note came back along with the check. The newly elected chief offered his congratulations and added, "It is a rare instance when I find a man who remembers his commitments and meets them on the dot. Harry S. Truman."

There wasn't time to revel in his new fatherhood; Humphrey immediately went back to work on *Knock on Any Door*. Professionally written, acted, and directed, the film followed the novel's simplistic approach, evident in Humphrey's valedictory lines: "Until we do away with the type of neighborhood that produced this boy, ten will spring up to take his place, a hundred, a thousand. Until we wipe out the slums and rebuild them, knock on any door and you may find Nick Romano." Reviews were mixed. They could hardly have been otherwise. A youth whose credo is "Live fast, die young, and have a good-looking corpse" exerted little appeal for journalists over thirty. Few bought the then-trendy argument that criminals aren't responsible for their actions — they've been trapped by poverty, peer pressure, and absentee parents. In the end, *Knock on Any Door* did more to establish Nicholas Ray as a director to watch, and John Derek as the latest teenage idol, than it did to augment Santana's bottom line.

Next up for the company: *Tokyo Joe,* a feature whose attractions were obvious — a little too obvious. This time out Santana took no chances. The director was Stewart Heisler, who had been in the business since the 1920s when he had edited such vaudeville films as *In Hollywood with Potash and Perlmutter.* Since Humphrey had no intention of going to Japan for the filming, a second unit was assigned to take footage of the Japanese capital. An actor with Humphrey's trademark trench coat was shot from behind; in the editing process, matching shots were lined up showing the hero against a rear-screen projection of Ginza streets.

The story follows the trail of war veteran Joe Barrett. Before Pearl Harbor he and his wife, a White Russian named Trina, ran Tokyo Joe's gambling joint. When Joe returns to occupied Japan, he finds that Trina, reported as slain during the war, is not only alive but living with a new husband and their little daughter, Anya. Joe is the child's father, however, and he wants her to go back with him to America. The trouble is, Trina won't give her up and too many laws stand in Joe's way. To achieve his goal he strikes a deal with a gang leader, Baron Kimura. Joe will front for an airfreight service smuggling war criminals back into Japan, and the baron will get him the child. Betrayal, kidnapping, and violence follow. Before the finale, Anya is rescued and the fascists are caught, thanks to the American's valor. But Joe pays for all this with his life.

The international movie star Sessue Hayakawa played the gang leader; the slender, austere Alexander Knox was Trina's new husband; and Trina herself was the thirty-year-old Czechoslovakian actress Florence Marly. Resemblances to *Casablanca* were everywhere, with Knox standing in for Paul Henreid, Marly for Ingrid Bergman, Hayakawa for Conrad Veidt, and Tokyo Joe's for Rick's Café Américain. But as many filmmakers have learned the hard way, there is only one *Casablanca.* This imitation looked particularly jerry-built and inadequate, even though both films starred Humphrey Bogart. Reviews were gloomy across the board. Once again Humphrey Bogart was doing an impression of Humphrey Bogart, delivering the lines professionally, tough and terse as always, but showing none of the inner life that had invigorated so much of his recent work. No amount of promotion would make the film a hit. Still, Humphrey was about to turn fifty. He was not just the star of *Tokyo Joe,* his company had produced it. Wearing two hats was not his style, but there was no way out of his obligations to Santana. He grimaced at the schedule of meetings the publicity department had set up. The palaver would have to be gone through all over again — the stories about his youth, his school, his early years in the movies. But the interviews had to be done. He flew east to the paparazzi, who, with any luck, would give him valuable column inches. He got the inches, all right. Every one of them was injurious to his image, and served to blight Santana's future. Humphrey would have been far better off at sea or at home. Anywhere but in New York.

Chapter 6
Cut the Gab and Bring Me an Order of Fried Rabbit

I

Since the release of *The Squaw Man* in 1914, the public appetite for Hollywood gossip has been insatiable. Originally journalists reported what they saw and heard. In time public relations specialists stepped in, feeding items to columnists, fending off reporters, carefully shaping the images of their clients. Skilled as these experts were, though, they couldn't bottle up scandals forever. Bad news always had a way of leaking out. But sometimes, to the studios' astonishment, that news turned out to be good for business. In 1932, for example, Jean Harlow's second husband, Paul Bern, killed himself. The reason, said investigators, was because of an inability to satisfy a wife twenty-two years his junior. After the suicide, the movies' first blond bombshell was offered her biggest and most popular roles. In 1942 Errol Flynn, who liked to boast, "I like my whisky old and my women young," was accused of statutory rape by a seventeen-year-old girl. He was cleared of the charge; nonetheless, the durable phrase "In like Flynn" was coined. Errol became the movies' quintessential womanizer, as irresistible on-screen as he was in the boudoir. In this tradition, Humphrey was involved in an incident at El Morocco that burnished his reputation as a treat-'em-rough romantic lead.

Nightclubs flourished in the immediate postwar period — the Stork Club, El Morocco, and 21 were special favorites of hard-drinking New Yorkers, and of tourists who paid high prices to gawk at celebrities. On the evening of September 25, 1949, Lauren and Humphrey were joined by his old drinking buddy Bill Seeman, a prosperous wholesale grocer. The trio stopped off at 21 for a few glasses. By midnight Lauren had consumed more than enough liquor and retired to the Bogarts' suite at the St. Regis Hotel. Humphrey and Bill, noisily advertising their thirst for more, went on to the Stork Club. On a drunken whim they sent a waiter out to purchase two enormous stuffed pandas, souvenirs sold at Reuben's Broadway delicatessen. After a few more drinks, the pals and their pandas taxied to

El Morocco on East 52nd Street. They secured a table for four, set up the big toys in chairs, and ordered some adult beverages. Around 3 a.m., twenty-two-year-old Robin Roberts, a self-described "model," rose from her own table and tried to grab Humphrey's panda. He saw what she was doing, and pulled the toy in his direction. Roberts lost her footing and fell down awkwardly and hard. Robin's friend Peggy Rabe rushed to Roberts's rescue. She, too, wound up on the floor. The ladies' dates rose to defend them, saucers and plates were thrown; security personnel intervened; threats to sue followed a few minutes later.

That was on Saturday night. Four days later Humphrey was served with a summons to appear in Mid-Manhattan Court early on Friday morning — "too damn early," in his opinion. Nevertheless, he showed up on time. By then the tabloids had covered the "Panda Fracas" in lurid detail. There were photos of Roberts in a dress that showed plenty of poitrine, and quotes from Humphrey abjuring any thoughts of violence. He had socked no one, he reminded reporters, and would never hit a woman in any case because "I'm too sweet and chivalrous. Besides, it's too dangerous." He did confess to being drunk at El Morocco, "but who isn't at three o'clock in the morning?" Covering the courtroom procedure for the *Guardian,* journalist Alistair Cooke described Humphrey as looking tight-lipped and melancholy, sober as a judge. A lawyer accompanied the actor, who was now wearing a gray suit, white shirt, and tie of subdued colors. "Tapping behind him on limb-breaking high heels came a sultry brunette, her lawyer and a bosom companion, a round-faced blonde."

After hearing both sides, the court issued an opinion. This was a case of attempted extortion; the testimony of Misses Roberts and Rabe was not to be taken seriously, hence the case had no merit and was rejected. "Mr. Bogart nodded his expert appreciation of American court proceedings, and the lawyers, the blondes and brunettes swept out to the grinning crowd outside. . . . Once again, justice had triumphed." Justice notwithstanding, the club owners got righteous. El Morocco declared Bogart persona non grata, and some two hundred and fifty "niteries" gave out the word that they would tolerate no more outrageous behavior from a customer — any customer, no matter how high he was on the movie marquees. The incident gave rise to a remark by Dave Chasen, proprietor of Chasen's restaurant in Beverly Hills, where Humphrey was known to knock back a few: "Bogart's a hell of a nice guy until around 11:30 p.m. After that, he thinks he's Bogart."

Warners executives were unhappy about the rumble in New York. Granted, bad attention was better than no attention. However, this was not the Prohibition era and alcoholism had lost the power to amuse long, long ago. But to Jack Warner, booze was only a secondary annoyance. The basic problems were effrontery and ingratitude. Warner considered the possibilities, and devised a way to strike back. His revenge was the downside of the panda affair, and it damaged the man who was still teetering between celebrity and serious actor.

At the half-century mark, Humphrey still had trouble defining his persona. On one hand he was a serious and versatile film actor who had paid his dues in scores of plays and dozens of B movies on his climb to the top. On the other hand, he was a wise guy, a drinker, a persistent annoyance to authority figures — in short, a case of arrested development. This conflict arose from a lifelong ambivalence about celebrity. Stardom had brought him money, status, glamour, love. But it had also robbed him of privacy and a chance to reflect on it all. He was not comfortable with many actors on his level; he preferred the company of writers and artists. But in the Hollywood caste system, stars were expected to live in a certain neighborhood and entertain in a prescribed manner, no matter how alien to their wishes and yearnings. In the coming years Humphrey would find more solace aboard the *Santana* than he did on dry land. Bobbing about Catalina, he was not fleeing the business, he was seeking himself.

Warner's payback was just the sort of insult that drove Humphrey wild. It took the form of two second-rate vehicles, *Chain Lightning* and *Murder Inc.,* later retitled *The Enforcer.* Bogart, the studio pointed out, was contractually obliged to do both of them. For the first picture, Stuart Heisler functioned as a foreman rather than a director. Humphrey played Matt, a swaggering, onetime bomber pilot. His ex-girlfriend, Jo (Eleanor Parker), works for Mr. Willis (Raymond Massey), an unscrupulous manufacturer reminiscent of the executive in Arthur Miller's *All My Sons.* Anxious to sell a jet plane to the air force before it's been properly tested, Willis hires Matt to do some airborne experiments. But the company's designer, Carl (Richard Whorf), takes an intense dislike to the new man and flies the plane himself — only to perish when an escape device fails. Guilt-stricken and humbled, Matt takes a new plane for a long, risky flight. He accomplishes his goal and, for lagniappe, wins back Jo's affection.

Chain Lightning was efficient hackwork, nothing more. Bogart did a lot of grimacing; Massey matched him scowl for scowl; Parker went through her scenes with one expression — weariness. Aloft, the film displayed a certain tension and style; back on planet Earth it turned into a stodgy, dated, by-the-numbers melodrama.

There was nothing inherently wrong with the other Warners project. *The Enforcer* was based on the true story of Murder Inc., a group of killers who worked for the mob in the 1930s. New York detectives closed in, working with victims and stool pigeons to track down the leaders. One of the informants, a thug named Abe Reles, promised to give state's evidence against his employers. Reles was in police custody when he mysteriously "threw" himself out a window, thereby weakening the prosecutor's case. Surrounded by corrupt cops, the enforcers found other ways to nail the criminals. By the end of the decade Murder Inc. was defunct.

The cinematic Bogart had visited this

underworld many times, first as a criminal, then on the other side of the law. The remorseless private eye of *The Maltese Falcon,* the wisecracking shamus Philip Marlowe of *The Big Sleep,* the street-smart defense attorney of *Knock on Any Door* were unforgettable. That was their trouble. Those film noir types were familiar not only to Humphrey but to moviegoers. As crusading district attorney Martin Ferguson, the star could add little to such a retrograde feature. Ironically, what saved *The Enforcer* from ignominy were the supporting characters. The Broadway director Bretaigne Windust (*Life with Father; Arsenic and Old Lace*) was supposed to make his debut with this film. But several weeks into production Windust was hospitalized. Raoul Walsh took over. The seasoned old pro refused credit — this was Windust's first film opportunity, and he wasn't going to spoil the debut. Nevertheless, it was Walsh who coaxed outstanding performances from Zero Mostel, shortly to go on the blacklist, and Ted De Corsia, a seasoned actor who had played racketeers so many times audiences thought he was a Mafioso gone straight. Humphrey was the one who suffered from their brilliance. Notes British film historian Jonathan Coe, "This is one of the few Bogart films where it is possible to believe — as you couldn't with *High Sierra,* say, or *The Big Sleep* — that it might have been just as good with a different star in the central role."

None of this sat well with Humphrey. "He knew damn well that in this town you're only as good as your last movie, and the last two movies were a lot less than great," observed a friend. The regression was demoralizing on two counts. It meant that Jack Warner had won the battle, and it meant that fewer first-class scripts were going to be sent to the recalcitrant Bogart. The backslide could be measured off-screen as well. Almost all major movie stars repeated their big roles on radio, the dominant electronic medium of the time. *Lux Radio Theater,* for example, used such Hollywood luminaries as Fredric March, Barbara Stanwyck, Clark Gable, Joan Crawford, and Gary Cooper. On other programs Humphrey voiced his parts in *High Sierra, Casablanca,* and *The Maltese Falcon;* in addition, he had been the male lead in *A Farewell to Arms* opposite Joan Fontaine. But now Humphrey and Lauren made plans to act in their own radio program, set in a shady Havana hotel. It would do very little to burnish the Bogart image — but then, what was the Bogart image these days? Humphrey was no longer sure whether the radio show was a smart move or an act of desperation.

In *Bold Venture* he would play Slate Shannon, hotel proprietor and sailor; Lauren would be his ward, a sultry young woman named Sailor Duval. The script called for Shannon's boat to encounter pirates, counterfeiters, and assorted lowlifes. The "adventure, intrigue, mystery and romance" would take place "in the sultry settings of tropical Havana and the mysterious islands of the Caribbean." There was nothing inherently wrong with this idea — except that it bordered on self-parody, and that other caricatures were already at work sullying the Bogart brand name.

Two animated shorts, for instance, mocked Humphrey as they amused audiences. In the racist "Bacall to Arms," a cartoon Bogart and Bacall flirt with each other. She lights her cigarette with a blowtorch and he gets covered with charcoal. In blackface, Humphrey does an imitation of the hoarse-voiced Eddie "Rochester" Anderson, Jack Benny's African American butler. In "Slick Hare," another Humphrey caricature bosses Elmer Fudd around in a restaurant ("Cut the gab and bring me an order of fried rabbit"). Bugs Bunny eludes them both, and the intimidator meekly settles for a ham sandwich.

A novelty song followed. "All Right, Louie, Drop the Gun" was written by the husband-and-wife team of Ray Carter and Lucile Johnson. A man sings about his failed romance — every time he approaches his girlfriend, she hollers the title words, "All right, Louie, drop the gun," a misquote from *Casablanca*. (What Rick actually says is "Not so fast, Louie.")

Humphrey's company added to the general depreciation. *Sirocco* was Santana's attempt to recapture the magic of *Casablanca*. The period piece took place in French-occupied Syria, circa 1925. Everything in the film had a strained air about it, including the central performance. During its preparation Humphrey spoke to *New Yorker* reporter Lillian Ross. "I've been doing the role for years," he told her. "I've worn that trench coat of mine in half the pictures I've been in. What I don't like is business worries. . . . I'm bowed down with business worries." To cite one example, "Santana has had eleven writers on *Sirocco,* and none of them goons has come across with an ending yet." A conclusion was eventually provided, and Humphrey wrapped his trench coat around the part of Harry Smith, a man out for Number One at all times. The gunrunner is a man described by a French colonel as having "no morals, no political convictions." Smith remains that way until the finale, when he decides to act gallantly, takes the side of the good guys, and gets killed by a terrorist's grenade. The co-star was the beautiful but uncharismatic Marta Toren; other than a Swedish accent ("How can a man so ogly be so handsome?" she asks Humphrey), the actress had none of Ingrid Bergman's cinematic virtues. Lee J. Cobb, Everett Sloane, and Zero Mostel were supposed to lend the proceedings a raffish style, but their parts were underwritten and the performances fizzled. Curtis Bernhardt had previously directed *Conflict*. This time out, he provided little energy and no inspiration.

The picture was held at arm's length by critics on both sides of the Atlantic. To almost all of them *Sirocco* seemed a parody of a Bogart movie, studio-bound, the fez-topped costumes bogus, and the dialogue stilted and unconvincing. They got no argument from Humphrey; he was to acknowledge privately that *Sirocco* "was one we had to do. It stank, of course." But being candid about doing a bad movie did nothing for his morale or for his deteriorating career.

He had fallen from grace and he had done it while everyone was watching. And he had no one to blame but himself.

Ironically, Santana was to salvage the Bogart reputation. Sandwiched between Humphrey's bad choices was a modest noir thriller called *In a Lonely Place*. Nicholas Ray would go on to make some important films about loners and outsiders, among them *Rebel Without a Cause* and *The Savage Innocents*. But for many reasons this was his most personal work. Ray became an alchemist as he worked on *Lonely Place*, pushing Humphrey to the limit until he turned the star back into an artist. The actor who liked to affect the aura of a loner who insists on going his own way was in fact the neediest of all leading men. For without a gifted boss he was condemned to repeat himself in film after film. In this picture Nicholas Ray, like John Huston before him and after him, showed just how director-dependent Humphrey was.

In a Lonely Place is character-driven in every sense. Before he has spoken a word, the male lead is described as a troubled figure with nowhere to go but down. The mise-en-scène made Humphrey uncomfortable, perhaps because it seemed a little too close to home. The character he played was a Hollywood personality, wellborn yet insecure, edgy, defensive, teasing, with a streak of violence hidden beneath a mask of politesse. The script offers a concise description:

> Into the scene, headed for Romanoff's, comes Dixon "Dix" Steele. He is a tightly knit man with an air of controlled, spring-steel tension about him. He wears a well-cut, but well-worn tweed jacket and slacks.
>
> Mr. Steele — God help him — is a motion picture writer.

That contradictory writer hasn't had a hit in a decade. Dix makes a big point of putting down his colleagues for doing hackwork in the "popcorn business" — then tries to come up with a script based on a bestselling potboiler, even though he refuses to read it. The writer claims to have no interest in the human condition — but punches out a local hotshot for taunting his pal, a onetime movie star, now a washed-up rummy (played by Robert Warwick, an old pro who was in Humphrey's first important play, *Drifting*). Thus far, it's the Bogart of old — cynical, unyielding, yet with a patrician nobility winking just beneath the surface.

In fact this was an entirely new kind of role for Humphrey, more mature than Sam Spade and more complicated than Fred C. Dobbs. On a whim, Dix invites a hatcheck girl, Mildred Atkinson (Martha Stewart), back to his apartment. Although Mildred is a pretty brunette, the offer is literary, not sexual. She's read the novel and Dix wants her to tell him the story in easily assimilated form. Mildred is a simple girl; the screenwriter is bored to distraction. When she finishes talking, he sends her out into the night with barely concealed distaste. The next morning Mildred's body is discovered on a deserted roadside. The young woman has been bludgeoned to death. Witnesses saw her leaving the restaurant with Steele; police regard him as a prime suspect. But before Dix can be arrested, a starlet named Laurel Gray (Gloria Grahame, the real-life Mrs. Nicholas Ray) furnishes him with an ironclad alibi.

Laurel lives across the way from the Steele apartment and testifies that she watched Mildred depart, leaving Dix alone in his well-lit living room. For the moment, the cops are satisfied. Screenwriter and starlet soon find they have a lot more in common than show business. A torrid affair begins. So does Dix's new and inspired script, with a memorable self-portrait of the narrator: "I was born when she kissed me. I died when she left me. I lived a few weeks while she loved me." Even though Laurel falls under Dix's spell, a dark suspicion lurks in the back of her mind — especially when she sees her lover in one of his rages. During a drive the couple gets sideswiped by another car. Dix leaps out and savagely beats the other driver. Only Laurel's interference keeps him from killing the downed man with a rock. (Ray and Grahame were on the brink of divorce during the production and Steele is obviously a surrogate of Ray, forlorn, resentful, unable to assuage his grief or manage his rage.)

Would Dix be capable of homicide? Laurel is not the only one who thinks he is. Steele's agent, Mel Lippman (Art Smith), also believes his enigmatic client might actually be guilty of the Atkinson murder. By now Laurel is terrified of Dix — so terrified she agrees to marry him, fearing that he might kill her if she refuses. During one of his rare absences she tries to pack up and flee. Her fiancé comes to call, sees her luggage, and flies into an uncontrolled fury. Dix very nearly strangles Laurel, then pulls back, looking at his hands as if they belong to someone else. As the two catch their breath, the phone rings. A detective has some comforting words: Mildred's boyfriend has confessed to the crime. The information comes too late. Dix may be innocent of one killing, but he has murdered any chance for love or stability. His line has a new meaning now: "I was born when she kissed me. I died when she left me. I lived a few weeks while she loved me."

Humphrey had wanted to cast his wife as Miss Gray. This presented Jack Warner with an opportunity for revenge. He was always furious with the rebel for something; this time it was because Santana's films were being released through Columbia instead of Warner Bros. He struck back. No, Mrs. Bogart would *not* be sprung from her contract with Warners, not even for this one picture. Jack had inadvertently done Humphrey a favor: Gloria happened to be ideal for the part. Had Lauren been cast, the film would have been a Bogart-Bacall product, with the leading lady reciting a lot of breathy lines and doing a series of long, suggestive poses —Vivian Rutledge in vamp mode. Grahame had a wide range and an edgy sense of humor that came across in every role.

In her memoir, Louise Brooks denigrated many Bogart movies (as well as Bogart himself), but she had good things to say about *In a Lonely Place.* "Before inertia set in," she wrote, Humphrey "played one fascinatingly complex character, craftily directed by Nicholas Ray, in a film whose title perfectly defined Humphrey's own isolation among people. *In a Lonely Place* gave him a role that he could play with complexity because the film's character, the screenwriter's pride in his art, his selfishness, his drunkenness, his lack of energy stabbed with lightning strokes of violence, were shared equally by the real Bogart." She had a point. Lauren Bacall's autobiography speaks of a time just before her marriage when she went aboard Humphrey's yacht. It could be a description of Dixon Steele at ebb tide: "I don't know what happened this time — when or how the click in his brain took place — but suddenly he was fighting with me. I got more and more frightened. He started slamming his fists on the table, crying 'You goddamn actresses are all alike. . . .' I'd never seen fury like that — unreasonable, lashing out. I hated it."

Humphrey's behavior was obviously inflamed by drink, but there was more to it than that. The constant needling he experienced in childhood continued to play out in situations where he felt cornered by others or confused by his own emotions. The best of Steele and the worst of Bogart criss-crossed several times in the movie. No doubt old memories were stirred up, and Humphrey didn't know how to handle them except by playing the part as honestly as he could — and then, as usual, dissolving his fears and memories in alcohol.

Lonely Place was not the only 1950 film to examine a self-loathing Hollywood. Every scene of Billy Wilder's deeper, darker, and more polished *Sunset Boulevard* reveals the downside of fame and illusion, as a vain old movie star is cosseted and deceived by her younger lover and her adoring ex-husband. And even though *All About Eve* took place around Broadway, it was, after all, a movie about a diva pursued and eventually toppled by an ambitious newcomer. Its subtext was the impermanence of acclaim and the ruthlessness of show business on any stage, theatrical or sound. These features cannot be separated from history; at the beginning of the decade the film business was beset by the political blacklisting of employees, the disintegration of the studio system, and an unstable geopolitical climate. Inevitably some of the tension spilled over into the directions and performances.

In many ways *In a Lonely Place* was the weakest of these three features. Yet Humphrey's star turn, even more than Gloria Swanson's in *Sunset Boulevard* and Bette Davis's in *All About Eve,* edged closer to the neurotic fear of failure that has always characterized Hollywood, but that was at its most intense in the early 1950s. The picture was so powerful that when producer-director Curtis Hanson made *L.A. Confidential,* which takes place during the same period, he screened it for costars Russell Crowe and Guy Pearce. "I wanted them to see the reality of that period and to see that emotion," Hanson recalled. "When I first saw *In a Lonely Place* as a teenager, it frightened me and yet attracted me with an almost hypnotic power. Later, I came to understand why. Occasionally, very rarely, a movie feels so heartfelt, so emotional, so revealing that it seems as though both the actor and the director are standing naked before the audience. When that happens, it's breathtaking."

In later years, Humphrey confessed that he never liked *In a Lonely Place.* It's not hard to see why. Dixon Steele and Humphrey Bogart might have been blood brothers. Both went through life as if they had sand under their skins; both were oddly attractive men with high IQs; both were capable of quixotic kindness and uncontrol-

306

lable rages that spilled over from difficult childhoods. Nicholas Ray was quick to take advantage of their similarities. Though many people claimed credit for the periodic resurrections of Humphrey's career, Ray's is the most credible: in creating Dixon Steele, he said, "I took the gun out of Bogart's hands."

At this moment, the Bogart mystique took an unpredicted turn. By an accident of timing, *Lonely Place* announced the sunset of the brute/hero in American film. In previous years the role of a cruel or domineering male provided a gateway to eminence. It involved a measure of misogynism as well, for women were often the ones who made an obscure actor a star once he behaved badly on-screen. *White Heat* broke from the pack of crime movies when James Cagney slammed a grapefruit in the face of Mae Clark. In *The Seventh Veil* James Mason played Nicholas, the crippled and jealous guardian of a talented pianist Francesca (Ann Todd). During one of his outbursts he argues with Francesca as she plays — and suddenly brings his cane down on her fingers. The movie won an Academy Award, was the biggest box office success in 1946 Britain, and established Mason as a major star.

A year later Richard Widmark made his

screen debut as the homicidal lunatic Tommy Udo in *Kiss of Death*. In his big moment, Udo sneaks behind an old lady in a wheelchair, pushes her down a flight of stairs, and giggles about what he has just done. "The sadism of that character," wrote critic David Thomson in *The New Biographical Dictionary of Film,* "the fearful laugh, the skull showing through drawn skin, and the surely conscious evocation of a concentration-camp degenerate established Widmark as the most frightening person on the screen." Widmark received an Oscar nomination, and began a illustrious forty-year career in which he played a series of romantic leads.

At the same time Robert Mitchum appeared in *Out of the Past,* the classic film noir that made him famous. Jeff, a laconic detective, is never less than blunt with females, deadly or otherwise: "You're like a leaf that the wind blows from one gutter to another." When an ingenue protests that she's innocent of a theft, his signature line is "Baby, I don't care." Toward the conclusion another woman pleads, "I don't want to die!" His reply: "Neither do I, baby, but if I have to, I'm going to die last."

Dixon Steele was just about the last of these protagonists. *Lonely Place* received mixed reviews: *Time* called it a "Bogart melodrama that seems to take forever getting to the point," but other important publications praised the film. Humphrey took special pleasure from the *New York Times* critique. Bosley Crowther, who had detested *Knock on Any Door,* proclaimed, "Humphrey Bogart is in top form in his latest independently made production, and the picture itself is a superior cut of melodrama." As a quick-tempered screenwriter suspected of a capital crime, "Mr. Bogart looms large on the screen of the Paramount Theater and he moves flawlessly through a script which is almost as flinty as the actor himself."

Variety indicated that, short fuse and all, Dix Steele was sympathetic because "he favors the underdog; in one instance he virtually has a veteran, brandy-soaking character (out of work) on his very limited payroll. . . . Director Nicholas Ray maintains nice suspense. Bogart is excellent. Gloria Grahame, as his romance, also rates kudos."

The feature had great importance for Humphrey. For the first time in more than a year he had truly acted a part instead of walking through it. He took satisfaction in the praise of journalists and colleagues, but worried anew when the public failed to share their enthusiasm. Was it time to sell off Santana, get the company off his back? Soon, maybe; right now he had other things on his mind. Lauren was unhappy at Warners. The scripts she was being offered were never up to snuff; it was as if the studio was trying to get back at him through his wife. Well, the hell with Jack Warner. There was another studio and a new script out there for Humphrey. The trouble was, it involved something he hated: travel. To Africa, no less.

II

The journey began with a call from John Huston. Always one for the idée fixe, the director had become obsessed with a novel published back in 1935. "Bogie," he began, "I've got a helluva property — with the worst low-life character in the world as the hero — and you're Hollywood's worst form of life. How about it?"

The leading lady had already been enticed, thanks to a producer who never took maybe for an answer. She remembered their first conversation. "Hello, Miss Hepburn," said the purling voice on the other end of the phone. "I'm Sam Spiegel. I'm going to do a picture with John Huston — it's by C. S. Forester and it's called *The African Queen*."

There was a backstory here. There was always a backstory with Spiegel. Born in western Galicia in 1901, the bright Jewish boy joined the Zionist movement in adolescence, married, and settled in Palestine. Seven years later he abandoned his wife, daughter, and assorted debts to assume a new life in the United States. Claiming to be a diplomat, he was investigated, found to be a fraud, and wound up serving a nine-month prison sentence. Upon release he fled to Europe. There, with a combination of chutzpah and charm, he managed to produce three films, none of any note.

Reentering the States, Spiegel worked his way to Los Angeles, where he devised his own way to Hollywood prominence: hosting A-list parties. He borrowed funds, crashed other people's fetes, and worked the rooms, making contacts and eventually staging his own bashes. These made Spiegel notorious but difficult to resist; the food and drink were incomparable, and he allowed — in fact encouraged — gambling and unrestricted sex on his rented premises (Marilyn Monroe was said to be one of his "house girls"). Ultimately he convinced investors to back two pictures, one made by Orson Welles. In later years Welles disavowed *The Stranger* because his artistic flourishes were sharply edited by Spiegel, turning an experimental film into a conventional thriller. Nevertheless the movie made a profit and convinced major studios that Welles was a bankable talent.

From the start Spiegel had been unhappy with the script of *The Stranger;* he had hired John Huston to help with the rewrites. A friendship developed between the two aggressive seducers. In 1949 they founded a production company, Horizon Pictures. Their first film, *We Were Strangers,* directed by Huston and produced by one S. P. Eagle, miscast John Garfield and Jennifer Jones as Cuban revolutionaries. "It wasn't a very good choice," Huston was to concede, "and it wasn't a very good picture." The partners had learned their lesson, however. Next time out they would be more careful in their choice of material and performers. Huston learned that Forester's Congo romance had a history of options that had gone nowhere. Columbia wanted to adapt *African Queen* for their husband-and-wife team of Charles Laughton and Elsa Lanchester. Nothing came of it. Warners acquired the property with David Niven and Bette Davis in mind. Nothing came of that, either.

No studio had ever really believed in the project. For at its center was a love story set in 1915 between two rapidly aging cranks. Charlie Allnut is a gin-soaked Cockney skipper plying the Ruki River; Rose Sayer is an uptight British spinster who aids her brother, the Rev. Samuel Sayer (Robert Morley), in his vocation: converting the local animists to Christianity.

Charlie is the siblings' only link with the outside world, irregularly bringing them packets of mail from their native England. This time he brings cataclysmic news along with the letters. German armies have invaded East Africa; the kaiser's troops are only hours away. The Sayers refuse to move. Charlie shrugs and goes upriver, whereupon enemy soldiers invade the Sayers' turf as predicted, burning down huts and forcibly conscripting the villagers. The reverend protests and gets savagely beaten by a German officer. Wounded and in shock, he succumbs to jungle fever. Not long afterward, Charlie returns. He helps the grieving Rose bury her brother, and invites her to come aboard his little craft. The reprobate will take her downriver to a safe haven, then move on to his own hiding place where he can wait out the war in drunken tranquillity.

But Rose is made of stronger stuff. She wants her brother's death avenged, and conceives a plan to make the Germans suffer. The river is a tributary to Lake Albert, where a German ship, the *Louisa,* is known to be anchored. She and Charlie can make their way to the lake, convert the *African Queen* into a torpedo boat, and head it toward the *Louisa,* diving off just before it hits. Charlie regards her plan as insane: "There's death a hundred times over," he warns. Hazards include an enemy fort facing the river, as well as three sets of dangerous rapids.

A war of nerves begins, with Charlie grousing about Rose's lofty, teetotaling attitude ("Nature," Mr. Allnut, "is what we're put on earth to rise above") and Rose getting revenge for Charlie's drunkenness by spilling every last drop of his precious Gordon's gin into the black water. Nonetheless, with each hazardous nautical mile they draw closer and closer. Despite themselves, the virgin and the reprobate fall in love. In the novel their mission fails, the Germans capture the couple, decide that it would be uncivilized to order their execution, and, flying a flag of truce, hand them over to the English. Forester's ending was the weakest part of the novel. Rose and Charlie plan to get married by the local British consul. Having created an unusual romance, the author denigrated it in the final line: "Whether or not they lived happily ever after would be difficult to say."

A reader at RKO found the principals of the story "physically unattractive" and the tale itself "distasteful and not a little disgusting." At a previous time that judgment would not have been made. But as the postwar era came to an end, youth received a new emphasis — in fashion, in business, in ads, and, inevitably, in films, old was out. Men and women were marrying younger, starting families earlier, establishing themselves in their twenties and thirties. It was assumed that when they went out to the movies, they wanted to see reflections of themselves and their generation. The idea of love between two expatriates who appeared to be in late middle age was clearly unacceptable. It would be like watching their grandparents canoodling. "A story of two old people going up and down an African river?" scoffed producer Alexander Korda. "Who's going to be interested in that? You'll be bankrupt."

Something else weighed down the material as well, though it went undiscussed. Miss Sayer is a deeply pious Methodist, bent on saving souls. For her the New Testament is not a series of homilies and metaphors, but the revealed and literal truth. America in midcentury was on the cusp of a secular age, and religious movies like *The Miracle of the Bells* and *Going My Way* were no longer big at the box office. Yet there remained millions of Christians who wouldn't stand for ridicule or irreverence on-screen. Thus *The African Queen* would be forced to please both camps, the believers and the fallen away, a tightrope walk if ever there was one.

In 1950 Huston, almost alone, saw great possibilities in a screen adaptation. (Spiegel was the other true believer. He went on record in the *The New Yorker,* burbling to Lillian Ross that *The African Queen* would "give John the kind of commercial hit he had when he made *The Maltese Falcon* in 1941.") There were a few provisos. Horizon would have to wrest the property from Warner Bros. at a bargain price. Huston would have to shoot on location — none of those bogus rear-screen projections of hippos and natives Hollywood was so fond of. He would have to devise a more appropriate and cinematic ending. And most important, the partners would have to have major stars for this production. The first obstacle seemed insurmountable. Warners named what they considered a reasonable sum. But in the early 1950s, when the average yearly income was about three thousand dollars and the Dow Jones average seldom rose above eleven hundred, fifty thousand dollars was more than Huston and Spiegel could pay. Rising to the occasion, Sam worked out a deal with Sound Services, Inc., a company that rented sound equipment to filmmakers. The partners guaranteed to pay back the loan with interest in a year's time. As a sweetener Horizon also promised to use Sound Service equipment to make *African Queen,* with a big listing in the screen credits.

As soon as he acquired the rights, Sam went after financing for the movie. Though its cast was small, its locations were hazardous and far away. An arrangement was made with James and John Woolf, the brothers who ran the British production company Romulus Films. In her lively biography of Spiegel, Natasha Fraser-Cavassoni points out that Romulus had failed with its previous production, *Pandora and the Flying Dutchman,* starring James Mason and Ava Gardner. "British films were doing no good," recalled John Woolf, "and the idea of making films with Hollywood actors greatly appealed." Once the money was in place, Huston snagged Humphrey. "Before I met

John," Humphrey told a reporter, "my range was Beverly Hills to Palm Springs. Now the Monster wants me to fly twelve thousand miles into the Congo. And the crazy thing is that I've agreed to go."

Spiegel took it upon himself to deliver the female lead. He sent Katharine Hepburn a copy of *The African Queen.* Several days later it was she who called him.

Her voice thrummed. "It's fascinating. Who's going to play what's his — yes — Charlie Allnut."

She was informed that it was to be Humphrey Bogart. Her reaction: immediate delight. He's "the only man who could have played that part." Her co-star was equally pleased. Recalled Huston: Bogie's "idea of doing it with Katie Hepburn — instantly appealing."

C. S. Forester, né Cecil Louis Troughton Smith, had gained international recognition with the seagoing tales of Captain Horatio Hornblower. These led to a Hollywood contract, and until the beginning of World War II the author spent thirteen weeks of every year working as a screenwriter. He had his own plans for *The African Queen.*

But Forester's health broke down in the late 1940s. Having created the story, he was forced to make way for younger and healthier writers to bring it to the screen. An early version was prepared by the British short story writer John Collier (*Fancies and Goodnights*). Huston now brought in James Agee. The forty-two-year-old critic and author had singled out *Maltese Falcon* and *Sierra Madre* for special praise in *Time* and the *Nation,* but had never attempted a screenplay. Even so, Huston looked upon Agee with favor — especially after a series of interviews, followed by the publication of "Undirectable Director" in *Life* magazine. Huston's movies, observed the writer, "continually open the eye and require it to work vigorously, and through the eye they awaken curiosity and intelligence. That, by any virile standard, is essential to good entertainment. It is unquestionably essential to good art."

Agee fancied himself a rebel, and Huston actually was one, so they got along famously from the beginning. Both men were drinkers and smokers; both liked intense conversations deep into the night and serious tennis in the afternoon. It was the last predilection that kept the screenwriter from completing his project: he suffered a severe heart attack after playing a set with his new boss, and was sidelined for the production. Peter Viertel, a well-traveled scenarist who

319

had written the script for *We Were Strangers,* took his place. Agee's effort, Viertel recalled, "was laden with brilliant descriptions, but there were practically no dialogue scenes." He flew off to the Congo to get a feel for the place.

Meantime, Humphrey and Lauren made ready for the voyage. Not since World War II had Humphrey been overseas. These days his idea of an out-of-town trip was taking *Santana* beyond the three-mile limit. To get him to go to the Congo and Uganda required more than Huston's considerable powers of persuasion. It also required financing. After much negotiating, Horizon agreed to pay Bogart a deferred payment of $125,000, and of greater significance, 30 percent of the gross. (Hepburn would receive $65,000 in cash, plus 10 percent of the gross.) Humphrey gave in on any number of points, but he remained inflexible about one: Lauren would have to accompany him every mile of the way. His first and second marriages had suffered because he and his wives pursued separate careers. Not this time. Lauren was happy to accede to her husband's wishes, and Huston, scamp though he was, knew better than to come between the Bogarts.

Taking a two-year-old to the oppressive

conditions in Africa would have been unthinkable. So young Stephen was left behind in the care of a nursemaid, Alice Hartley. She took the boy to the airport to wave good-bye to his parents. Shortly after the plane ascended Hartley gripped the child, moaned, and slumped to the ground. She had suffered a massive stroke and died that night. From New York, Lauren arranged for her mother to assume the caretaker role. The Bogarts had made their commitment to the film; now they wondered whether they were sailing under a curse. Concerned and fearful they pressed on, boarding the *Liberté* and heading for Britain.

Although Hepburn and Bogart were both major stars, they had only met en passant in Hollywood. In London they got the chance to speak at length. As it turned out, they had much in common. Both had been hellions from childhood onward. Their mothers were militant feminists. Their fathers were medical men — Humphrey's a surgeon, Katharine's a urologist. Both stars were known for their intense romantic involvements; although four of Humphrey's led to the altar, Katharine had only been a wife once. She was now intimately involved with the married Spencer Tracy. The pair had already co-starred in half a dozen movies.

Following a script conference — the film still had no ending — the actors left for Italy. Neither of them had been to Vatican City before, and it was very much a when-in-Rome proposition. Humphrey, born Episcopalian, and Lauren, born Jewish, met a starstruck priest in the city. Monsignor John Patrick Carroll-Abbing promised to arrange an audience with Pope Pius XII, and the Bogarts did nothing to discourage him. The next day they received an invitation to Vatican City, where His Holiness scrutinized the actress and remarked fluently, "You are Miss Lauren Bacall!" As he went on, the pope-struck Humphrey remembered, "I was so overwhelmed that I don't know now whether someone said I was Miss Bacall's husband." He suddenly became aware that Pius XII had turned to address him. "He asked, 'Where do you come from?' And you know what I heard myself saying? 'San Francisco.' I don't know if my subconscious thought the word 'Hollywood' too tawdry or what. I simply said 'San Francisco,' and then was too stunned to say another word."

While the Bogarts toured the churches and museums, Katharine went on a clandestine tour with Spencer, who had flown in unannounced. "We drove all over the place," she recalled, but the press "never got a picture of us together." He flew out, also unannounced. When it came time for Katharine to depart, she outwitted the paparazzi at the airport, arriving early and hiding in a ladies' room until they went away. It was left to the Bogarts to smile and pose for photographers.

All three expected to be greeted by Huston when they arrived at Stanleyville, in the Belgian Congo. They were met instead by screenwriter Peter Viertel. Their director had gone on a hunting expedition. Or so it was implied. Katharine thought otherwise. In her memoir she theorizes that Huston "was absolutely horrified at the thought of beginning the picture, and the sight of us was the knell of doom. It was an utterly piggish thing to do and it makes me mad to think of it even now — goddamn — goddamn. . . ."

Much worse lay in store. Scorpions and spiders took up residence in the sinks; mosquitoes and tsetse flies swarmed in the humid ninety-degree air; poisonous snakes and crocodiles threatened the paths and riverbanks. When Huston finally did show up he was delighted at the plethora of creatures and the lack of creature comforts. In his view, *Treasure of the Sierra Madre* gave audiences a sense of the heat and hazards of Mexico because it was shot on location, and by God, if he had anything to do with it *African Queen* would convey the overpowering might and menace of the Congolese jungle.

Once the director, writer, cast, and technicians got to the set, a series of routines began. First, the ladies took stock of each other's looks and abilities. Lauren was wary at the start, noting that Katharine "talked compulsively," quite often about herself. But the younger actress acknowledged that it "really took guts to travel so far without a friend or companion." For her part, Katharine admired Lauren's "fund of pugilistic good-nature." Years before, a drunken Mayo Methot had mocked Lauren's inability to wash Humphrey's socks. Yet in Africa that's exactly what Lauren did, in addition to laundering her husband's shirts and underwear and pressing his garments. Katharine could only gaze in wonder.

She was not so indulgent when she got around to her director. The important people had their own huts, but had to use outdoor privies. Huston's dwelling place was the grandest, because it had a private shower. "I never did see him go to the outhouse," Katharine maliciously remarked. "Maybe he never did. Wouldn't surprise me a bit. Would explain a great deal."

She was also wry about an incongruous, potbellied figure who periodically popped in, wearing outfits better suited to Palm Beach. This was the impresario Sam Spiegel (S. P. Eagle). "I watched him in his shorts and colored shirts rushing around that camp in the rain," Katharine wrote, "and I thought: The man who has to pay the bills — terrifying." Yet she quite liked him because she believed, as William Blake did, that energy is eternal delight: "He loves his work and he loves his life. He's a doer."

And gradually, almost in spite of herself, she came around to admiring Huston. There was no romantic involvement — Katharine only had eyes for Spencer — but she watched John having the time of his life, sightseeing from the air, hunting big game, while around him all were sweating. She decided to get in on the act. Spiegel learned of her plans and became splenetic: "Katie — setting off with John in a little plane — how can you — *how?* You may be killed. Then what . . ."

When she refused to alter her plans, Spiegel appealed to Humphrey. He confronted

Katharine. These were wild animals that deserved to live out their lives undisturbed by interlopers. "Katie, what's happened to you? You're a decent human being."

"Not anymore I'm not. If you obey all the rules you miss all the fun. John has fun."

"John. That son of a bitch has gotten to you."

"He's seeing Africa."

"You're making a picture."

"Yes, I'm making a picture, but I'm seeing life at the same time."

Humphrey gave up. "She's gone," he told Spiegel. "Under the spell."

He kept referring to Huston as the Monster, but with diminishing conviction. For if he disliked the director's manipulation of Katharine as if she were a Bryn Mawr junior, he admired the way he helped her create the leading lady of *The African Queen*. Early on in the filming, Katharine had trouble getting a hook on Rose Sayer's character. Was she just a dry stick in a long skirt, a fundamentalist prude who took joy in correcting others? In that case, how could an audience find her sympathetic? The rehearsals were unsatisfactory; they discomfited John, Humphrey, and Katharine herself. And then, from out of nowhere, the director made a suggestion. What if Rose

Sayer's tone and diction were to suggest Eleanor Roosevelt's? FDR's lovably naïve, somewhat censorious widow was famous for her all-purpose expression and lofty diction. Servants, heads of state, journalists, northern liberals, and hostile Republicans received the identical toothy "society smile," and a grand statement delivered in her unique, unsteady soprano. Katharine thought about John's idea, brightened, and concluded, "That is the goddamnedest best piece of direction I have ever heard." From that point on she impersonated the former first lady and, at the same time, slyly commented on Eleanor's refusal to recognize adversity. It was the turning point of her midlife career.

Humphrey had an easier time getting into the cranky persona of Charlie Allnut. He was incapable of doing a Cockney accent, so the Londoner became an all-purpose Canadian and Charlie's age was adjusted upward. His "uniform" — canvas shoes, hat and trousers that once were white, horizontally striped shirt — was set off with a bright red neckerchief. This gave him an eccentric, jaunty style. But he fought against any hint of movie star glamour. With films like *The Red Shoes* and *Black Narcissus,* cinematographer Jack Cardiff had built a strong reputation for making actors look more attractive than they actually were. Humphrey was having none of it. He warned Cardiff that the famous Bogart "lines and wrinkles" had been cultivated for years. "They are me," he continued, "so don't try to light them out and make me look like a goddam fag." If nothing else, Charlie Allnut was all male, like the Fred C. Dobbs of *Sierra Madre* and the Dixon Steele of *In a Lonely Place.* The difference was that those men began with some appeal, then descended into paranoia and self-destruction. Charlie would reverse the process, starting off as Miss Sayer's irritable antagonist and winding up as a lover who would prove alluring not only to Rose but to the audience. "I slowly got him into it," Huston said, "showing him by expression and gesture what I thought Allnut should be like. He first imitated me, then all at once he got under the skin of that wretched, sleazy, absurd, brave little man. He realized he was on to something new and good. He said to me, 'John, don't let me lose it.' " In making that appeal, Humphrey was sharply aware of Ernest Hemingway's observation about writing. He felt it applied doubly to acting: "When you've got it you've got to keep going because when you've lost it you've lost it and God knows when you'll get it back." John made certain that Humphrey stayed on key; the surrounding conditions did the rest.

The director had logged twenty-five thousand miles of air time in an attempt to find just the right landscape. One place he selected was an isolated bank of the Ruiki River, an inky, slow-moving tributary to the Lualaba choked with decaying vegetation. Other parts of *The African Queen* were shot in and around Uganda, Murchison Falls on the border of Lake Albert, and the Belgian Congo, identified in the film as German East Africa, its name during World War I. (Subsequently the country was known as Zaire, before the name was changed to the Democratic Republic of the Congo.) "I wanted those characters to sweat when the script called for it," Huston was to recall. "On a sound stage you fake it, but in Africa you don't have to imagine that it's hot, that it's so humid and wet that cigarettes turn green with mold; it really is hot and clothes do mildew overnight — and when people sweat it isn't with the help of a makeup man."

The gradations of local color came at a steep price. Katharine described some daily catastrophes: "John would scream — Bogie and I would jump — and the boiler would be tipped over, or nearly. The canopy would be torn off. The camera or lamps or whatever was caught by the overhanging shrubbery on the banks. . . . The hysteria of each shot was a nightmare." The director, who played up his bwana role to the Africans, zealously guarded the boat during the daytime, but relied on laborers to look after it at night. They listened carefully to his instructions: nothing must be taken from the vessel, no one must be allowed on until he gave the say-so. One evening they observed with particular interest as the *African Queen* sprang an internal leak. Huston's orders were obeyed to the letter. Noted Lauren: "The Natives had been told to watch it and they did — they watched it sink." It took three days to haul the boat to the surface of the Ruiki, and a few more to make it buoyant again.

Most of the crew became ill during the shooting. Katharine joined the walking wounded; because of severe digestive problems she lost some twenty pounds, a great deal of weight for someone constitutionally thin. At times she was forced to throw up between takes, but she never took a sick day. Dysentery was common, as were malaria and a general malaise. The only ones who escaped the misery were Humphrey and John, who made a point of staying away from bottled water, eating only canned food, and drinking nothing but beer and straight whiskey from a makeshift bar set up under the trees. Katharine learned too late that those water bottles were contaminated. She remembered bitterly, "I — the queen of water drinking — the urologist's prize — was the sickest. And those two undisciplined weaklings had so lined their insides with alcohol that no bug could live in the atmosphere."

All along, the undisciplined weaklings teased Katharine, writing obscenities on the mirror in her hut and cavorting loudly even when they were cold sober. John claimed that anything that bit him soon dropped dead of alcohol poisoning. "Nothing bites me," Humphrey liked to boast. "A solid wall of whiskey keeps the insects at bay." Yet she found both men irresistible. "Katie has a weakness for wastrels," the director observed, twinkling. After all, look at Spencer Tracy . . .

In theory, *The African Queen* was an epic drama writ small, a story of human endurance against the formidable odds of weather, topography, and war. In practice, it was all that and more; it was a human comedy, a bright look at the battle of the sexes. The film wasn't planned that way, but the Bogart-Hepburn chemistry surprised everyone — most of all themselves — by becoming humorous rather than erotic. Humphrey had a natural gift for leavening his hardnosed characters with a sardonic expression, and Katharine had played opposite some of American cinema's great light comedians, including Cary Grant, James Stewart, and, of course, Spencer Tracy. Humphrey proved to be their equal. When Hepburn came to appraise him she wrote, "Bogie was funny. A generous actor. Always knew his lines. Always was on time. Hated anything false. He was an extraordinarily decent fellow. Fair — forthright — uncomplicated. Fun too — a good sense of humor. Devilish if he thought you were a phony. Like a cat with a mouse, he'd never let you off." She was particularly taken with his performance after the *African Queen*'s odd couple enjoy one discreet night of love. Rose asks, "Dear . . . dear, what is your first name?" After he informs her, Charlie walks away. "I'll never forget that closeup of him after he kisses Rosie," she wrote, "then goes around the back of the gas tank and considers what has happened. His expression — the wonder of it all — life."

The only time Humphrey locked horns with John was during the film's "leech scene," when Allnut clambers aboard the *African Queen* after immersing himself in a particularly bad stretch of water. At this point John brought a leech breeder to the set — after all, what was the point of being on location, sweating real sweat, suffering real fever, if you weren't going to use real bloodsuckers? Humphrey adamantly refused to permit a single leech on his body. The director fumed, threatened, wheedled, charmed. No sale. "So the rest of that day," Katharine recalled, "was spent trying to find — invent — a material that would stick to Bogie's skinny frame." Tight closeups were taken of the breeder's flesh loaded with parasites. When Humphrey was shown in a full body shot, he struggled with rubber leeches. This was one of the few inauthentic sequences in the film. Others included a few rear-screen projections and some model shots of the boat bobbing in rough water. But these were minor in a poignant comedy whose final touches were completed in London and Hollywood. Huston was immensely pleased with the result, especially since he and Viertel had concocted the finale at the last minute, much as the writers of *Casablanca* had done in 1944. Alternate conclusions had the couple rescued by a British warship; a proposal of marriage by Rose, before the British consul; and the vanishing of Charlie, when he suddenly recalls the wife he had abandoned in England twenty years before. None of them would do; the picture demanded a happy ending, and an ingenious, if implausible, deus ex machina supplied it.

Now that the ordeal was over, everyone was free to let off steam. Huston was vastly amused with some Bogart interviews. In one, Humphrey looked over the new crop of slovenly dressed Method actors, men who tended to make up their lines as they went along. The established star picked on the newbie. "I came out here with one suit and everybody said I looked like a bum," Humphrey recalled. "Twenty years later Marlon Brando came out with only a sweatshirt and the town drooled over him. That shows how much Hollywood has progressed." Yet when he spoke of the way he and Katharine had worked, it seemed right in line with Brando's belief that actors uttering memorized speeches were about as convincing as a child reciting "Mary Had a Little Lamb." You had to get the gist of the scene and make up the rest. "We seldom learned our lines for *The African Queen,*" Humphrey stated in a different interview. "Instead we just got the general idea and talked each scene out overlapping one another, cutting one another off, as people do in everyday conversation." That technique, Huston observed, was right out of the hated Actors Studio manual. It would have been unlikely for Humphrey to acknowledge his debt to the Method actors, leading men who refused to learn their parts by rote. But despite his grumbles and put-downs, Humphrey's technique had evolved over the years, and he had shrewdly kept pace with the latest performing styles.

While the film was wrapping two pieces of information came in, one heartening, the other heartbreaking. John Huston had become the father of a little girl, Anjelica, by his fourth wife, ballerina Ricki Soma. And Humphrey Bogart learned that the body of his third wife, Mayo Methot, had been found at a motel in Multnomah, Oregon, a suburb of Portland. The forty-seven-year-old actress had completely dropped out of sight, vainly struggling with alcoholism, depression, and more recently the results of a cancer operation. The corpse went undiscovered for several days. Humphrey shook his head when he heard the news. There was no schadenfreude here.

"Too bad. Such a waste," he lamented. "Mayo had real talent. She had just thrown her life away."

Once the Bogarts returned to their house, Humphrey's spirits picked up. He had paid his dues, roughed it in deepest Africa, made a film, and returned in one piece. He was back where he belonged, in his house, with Lauren and Stephen at his side and his boat bobbing at the yacht club. In February *The African Queen* opened in New York to qualify for the Academy Awards. By then it had received raves from most of the British papers. "You've probably seen the English reviews, which are, without exception, positively lyrical," Huston wrote Hepburn from his estate in Ireland. "It's as though one critic was trying to outdo the other in his praise." The *New York Times* was hardly lyrical, but after Bosley Crowther labeled the movie as a "slick job of movie hoodwinking," he went on to praise the leads: "Not since Elsa Lanchester and Charles Laughton appeared in *The Beachcomber* have the incongruities of social station and manners been so pointedly and humorously portrayed." The rest of the papers fell in line. The reviewers had been seduced by two old pros with decades of experience behind them. Humphrey and Katharine were at once durable and vulnerable, and knew how to use their thinness to great advantage. Rose Sayer was appraised as gaunt, proud, and lovely; Humphrey was considered skinny, coarse, and irresistible. As a pair they were like tennis pros who engaged in long rallies, not because they were trying to win the volley but because they wanted the sheer exhilaration of playing the game. And play it they did, to the full extent of their considerable gifts.

United Artists knew what it had. A quiet campaign got under way to get the star his first Academy Award; he had been nominated for *Casablanca* twelve years earlier. This was done with Humphrey's assent, an abrupt about-face from his stance delivered only a year before. In *Cosmopolitan* Humphrey had written an article declaring, "It's about time someone stuck a pin in the Oscar Myth and let out all that hot air contained in the Academy Awards." As he saw it, the only way performances could be weighed against one another was to have all actors play the same part — Hamlet, say — and for all actresses to play, for example, Mildred Pierce. But as 1953 began, Humphrey revised his thinking. He had made a sensational breakthrough with his first Technicolor film. How many other chances would he have at a trifecta: fine script, perfect co-star, ideal director? It was now or never for that little statuette.

And so provocative items began to appear in columns and features, quoting Humphrey or Katharine or both, and so Humphrey appeared as a guest on various radio shows, and so the academy nominated him in the Best Actor category, along with Katharine Hepburn for Best Actress. In his dark moments Humphrey considered the nomination to be a consolation prize. The hottest film under consideration was *A Streetcar Named Desire,* starring the new, new thing, Marlon Brando. Still, this was only Brando's second film; there was an outside chance for a sentimental favorite. The auguries were good; Spencer Tracy and Katharine Hepburn, who had a total of eight nominations between them, believed he would win. What's more, Lauren was pregnant. Prior to the ceremonies Humphrey did a lot of grousing; when people win they should be grateful to no one but themselves. They did the acting, why recite a laundry list of thank-yous? He maintained that attitude until the night of March 20, 1952, at the RKO Pantages Theater in Hollywood.

Streetcar was the big winner; Vivien Leigh had already won Best Actress, and Karl

Malden had been named Best Supporting Actor. Greer Garson came onstage to repeat the names of the nominees for Best Actor: Marlon Brando for *Streetcar,* Humphrey Bogart for *African Queen,* Fredric March for *Death of a Salesman,* Montgomery Clift for *A Place in the Sun,* Arthur Kennedy for *Bright Victory.* Lauren squeezed her husband's hand as the winner was announced: Humphrey Bogart. "A scream went up from the audience," Lauren remembered. "I leapt into the air — I thought I'd have the baby then and there." Humphrey kissed her, went up onstage, and proceeded to go against everything he had grumbled about to friends and in print, acknowledging the help and generosity of John Huston, Katharine Hepburn, and Sam Spiegel. "No one does it alone," he told the noisy, appreciative audience. "As in tennis, you need a good opponent or partner to bring out the best in you. John and Katie helped me to be where I am now."

A few weeks later, he assumed the old self-deprecating stance. "The best way to survive an Oscar is never to try to win another one," he told reporters. "You've seen what happens to some Oscar winners. They spend the rest of their lives turning down scripts while searching for the great role to win another one. Hell, I hope I'm never even nominated again. It's meat-and-potato roles for me from now on."

And a few weeks after that he made the news again, when his daughter was born. Humphrey supplied the infant's name: Leslie Howard Bogart, in honor of the man who had set him on the road to the Oscar. It could take years, but in the end Humphrey always managed to pay his debts.

CHAPTER 7
THERE'S NOTHING YOU CAN DO ABOUT IT. NOTHING!

I

Humphrey had been burned by past politics, and he had no wish to engage in any more public debates about issues or candidates. When the 1952 presidential campaign got under way, he quietly backed the Republican candidate, Dwight David "Ike" Eisenhower. Lauren was for Ike's opponent, Adlai Stevenson. The status quo didn't last very long. Lauren talked her husband into endorsing her candidate, and by early autumn the two were vigorously campaigning at "Madly for Adlai" rallies. In almost every case they proved to be a bigger draw than the Democratic candidate. Humphrey was more amused than impressed by the bright, well-spoken divorcé; not so Lauren. Adlai, she wrote, "did like to flirt, and he did like to be admired, and he did know that I was very young and had a wild crush on him." Her adoration and effort went for naught;

when the final tallies were in, Stevenson had suffered a stunning defeat — 89 electoral votes for him, 442 for Ike, ending twenty years of Democratic Party rule. Lauren's wild crush didn't please Humphrey, nor did the fact that she was depressed for weeks after the election. He could hardly wait to get back to work with a new director, Richard Brooks.

The men had first met after World War II, when Brooks was a crew-cut ex-Marine seeking to establish himself as a screenwriter. He amassed some good credits, particularly on *Key Largo,* the first time Richard and Humphrey worked together. By the winter of 1952 Richard had established himself as a novelist whose latest work, *The Producer,* was a roman à clef about the movie business. Recalled Brooks, "There is a character, an actor, in the novel who is very much Bogart. I asked Bogie if I should use the character. 'Is it an honest character?' Bogie asked. 'I think it is,' I said." He asked Humphrey if he wanted to read the manuscript. "If you say it's honest, I don't care," he told the author. "You have clearance." Actually, Brooks acknowledged, "it wasn't too complimentary a character. But Bogie went around after the novel appeared saying to people, 'That's me.' " At the same time, Brooks also established himself as an outstanding director, whose credits included *Crisis* and *The Light Touch*. The newspaper melodrama *Deadline U.S.A.* marked the first time he would hold the reins of a Bogart feature.

Save for the Stevenson business, everything had been going Humphrey's way since the Academy Award: the birth of Leslie, increasing star power, enough money to buy a grandiose fourteen-room house at 232 South Mapleton Drive in Holmby Hills, an exclusive neighborhood near Bel Air. According to Verita Thompson, Humphrey's hairdresser — and self-described inamorata — he was uncomfortable about moving into such a residence. ("What the hell good's a table you can't even set a goddamn drink on? I could put a down payment on an entire foreign country for the dough this joint set me back [$165,000], and I can't even set my drink down without having to go find one of those little fucking coasters!")

In fact, he relished the place, particularly a large alcove with a bar and a fireplace where the walls were covered with photos of friends. A racing trophy won by the *Santana* rested on the mantelpiece. All his friends were welcomed there; Brooks was a regular, and it was assumed that when *Deadline* went before the cameras, making the picture would be something of a lark. According to Warren Stevens, who played a reporter, Brooks made that impossible.

In *Bogart: A Life in Hollywood,* Jeffrey Meyers mentions an interview in which the actor recounted some difficult days on the set. "Brooks suddenly exploded on the first take. He had changed his mind about how to do the scene and took all day to get exactly the shot he wanted. Brooks was rude, unreasonable and hard on the crew, who once retaliated by dropping a dangerously heavy sandbag right next to where he was standing." At the same time, Stevens said, Humphrey was quiet and deferential, pleased with his role and delighted with his co-star, Kim Hunter, who had won her own Supporting Actress Oscar at the 1952 ceremonies for her work in *A Streetcar Named Desire.* After one scene he congratulated her — and himself: "By God, we winged it!," an echo of the way he and Katharine Hepburn had meshed.

Brooks had an entirely different take. Throughout the winter, Humphrey "was withdrawing," he maintained. "There was an impatience which was totally unlike him." On one occasion Humphrey was obviously hungover. He came to the set unprepared — a lapse unseen since his Broadway days — continually blew lines, and then blamed the script: "The thing doesn't seem to work." Brooks suggested that Humphrey had health issues that winter, even if there were no overt symptoms of any disease. In their biography, *Bogart,* A. M. Sperber and Eric Lax bring in script supervisor Kay Thackerey to speak about the star's edginess. When he continued to have trouble with his lines, she cued him, emphasizing certain words. He snapped, "Are you trying to tell *me* how to read a line?" After that, she said, "Anytime I threw him a line I threw it *in an absolute monotone without any inflection whatever.*"

For all these conflicts and recriminations, Humphrey's sixty-fifth picture turned out to be quite presentable — though perhaps not what one would have expected after *The African Queen.* Filmmakers have usually been partial to the subject of journalism, not least because so many of them started out on newspapers, among them Herman Mankiewicz, whose experience on the *New York World* enlivened the story of a press lord, *Citizen Kane;* Ben Hecht and Charles MacArthur, whose *Front Page* reflected their experiences on Chicago papers; and Richard Brooks, former sports reporter for the *New York World-Telegram,* whose love of journalism gave *Deadline U.S.A.* a palpable vigor and authenticity. (He was wise enough to shoot the interiors at the actual offices of the *New York Daily News.*)

The plot revolved around the future of a large metropolitan paper and its embattled editor in chief, Ed Hutcheson (Bogart). Three crises arrive at the same moment. The owner of the *Day* (Ethel Barrymore) is being pressured by her spoiled, avaricious children to sell the paper to its tabloid competitor, effectively putting it out of business. In the seventy-two hours before turnover is to take place, Hutcheson aims to change her mind, expose the dangerous head of a crime syndicate (Martin Gabel), and win back his ex (Kim Hunter). The countdown begins. At the end of three days, Hutcheson has a pair of personal victories and one major defeat: the old-time "tear up page one" newspaper business has had its *Day.* Along the way, he articulates the highs and lows of journalism: "It's not enough any more to give 'em just news. They want comics, contests, puzzles. They want to know how to bake a cake, win friends, and influence the future. Ergo, horoscopes, tips on the horses, interpretation of dreams so they can win on the numbers lottery. And, if they accidentally stumble on the first page — news!" Yet at a less cynical moment he tells a younger colleague: "About this wanting to be reporter — don't ever change your mind. It may not be the oldest profession, but it's the best." And, at the finale, threatened by enemies, he holds up the phone to catch the sound of the latest news being printed: "That's the press, baby. The press! And there's nothing you can do about it. Nothing!"

By the early 1950s this portrait of print journalism was caught in a time warp. Its "tear up page one!" vigor notwithstanding, *Deadline* was less film noir than film *crépuscule* — twilight. Network television had already made deep inroads, the notion of a TV news "anchor" was introduced to the public, and newspaper circulation started on its long and irreversible decline. Brooks's film posed as a valentine to print journalism; in reality it was an advance obit.

II

In the field of journalism Claud Cockburn had earned a place at the bottom. In 1936, the Englishman worked his way south from Britain to Spain in order to cover the Spanish Civil War. In *The First Casualty,* his classic study of war correspondents, Philip

Knightley notes that Cockburn couldn't help but notice the low morale in the ranks of anti-Franco Republicans. To counter their despondency he provided his Communist periodical, *The Weekly,* with an account from the front. In it, the high-spirited Republican militiamen acted with great courage, showing the world how bravely and effectively progressives could fight. The battle was a total fiction; Cockburn had made the thing up out of whole cloth. One of his leftist colleagues protested. Whatever the feelings of the journalist, readers were surely entitled to facts. Cockburn disagreed: what entitled them to facts? "When they have asserted themselves enough to alter the policy of their bloody government and the Fascists are beaten in Spain they will have such a right." Concludes Knightley, "There can be no validity in Cockburn's attitude. If readers are to have no right to facts, but only what a correspondent feels it is in his side's best interest to reveal, then there is no use for war correspondents at all."

Reporters came to realize that the righteous Englishman was simply a propagandist for Stalin. Notoriety and derision followed Cockburn after World War II, and he turned to writing humorous novels in which facts were superfluous. He retired to the west of Ireland in 1947. In the early 1950s John Huston bought and restored a Georgian house on the coast of Galway; the two became neighbors and pub mates. During this period John pulled up stakes in Hollywood. He had a revulsion for the House Un-American Activities Committee and for the blacklist that resulted from their headline-grabbing investigations in Hollywood. In his view the United States "had — temporarily at least — stopped being my country, and I was just as glad to stay clear of it." In his memoirs he acknowledged that "the anti-Communist hysteria certainly played a role in my move to Ireland."

The irony was that just as he settled into his new home, antihysteria forces were beginning to coalesce in California and New York in an effort to fight the blacklist. On his popular CBS-TV program, *See It Now,* Edward R. Murrow editorialized against Senator Joe McCarthy. ("The actions of the Junior Senator from Wisconsin have caused alarm and dismay amongst our allies abroad, and given considerable comfort to our enemies.") The senator, who had attacked the State Department and the U.S. Army as bastions of leftism and accused the Democratic Party of "twenty years of treason," was shown to be an irresponsible and dangerous fraud. *Frontier* magazine was soon to publish its blacklist exposé, "The Hollywood Story," and under the auspices of the Ford Foundation, John Cogley began work on his two-volume *Report on Blacklisting.* John Huston's voice would have been a welcome one in the still-small chorus of First Amendment defenders. But the "fight-or-flight" syndrome had taken over, and he chose flight. In the process this most American director lost his focus. It would be quite a while before he got it back.

While in Galway, John picked up a copy of Cockburn's novel *Beat the Devil,* written under the nom de plume of James Helvick. He immediately saw it as a "shaggy dog" movie. It had a ripe cast of international hustlers out to fleece an African nation. At stake were the rights to rich uranium deposits, and every one of the gang members was on the muscle, capable of betraying his or her associates at any moment. So there were laughs as well as adventures in the story. Cockburn was not doing particularly well. John smiled his usual smile, exuded his customary charm, and took an option for the bargain price of ten thousand dollars late in 1952. The money wasn't his; he persuaded Humphrey, through Santana, to finance the deal.

It was not a hard sell. For all the grumbling, Humphrey esteemed the man who had guided him through his best work. If John Huston was a monster he was a *monstre sacré*. "Since I've won the Oscar," Humphrey told John, "I have tremendous respect for your opinions, drunk or sober." Still, John had to be given a hard time whenever possible. At the time of the purchase, he had suggested Lauren for a leading role in *Beat the Devil*. Humphrey sent a pseudo-angry letter to Ireland: "I read your insidious and immoral proposals to my wife. I have instructed Miss Bacall to disregard your blandishments and as your employer I implore you not to further fuck up my home, which has already been fucked up like Hell by Adlai Stevenson."

He was not through complaining. John suggested that Billy Dannreuther, the Bogart role, should be a spiffily dressed dandy. "I'd like to see you a very Continental type fellow — an extreme figure in a homburg, shoulders unpadded, French cuffs, regency trousers, fancy waistcoats and a walking stick." A second fulmination issued from Holmby Hills. "As regards your brilliant conception of my wardrobe, may I say that you're full of shit. . . . As regards the cane, I don't have to tell you what you can do with THAT!"

Humphrey and John did agree that *Beat the Devil* should be shot in Ravello, Italy, a town above the Amalfi coast with spectacular views of the Mediterranean. "It's only money," said Humphrey blithely, and off he went to get a look at the place. Huston, as usual, was on his own. Humphrey was forced to go it alone because Lauren was back in Hollywood filming *How to Marry a Millionaire,* co-starring Marilyn Monroe and Betty Grable. Additional financing for *Beat the Devil* had been provided by an Italian concern, Robert Haggiag, and the Woolf brothers' Romulus, based in Britain. A Huston production was never without complications; because of three streams of revenue, now they came in triplicate. Humphrey, who preferred to steer clear of the nuts and bolts of the film business, found himself immersed in budgets, schedules, and salaries. Lines of apprehension began to show in his face and temperament. As the opening day for filming approached, outbursts grew more frequent. Some were for effect; most were not.

The Italian sex symbol Gina Lollobrigida signed on to play Humphrey's wife, with the proviso that in European theaters she would be billed over the title. Jennifer Jones, a delicate beauty married to producer David O. Selznick, agreed to be one of the schemers. To add color and eccentricity Santana hired Robert Morley, who had played Katharine Hepburn's doomed brother in *The African Queen*. Both Humphrey and John regarded Peter Lorre as a talisman — he had appeared in two central Bogart films, *The Maltese Falcon* and *Casablanca*. They were very pleased when he became the fifth piece in their plan to make a new classic.

Casting was to be the easy part, the script the most difficult. Cockburn's initial version was deemed unusable. Santana brought in a team of experienced screenwriters, Peter Viertel and Tony Veiller (*The Killers; State of the Union*). Their work went before the censorious Breen office, which found it wanton. As the scenario stood, *Beat the Devil* condoned the out-of-wedlock indecencies of the Bogart and Jones characters (he is married to a scheming Italian, she to an upper-class twit). Moreover, it made a "dashing, romantic and heroic" figure out of Billy Dannreuther, used scatological terms, and mentioned homosexuality — this at a time when director Otto Preminger was fighting for the right to have the words "virgin," "seduce," and "mistress" in the dialogue of his new comedy, *The Moon Is Blue*.

As it happened, Selznick was in Italy, completing the Jennifer Jones–Montgomery Clift vehicle, *Indiscretion of an American Wife*. Additional dialogue for that film had been supplied by the twenty-nine-year-old novelist and short story writer Truman Capote. The twee photograph of the author on the dust jacket of *Other Voices, Other Rooms* had attracted more attention than the prose within. Capote was still in Rome, living beyond his means. Selznick was impressed with the young man's work and advised Huston that "his is one of the freshest and most original and most exciting talents of our time — and what he would say through these characters, and how he would have them say it, would be so completely different from anything that has been heard from a motion-picture theater's sound box as to give you something completely fresh — or so at least I think."

Selznick's opinion was good enough for Huston. He hired Capote for fifteen hundred dollars a week, and suggested a new direction for the script. Recalled Truman, "Both John and I felt that the best thing to do was to kid the story as we went along.

The only trouble was that shooting had to begin the following week." In the few days before everyone went to work, the producer and director motored to the location in Ravello. On the way their chauffeur failed to make the proper turn and crashed into a stone wall. Riding without a seat belt, Humphrey was thrown forward, cracking a dental bridge and lacerating his tongue. The mouth wounds were stitched up sans anesthetic by a Neapolitan doctor. "Bogie had guts," Huston said admiringly. "Not bravura. Real courage." A week later a new bridge arrived from Los Angeles and everyone went to work, speaking dialogue that had been concocted on the spot.

That was not considered an insuperable obstacle. After all, *Casablanca* had been created under similar conditions, and everyone knew how well that had turned out. What people failed to realize was the simplest of truths: in *Casablanca,* human lives were at stake. As long as the protagonists were on the right side of the war, all sorts of morally questionable behavior could be permitted or excused. In *Beat the Devil* nothing was vital. It was all a game among thieves — and the writers of their dialogue. In Huston's overview, "the crooks; ostensibly heroic people; the romance; even virtue, became absurd."

But there was no other choice now; it was Capote or nothing. Truman made good on Selznick's promise. Something completely different was delivered on a daily basis, often only twenty-four hours ahead of the shooting schedule. "I didn't know how good it was, or how bad, or anything like that," Huston recalled. "We all knew that it was something. We just went with it." As Truman's biographer Gerald Clarke observes, he packed his dialogue with everything he found funny, from Lollobrigida's comic malapropisms to his favorite cinema clichés. Houston's assistant John Barry Ryan thought that "it was all perfectly obvious that he was making a movie for his own amusement. I always meant to sit down with him and ask, 'Truman, were you doing what we all thought you were doing? Was it all a game to you?' " Indeed it was, and the improvisatory form of the script was reflected in the private lives of everyone concerned with the movie.

The Lost One, Stephen D. Youngkin's entertaining biography of Peter Lorre, quotes cinematographer Oswald Morris on the atmosphere in and around the set. One night while Humphrey and John were playing poker, an emergency message was delivered to their table: Jennifer Jones was sitting atop the wardrobe in her room, glassy-eyed and hysterical. Humphrey went upstairs to find Lorre lying in Jones's bed, wearing a bright red flannel nightie, smoking a cigarette, and reading the paper. "She had come into the room, seen Peter there, screamed and leapt straight on top of the wardrobe and refused to come down until Bogart came up and got him out of her bed and apologized. So Bogie went up and fished Peter out of the bed. It was all a put-up job. That's the sort of thing that went on."

Ravello was not all that far from Rome, and a couple of celebrities passing through town took it upon themselves to make unannounced visits. Orson Welles dropped by, exchanged some words with his fellow director, and took off. Ingrid Bergman took the opportunity to say hello to her *Casablanca* co-star. Ingrid had scandalized Hollywood by abandoning her first husband and children to run off with Roberto Rossellini. Thereafter she became the lodestar of his movies. They had a minimal impact in Europe and none at all in the States. Yet she carried herself like a grande dame — as Alfred Hitchock had observed, Miss Bergman "only wanted to appear in masterpieces" All this made her ripe for Humphrey's reflexive needling, and he took full advantage of the opportunity. Was her conduct worth the price? Deep down, didn't she regret wrecking her career? Reviled in the United States, no longer important in Europe, who was she now? Ingrid answered coolly, "I am a very happy woman and maybe that is just as important as being a box office success in America." For once Humphrey had no comeback. When she left, he retreated to the jokey atmosphere around the set, trying to banish thoughts about profits and losses. But they wouldn't go away. The tension mounted, and the anxieties went public, showing up in his performance — in the tightness of the mouth, the weariness of the eyes, and the brusque, often unconvincing delivery of the lines.

Huston thought of the Robert Morley character as a latter-day Kasper Gutman, the Fat Man of *Maltese Falcon.* But Sydney Greenstreet had a twinkle and liked to mix with the other members of the cast. Morley detested practical jokes and found Lorre "an intensely tiresome little chap with quite the foulest vocabulary I have ever had the misfortune to listen to." Rather than hear a nightly cascade of scatological words and off-color material, Robert took his meals in his room.

Both leading ladies fell short of expectations. Gina Lollobrigida, the top-heavy Italian sex symbol, was of no interest to Humphrey. He professed himself "not a bosom man" and referred to her as "the Refrigerator." Gina's great rival, Sophia Loren, cannily if bitchily observed that Gina was "good playing a peasant, but incapable of playing a lady" — something she was required to do here. Although Jones had a finishing school beauty, hers had been an irregular career. After playing radiant heroines in films like *Since You Went Away* and *Cluny Brown*, she appeared in a series of unprofitable films. She was miscast as a fiery half-breed in *Duel in the Sun*, and seemed out of place in the title role of *Madame Bovary*. *Ruby Gentry*, the story of a swamp girl in the Deep South, might have been more of the same had it not been for King Vidor's strong direction. The feature pleased audiences and returned Jennifer to the elite group of bankable stars. Still, she had never been known for comic ability, and Capote's daily contributions threw her off balance for most of the shoot. "I always wanted to know where my character was going," Jones complained, "whether she was going to drop dead or jump in the ocean or be knocked over the head . . . so it sometimes threw me a little bit not to know from day to day what she was going to do or not to do."

On top of that, many of the Italian performers knew no English and spoke phonetically, giving their lines a strange, arrhythmic tone. Retake after retake was required. And then there was the business of the unions. When the shoot was over, Humphrey remembered that "Italian labor was divided into two camps: reds and whites. We weren't permitted to use the Commies, though they represented the best technicians."

Besides all this there was Truman, who made no attempt to hide his homosexuality, swishing around wearing a lilac scarf and an ankle-length camel's hair coat. Humphrey, who made a habit of railing about "fags," didn't know what to make of this short, flamboyant Puck. At first he gave Truman a wide berth, mocking his gestures and loudly referring to him as "Caposey." But as the filming went on, he found himself beguiled by the little man.

There were two reasons for Humphrey's turnaround. Truman could be outrageous, but he was a true professional, generating dialogue on a daily and sometimes hourly basis. He never seemed to need a break, save for eccentricities like phoning Rome to speak to his pet raven, Lola (who answered back), and going to a hospital to take care of an impacted wisdom tooth (where he turned out twelve pages despite the pain). Also, the little man was a lot more combative than he looked. One afternoon Humphrey was feeling particularly macho. Sitting in the lobby of the Hotel Palumbo, he kept challenging various crew members to arm-wrestle as they passed through. These contests were won handily and, spotting Caposey, the champ called out, "How would you like to take me on?" Truman accepted the invitation, pulled up a chair, and locked fingers with him. Seconds later, Humphrey's arm was down and it stayed there. "Would you mind doing that again?" Humphrey inquired. "Yes, for fifty dollars." Humphrey put money on the table — and lost again. "As we stood up," Truman remembered, "he caught me in a bear hug. He meant it affectionately, but there was also a certain kind of frustration-malice in the way he did it. 'Cut that out, Bogie!' I said. But he kept on squeezing me. 'Cut that out!' I said and hooked my foot behind his leg and pushed. Boom!" Humphrey tumbled back and suffered a hairline fracture of the elbow. As Huston observed, Truman was "a little bull." Unfortunately, his taurine prowess resulted in a delay of filming while the star-producer received medical attention. Yet the two men became fast friends. "I really liked Bogie," Truman insisted. "He was one of my all-time favorite people." Humphrey had similar feelings; he wrote to Lauren, "Wait till you meet our screenwriter. You have never seen anything like him. At first, I didn't think he was real — but he grows on you, and now I'd like to carry him around in my pocket, and take him out whenever I need a laugh."

He would need a lot of laughs to offset the feelings of imminent disaster. During one sequence, Huston planned to film Morley in a car. At the last moment he decided that a long shot could be used, making the actor superfluous. Heading downhill, the automobile crashed as the cameras rolled. Morley looked on, appalled: "I might have been killed." Replied the director, "Yes, but you weren't, were you, kid? So now you're fine, just fine." That was the trouble. With Huston, everything was always first-rate. That was his party line, no matter how dubious the weather, the work conditions, the picture itself. According to Morley, some years back Huston had been strolling down Fifth Avenue when he encountered a corpse lying on the pavement. Every other passerby ignored it; not John. He bent over and felt the man's wrist for a pulse. There was none. As an ambulance pulled up, he assured the stretcher bearers, "He'll be just fine . . . just fine." Humphrey wanted to share in John's general euphoria, but now his instincts told him otherwise. When the picture wrapped, he returned home full of forebodings. A special screening was set up so that he could consider the film objectively. Before the first reel ended Humphrey saw what was wrong: *Beat the Devil* was an unattractive mélange of styles and genres. And there was actually footage in which the voice of a Bogart imitator could be heard. During the weeks of postproduction in London, Huston felt that the star didn't sound like himself in certain scenes. Without asking permission, the director hired a versatile young actor named Peter Sellers to do some dubbing. (Save for those three men, no one could tell the difference.)

Humphrey felt certain that the critics would crucify the picture, that audiences would then pass it by, and that Santana would have to eat the loss. He consulted an old friend, Nunnally Johnson, a veteran producer, who had been associated with drama (*The Grapes of Wrath*), farce (*Mr. Peabody and the Mermaid*), and musical comedy (Lauren's latest, *How to Marry a Millionaire*). Nunnally thought the film might be salvageable. He screened the print for two veteran film cutters, Gene and Marjorie Fowler. They agreed; *Beat the Devil* had possibilities — if it could be reconstructed. As it stood now, the first half hour was a straight caper picture. Then, without warning, it lurched into self-satirizing farce. From long experience, the Fowlers knew that a confused viewer is a hostile viewer. They went to work, rejiggering some interior scenes and front-loading the final one. *Beat the Devil* now opened with some of the conspirators in chains, on their way to prison. Johnson furnished a line for Humphrey, speaking over the footage: "These are four *brilliant* criminals at the climax of their most magnificent effort." That would give audiences the necessary signal: a monumental send-up was about to be unreeled. Or so it was hoped. But in a letter to Humphrey, John Huston seemed to have lost his trademark buoyancy. "If the humor comes off — as I pray it will — I believe it will make some very tidy sums. On the other hand, if the joke should fall flat — well, God help me."

Flat is what it fell. The distributor, United Artists, had no idea how to promote the thing. One campaign pushed its dramatic side: BOGART MEETS HIS MATCH IN THE WORLD ADVENTURE THAT BEATS THEM ALL! Another, acknowledging that movie studios were frantically trying to woo audiences away from their television sets, struck a self-mocking pose: YOU HAVE SEEN COLOR — DIMENSION — CINEMASCOPE BUT NOW — WE PROUDLY PRESENT ON THE SMALL FLAT SCREEN BEAT THE DEVIL IN GLORIOUS BLACK AND WHITE!

When he wrote his memoir some two decades later, Huston's memory proved faulty. "A few critics hailed the film as a little masterpiece," he claimed, "but they were all European. There was not an American among them." Actually several U.S. reviewers admired Huston's movie. *The New Yorker* found it "a hugely entertaining work," comparing its "bright lunacy" to the novels of Evelyn Waugh. And *Time* was amused: "as elaborate a shaggy-dog story as has ever been told." For the most part, though, *Beat the Devil* was accorded a lukewarm reception. The big names in the cast made it seem like an expensive home movie, a sniggering in-joke for the kind of people who lived in Malibu Beach Colony.

The same held true for the European reviewers. A few enthusiasts made themselves heard. But the majority of journalists and cinéastes considered *Beat the Devil* a filmed charade, made for the amusement of its participants. The public was advised to stay away. It was just as Humphrey and John had feared. Audiences were bewildered and angry, and the word of mouth was terrible. "It should have been called *Beat the Customer,*" griped one viewer. Fearing a week of empty theaters, a Detroit chain canceled bookings of the film. The owner of a Baltimore movie house promised to give ticket holders their money back if they didn't like the picture. He had plenty of claimants.

Yet the saga of *Beat the Devil* still had far to go, and so did its star. In the early 1950s, the Eisenhower presidency represented the sunset of the war hero. Just as an emerging generation stood ready to take over the political scene, a group of ambitious young actors waited in the wings. Marlon Brando, Montgomery Clift, James Dean, and Paul Newman were on the rise, ready to take over the leading roles once played by the likes of Gary Cooper, Henry Fonda, Cary Grant, Spencer Tracy — and Humphrey Bogart. By the time *Beat the Devil* appeared Humphrey should have been considered the Ike of film actors, honored, appreciated, but growing more obsolete by the day. (After all, he was only nine years younger than the chief executive.) That was not the way it played out.

Somehow, Humphrey always managed to ride the wave of popular culture. It was not an accident. Luck played its part, of course, and he appeared in many a loser in the theater and on film. But when a pivotal role came his way, he always managed to seize the moment and move his career to the next level. The Bogart reputation took off in the 1930s when Broadway plays like *The Petrified Forest* crystallized the national angst. In the 1940s, *The Maltese Falcon* and *Casablanca* established Humphrey's reputation as the American male par excellence, operating in a compromised and often evil world, a man without illusions. "I don't mind a parasite," Rick tells Ugarte. "I object to a cut-rate one." Even so, this hard-bitten cynic has a heart — a vulnerable one, protected by a screen of acrimony and wisecracks: "Tell me," he asks Ilsa, "who was it you left me for? Was it Laszlo, or were there others in between? Or aren't you the kind that tells?"

And now, in the 1950s Humphrey was about to be plunged into an entirely new genre, a category that, at that point, had no name. A generation later, film critic Roger Ebert argued that *Beat the Devil* was the first "camp" movie, an accident waiting to happen. He praised Capote's elliptical dialogue, singling out Jones's line "They're desperate characters. Not one of them looked at my legs" and Lorre's description of time: "The Swiss manufacture it. The French hoard it. Italians want it. Americans say it is money. Hindus say it does not exist. Do you know what I say? I say time is a crook." Ebert also took delight in the film's improvised style, "half-serious" attitude, and patent absurdities: the ex-Hungarian Lorre, his hair dyed blond, is named O'Hara; the heavily accented Lollobrigida declares, "Emotionally I am English"; Humphrey claims, "I was an orphan until I was twenty. Then a rich and beautiful lady adopted me." There is a scene, Ebert points out, on a veranda overlooking the sea, "where Bogart and Jones play out their first flirtation, and by the end of their dialogue you can see they're all but cracking up; Bogart grins during the dissolve. The whole movie feels that way."

That style was off-putting in the 1950s, the mark of the unprofessional, the bum. Over the years, though, *Beat the Devil* made money by becoming a cult favorite. That cult had many members, but Humphrey was never one of them. "Only phonies think it's funny," he insisted. "It's a mess." True enough; even so, camp followers delighted in that mess. In her celebrated essay "Notes on 'Camp,' " Susan Sontag offers some definitions. "Camp proposes a comic vision of the world. But not a bitter or polemical comedy. . . . The ultimate Camp statement: it's good *because* it's awful." In a triumph of irony, the flamboyant, sibilant Capote had taken two unassailable symbols of ur-masculinity, John Huston and Humphrey Bogart, thrown them both to the ground, and then helped them to their feet.

III

Herman Wouk spent four years in the navy aboard destroyer-minesweepers, and his fourth novel grew out of that experience. Published in 1951, *The Caine Mutiny* hit the best-seller list and stayed there for nine months. Three years later he turned the courtroom portion of his tale into a stage play. *The Caine Mutiny Court Martial,* directed by Charles Laughton, and starring Henry Fonda and Lloyd Nolan, toured the country before settling in for a long run at the Plymouth Theater in New York. Meanwhile, the book had been sold to Columbia Pictures.

The film adaptation had a troubled beginning. Humphrey hungered for the role of Captain Queeg. Harry Cohn, head of Columbia Pictures, knew the situation and took full advantage. On the surface, all seemed well, but privately Humphrey told Lauren, "This never happens to Gary Cooper or Cary Grant or Clark Gable, but always to me. Why does it happen to me? Damn it, Harry knows I want to play it and will come down in my price rather than see them give it to somebody else." And so he did, settling for much less than his customary $200,000.

Then there was the matter of Edward Dmytryk. One of the Hollywood Ten, he had been given a six-month sentence for contempt. In jail he had griped to his fellow ex-Communist Ring Lardner, "You writers can write under other names. What the hell can a director do?" It was the first hint that he was about to jump-start his career by getting off the blacklist. After four and a half months behind bars (about a third of the time he had spent in the Party), Dmytryk let it be known that he wanted to meet "the toughest anti-Communist in town." That was Roy Brewer, leader of the International Alliance of Theatrical Stage Employees and one of the most adamant right-wing union chiefs in America. Brewer believed in rehabilitation at a price. For Dmytryk the price was a total repudiation of his past and the naming of names for the House Un-American Activities Committee. Appearing voluntarily before the committee in 1948, he filled the air with big names and small ones. These included screenwriter John Howard Lawson, whom he accurately described as the "high lama of the Party"; Jules Dassin, director of *The Naked City;* and Frank Tuttle, who had directed seven Bing Crosby hits. After naming twenty others as one-time Communists, Dmytryk was deemed fit to direct a film about the War of 1812.

Four pictures later he was hired to direct *The Caine Mutiny,* but he was still not sanitized enough for the U.S. Navy. Fortunately for Dmytryk, the film's technical adviser, Commander James Shaw, had impeccable credentials: he was a decorated veteran of Iwo Jima and Guadalcanal. The commander intervened on behalf of Columbia Pictures, persuading his superior officers that Dymytrk was now an impeccable patriot, as were producer Stanley Kramer and the entire cast. Columbia offered other assurances. The movie would provide a spirited endorsement of career officers and their crews, and the screen would show a paragraph stating that the U.S. Navy had never experienced a mutiny. (In fact there had been two mutinies. The first, in 1842, resulted in the hanging of three men, one of them the eighteen-year-old son of the secretary of war. The second occurred in 1944, when military workers at a northern California dock refused to resume loading ammunition after a merchant ship blew up, killing more than 300 men. The assembled officers found 258 protesters guilty, imposed bad-conduct discharges on 208, and court-martialed the remaining 50, who were found guilty and sentenced to lengthy prison terms. The sentences were commuted shortly after the Japanese surrender in August 1945.)

There were other difficulties, however, and these could not be managed so easily. In the Wouk novel, Captain Queeg is an interesting, conflicted man. By the last year of the war, the faithful husband and father, a valiant leader under fire, has become a burned-out by-the-book martinet. Does his failure of nerve threaten the *Caine* and every man aboard her? Or is he merely going through a bad patch like many another battle-weary combat veteran? It was up to the reader to decide. The other officers were also given dimension and complexity. The theatrical version kept that complexity because it only included the court-martial. Thus the two-hour running time could be spent on character as well as on plot development. The film ran about the same length, but included a long preamble and a postlude concentrating on Ensign Willie Keith (Robert Francis), a wellborn Princetonian in love with a club singer, but afraid to tell his haughty, dominating mother. As in many another oceangoing tale, from *Captains Courageous* to *The Rover Boys,* Keith grows up at sea. Unfortunately, the male ingenue and his story consumed valuable footage and minutes without adding much to the proceedings. The story of Captain Queeg had to be confined to the middle third of the movie, and it was up to Dmytryk and his cast to make the drama come alive in the time allotted to them.

No screen actors of this period could have done more with their parts. Even the smallest roles were filled by men with real faces and personalities. As the barely able seamen Meatball and Horrible, Lee Marvin and Claude Akins provided memorable comic relief. Fred MacMurray had spent his early career impersonating genial, all-American types. But he reversed course in 1949, playing a heel in the classic film noir *Double Indemnity.* At the age of forty-six he assumed another unsympathetic role. Lieutenant Tom Keefer, a novelist in civilian life, is a weak man with a glib tongue and a façade of good fellowship. Ever the agent provocateur, Keefer persistently labels Queeg a "classic paranoid," a "Freudian delight" who "crawls with clues," encouraging Lieutenant Steve Maryk (Van Johnson) to seize control of the *Caine.* Johnson, the blond, freckled "boy next door" in a dozen MGM pictures, had suffered a horrific automobile accident in 1943. For the rest of his life he wore a metal plate in his skull, and his still-handsome face was left with discernible scars. They gave the thirty-eight-year-old a hard-worn and serious demeanor he had lacked in earlier films. Johnson displayed an unaccustomed authority in *The Caine Mutiny,* especially during the typhoon scene, where Maryk deposes the glassy-eyed captain, assuming full charge of the ship.

Once ashore, Lieutenant Maryk and his fellow officers are arrested. At the tense court-martial they're reminded that mutiny is a capital crime; the only thing standing between them and the noose is an effective defense attorney — *if* Lieutenant Barney Greenwald is up to the job. As the court-appointed lawyer, the forty-two-year-old José Ferrer used his rolling bass and contemptuous glare to great effect.

Each officer testifies about the condition of the ship, the captain's fitness, whether they thought the mutiny justified. All but one backs Maryk. To save his own skin Tom Keefer denies the truth and states that he wanted no part of the takeover. Yes, he worried about Captain Queeg's stringent orders, but never, ever thought him incapable of command. As the *Caine*'s Iago, MacMurray might have stolen the film, had it not been for Humphrey's towering performance as Queeg. Reaching back to the Fred C. Dobbs of *Sierra Madre* and the Dixon Steele of *Lonely Place,* the fifty-five-year-old added his own experiences in the navy, as well as his knowledge of human behavior, closely observed. "Queeg was not a sadist, not a cruel man," he was to write. "He was a very sick man. I don't know whether he was a schizophrenic, a manic depressive or a paranoiac — ask a psychiatrist — but I do know that a person who was any one of those things works overtime at being normal. In fact he's super normal until pressured. And then he blows up. I personally know a Queeg in every studio." Audiences saw none of the overstatements and tears

Lloyd Nolan had employed on Broadway. Queeg begins his testimony in a reasonable tone and then, as Greenwald inexorably leads him on, descends into an angry, pitiable figure hovering on the threshold of madness.

One outburst would be mimicked by impressionists for the next fifty years. To corner Queeg, Lieutenant Greenwald refers to several incidents over the past year. The captain ran over his own towline. The captain put a yellow dye in the water to guide the small boats carrying invading GIs to shore — and then turned tail rather than face enemy fire. The captain was informed that a quart of strawberries had been stolen by the mess boys but refused to believe it. When he was a mid-shipman, he had caught a man with a makeshift key to the kitchen, and insisted that a seaman had done the same thing here. Queeg therefore ordered his officers to do a full-scale investigation from midnight to dawn. Ruthlessly prodded by Greenwald, he lurches into a monologue about past transgressions and accusations:

But they encouraged the crew to go around scoffing at me and spreading wild rumors about steaming in circles and — and then "Old Yellowstain" — I was to blame for Lieutenant Maryk's incompetence and poor seamanship. Lieutenant Maryk was the perfect officer, but not Captain Queeg. Ah, but the strawberries! That's where I had them. I proved with . . . geometric logic that a duplicate key to the wardroom icebox *did* exist, and I'd have produced that key if they hadn't pulled the *Caine* out of action. I-I-I know now that they were only trying to protect some fellow officers.

Queeg suddenly snaps out of his trance and looks around him, as if he, along with the court, had been listening to an obsessive and irresponsible commander. "Naturally," he says in a chagrined and melancholy voice, "I can only cover these things from memory. If I've left anything out, just ask me specific questions and I'll be glad to answer them one by one."

Lieutenant Greenwald has accomplished what he set out to do: destroy the captain's credibility and, in the process, the captain himself. No further questions are required; Queeg has been revealed as unstable and unfit to command. The court-martial is over. But not the drama. At a party celebrating their vindication, Keefer appears. "I didn't think you'd have the guts to show up," Maryk mutters. Replies Keefer, "I didn't have the guts not to."

Greenwald also shows up, drunk and angry at himself for breaking Queeg: "I had to torpedo him. And I feel sick about it." When one of the officers demurs, he rambles on. "When I was studying law, and Mr. Keefer was writing his stories, and Willie was tearing up the playing fields of Princeton, who was standing guard over this country of ours? Not us. We knew you couldn't make any money in the service. Who did the dirty work for us? Queeg did." When one of the acquitted men argues that Queeg endangered the lives of the crew, Greenwald counters, "He didn't endanger any lives. *You* did. At one point Queeg came to you for help, and you turned him down. He wasn't worthy of your loyalty. So you turned on him. You made up songs about him. If you'd been loyal to Queeg, do you think all this would have come up?" Greenwald exits with a histrionic gesture, flinging the contents of his glass in Keefer's face. The only reason the scene works is because Humphrey has given Queeg a tragic stature. Although the captain is absent, his disintegration marks everyone in the room.

The *Hollywood Reporter* judged Bogart's

"infinitely pathetic performance" to be "a high point in the history of screen acting." *Time* had put Humphrey on its cover during the making of *The Caine Mutiny*. The article, headlined THE SURVIVOR, stated that in the process of making sixty-eight pictures, Bogart had acquired a brassy air of confidence and command. "He deliberately gives Queeg the mannerisms and appearance of an officer of sternness and decision, then gradually discloses him as a man who is bottling up a scream."

Humphrey needed this film more than he was willing to say to Dmytryk or to his fellow actors. He considered his last movie to be a cringe-making loser, and though he liked to scoff at reviewers, he secretly believed they were right about *Beat the Devil*. When the raves came in about his performance as Captain Queeg, he could no longer pretend that critics didn't count, that the only important things were the rapt attention of audiences and the sum total of box office receipts. He collected the reviews and showed them around. One afternoon he and Spencer Tracy were knocking a few back. Tracy provoked him as usual: "Hey, you're not an actor." Humphrey rose to the bait, but this time he let others answer for him. "Here," he said, producing his good notices. "Look at these." Tracy pretended not to be impressed. But he was, and so was the friend he had been kidding. Humphrey began to feel a new surge of confidence. All right, he had made a mistake with the Huston-Capote movie, but that was just a speed bump. He breathed easier these days; *The Caine Mutiny* had proved that he was still box office material. He had some doubts about his next movie. Was a comedy the right thing to do after a wartime melodrama? Certainly it would test his versatility, but did he really need to take another test at the age of fifty-five? Maybe so.

IV

Sabrina fair,
Listen where thou art sitting
Under the glassy, cool, translucent wave,
In twisted braids of lilies knitting
The loose train of thy amber-dropping
   hair;
Listen for dear honor's sake,
Goddess of the silver lake,
Listen and save!

John Milton's lines flattered those who bought tickets to Samuel Taylor's sophisticated Broadway comedy. Starring Margaret

Sullavan and Joseph Cotton, *Sabrina Fair* was one of the bright spots of the 1953 season. The sprightly dialogue and time-worn plot were in the tradition of Philip Barry's *Philadelphia Story* and *Holiday,* and S. N. Behrman's *No Time for Comedy.* The daughter of the Larrabee family's chauffeur leaves for Paris as a gawky teenager and returns as a lovely young woman. Once she had a crush on the Larrabees' flamboyant son David; now she falls for his older brother, Linus, a stuffy businessman whom she liberates and brings to life — all very well for a 1930s play, but hardly the material for a midcentury Hollywood smash.

Nonetheless, Billy Wilder bought the play in the belief that it only needed his touch to become a commercial property. Wilder was one of the shrewdest writer-directors in the business; one of his tricks was to use an actor in an unaccustomed role: silent-movie queen Gloria Swanson as a self-deluding star in *Sunset Boulevard,* for example, or Barbara Stanwyck as a steamy, lethal blonde in *Double Indemnity,* along with the all-American Fred MacMurray as her dupe. Wilder's first choice for the role of the senior Larrabee was Cary Grant, who would have given Linus his inimitable jaunty style. Late in the game, Grant turned out to be unavailable. Billy chose to cast against part yet again, and asked Humphrey Bogart to take the role. Humphrey was well aware that he was the director's second choice and dragged his feet for more than a month. Ultimately he allowed two agents, Sam Jaffe and Irving Lazar, to talk him into it. They reminded him that Paramount was not Columbia; the studio was quite willing to pay the full Bogart salary of $200,000.

Humphrey would have many reasons to regret this decision. In the first place, his co-stars and director were cliquish and unfriendly to those outside their circle. The year before, Audrey Hepburn had won an Academy Award for Best Actress for her performance in William Wyler's brief, delirious romance of a princess and a commoner, *Roman Holiday.* The same evening William Holden took home the Best Actor Oscar for his gritty performance as the hero of *Stalag 17,* a prisoner-of-war picture directed by Wilder. Hepburn, Holden, and Wilder formed a triumvirate, with private jokes and references that rendered Humphrey an outsider. The camera loved Hepburn's delicate beauty, and she enchanted almost every male on the set — except for Humphrey. He considered her a novice, vastly overindulged by her director. Audrey was "all right," he observed flatly, "as long as you like to do thirty-six takes." He also had very little use for Holden, whom he regarded as a flat-out hypocrite. Despite the fact that William was married, he liked to carry on with his co-stars, including Hepburn. He also let it be known that he didn't like Humphrey's drinking habits (although he later became an alcoholic himself), and made it clear that as a conservative Republican he considered his co-star's politics to be both naïve and radical.

In the second place, Humphrey thought the script had an arch tone that did nothing to enhance the Bogart image. It was all very well for Cary Grant to play opposite a kid; he was only four years younger than Humphrey, but as everybody knew, Cary was ageless. Every one of Humphrey's fifty-four years showed in the topography of his face. At twenty-four, Audrey Hepburn had the affect of a gamine barely out of her teens. Humphrey considered the April-November romance unseemly, even though Audrey was only five years younger than Lauren.

And then there was the matter of the Bogart wardrobe. The man who once exploded when John Huston tried to turn him into a toff was now required to wear dark suits and a homburg for the role of Linus. Discomfort became a constant companion through seven weeks of shooting.

Like Humphrey, the forty-eight-year-old Wilder had a penchant for needling anyone in a position to challenge his authority. After a difficult moment, the director confronted Humphrey: "I examine your ugly face, Bogie; I look at the valleys, the crevices, and the pits of your ugly face, and I know that somewhere under the sickening face of a shit — is a real shit." Humphrey retaliated with deeds as well as words. At precisely 6:00 p.m., as his contract stipulated, he had a Scotch and water and walked off the set even if he was in the middle of a scene. The two men might have made interesting dinner guests or debaters on a talk show, but as colleagues they were a disaster. Wilder was the kind of director Humphrey found difficult to work with: "He works with the writer and excludes the actor." In his customary style, Wilder constantly brought new pages of dialogue to the set. One scene was written by the three collaborators, Wilder, Ernest Lehman, and Samuel Taylor, during their lunch hour. It was shot that afternoon in seventy-two takes. As the pages arrived, Humphrey went into attack mode. He did bad imitations of Wilder's Viennese accent ("Vould you mind translating that into

English? I don't shpeak so good ze Cherman") and asked whether the director had any children. Informed that Billy had a thirteen-year-old daughter, he inquired, "Did she write this?" Humphrey condemned the entire script as "a crock of shit" and said that now he understood how Ingrid Bergman felt in *Casablanca.* "I didn't know what the end of the picture would be," he was to recall. "I got sick and tired of who gets Sabrina."

Billy began by labeling Humphrey "evil, a bore, a coward, a man who would run like a weasel." As the weeks ground on, though, the director acquired a grudging respect for the actor. Bogart, he told a reporter, is "an extremely competent s.o.b." He shows up "on time, but completely unprepared," yet, "having looked at the particular scene about to be shot for a few minutes, he knows his lines. He never blows them." His work emerges "in short spurts and it looks like a whole thought-out conception when it comes out."

Wilder might have been discussing his own contributions. They were also delivered in short spurts — the rewriting got to be so intense that Samuel Taylor walked out — but seemed to be all of a piece once the film had been edited. What the director could not remove was his penchant for bizarre casting, no matter how inappropriate the performer. Only two years after making *Sabrina* he co-wrote and directed another film about the pursuit of a young woman by an older man. *Love in the Afternoon,* also starring Audrey Hepburn, did nothing for her career and made the fifty-five-year-old Gary Cooper look uncomfortable and embarrassed in the role of an international playboy.

Instead of presenting the comedy in a straightforward manner, Wilder forced *Sabrina* into a coy fairy tale. His version began with Hepburn's soft voice intoning, "Once upon a time on the North Shore of Long Island, some thirty miles from New York, there lived a small girl on a large estate. . . ." Audrey had little experience before the camera — this was only her second American movie — and Billy had no wish to change her in any way. In *Sabrina* she was the same self-consciously dewy-eyed ingenue of *Roman Holiday,* except that in the latter film she wore costumes by Edith Head; in the former her wardrobe was designed by Hubert de Givenchy.

Humphrey, on the other hand, was bullied into abandoning his assertive style in favor of a light, sardonic delivery. In the end, he reluctantly did as he was told; in Wilder's words, Bogart "took it, played it, and bitched." Not that it mattered. Wilder's reputation preceded him, and Humphrey was essentially given a pass by the reviewers. They were too kind. For despite the appearance of two older men — John Williams as Sabrina's father, former silent-screen icon Francis X. Bushman as a tycoon — Humphrey never appeared to be rejuvenated by Audrey. From the opening shot to the final credits there was not a scintilla of a spark between them. He looked too stiff and old for her; she looked too lithe and young for him. It was impossible to imagine them in bed. Yet in 1954, when the Lone Ranger was making his farewell radio appearance, the Miss America pageant was broadcast on television for the first time, and the words "under God" were officially inserted into the Pledge of Allegiance, *Sabrina* passed for urbane entertainment. Despite its creaky foundation, despite Audrey's arch portrait of a female faun and Humphrey's unpersuasive impersonation of a workaholic executive, it turned a neat profit. Rather than continue a feud that would only serve to damage their reputations, Bogart and Wilder found a way to reconcile. They acknowledged a mutual, if grudging, respect, and in time were seen at the same parties chatting away as if neither had ever uttered a cross word. But they never worked together again.

Whatever the shortcomings of his most recent film, Humphrey was by every measure a pantheon figure with wealth, celebrity, and an important body of work. He could easily have taken a break, played with his young children, sailed leisurely to Catalina and back, visited old friends in New York. Perhaps if he had paid more attention to his racking cough, he would have slowed down. But that was not Humphrey's way. He felt the need to secure his position. Joseph Mankiewicz provided the opportunity. The writer-director's 1950 film, *All About Eve,* had received six Academy Awards, including Best Picture, and Mank, as he was known around the studios, believed he had come up with another big winner.

The Barefoot Contessa, scripted by Mank, is a fictive biography of a recently deceased Spanish actress, Maria Vargas, charting the pleasures and sorrows of her rise from peasantry to royalty. Told in the manner of *Citizen Kane* (perhaps not coincidentally, Joseph's brother Herman Mankiewicz had co-written the screenplay for that picture), *Contessa* uses flashbacks and eyewitness accounts to recollect Maria's jumbled life. Mank gave nothing away, but as various members of the cast signed on, Humphrey — and many another reader — saw *Contessa* as a scenario à clef. The title role would be played by Ava Gardner. It was not hard to imagine her as Maria: her father had been a North Carolina sawmill worker and her mother a domestic, yet before the age of thirty Ava had married three times and become a major film star as well as an international sex symbol; as if to remind herself of her humble origins, she delighted in going barefoot at toney restaurants and nightclubs.

But Ava's life and career did not really run parallel to the contessa's. True, both women had many affairs and husbands; both drank too much; both were suffocated by their celebrity. But the basic model for Maria was Margarita Carmen Cansino, the Latin vaudeville dancer who changed her name to Rita Hayworth, became a major film actress at the age of twenty-five, and stayed in the front ranks for years, briefly abandoning her film career to wed Prince Aly Khan.

Two unknowns were considered for the part, but neither the Briton Joan Collins nor the Italian Rosanna Podesta had the quality Mank was looking for. *Contessa* needed someone with an exotic beauty, talent to match, and proven box office appeal. It soon became clear that only one woman would do. The problem was, Ava Gardner was under contract to Metro-Goldwyn-Mayer. The year before, Mank had directed *Julius Caesar* for that studio and during the filming had clashed with production executives over budgets and timetables. Now they struck back. He could have Ava, *if* he paid MGM $200,000 plus 10 percent of the gross. They got what they wanted. So did Mank. With Humphrey Bogart playing Harry Dawes, a washed-up director newly on the wagon, Edmond O'Brien as the sycophantic publicist Oscar Muldoon, and an experienced cast of character actors, he was ready to make a mordant commentary on the wasteland of Hollywood and the playgrounds of international high society.

The film opens on the rain-soaked funeral of Countess Maria Torlato-Favrini, set in a Roman cemetery. In flashbacks, Harry and Oscar summon up Maria's early, middle, and late days. They begin with a low point in Harry's professional life. He has one last hope: Kirk Edwards (Warren Stevens). The billionaire is on track to produce his first movie, and allows Harry to come along for the ride. All that it costs the director is his own dignity and self-respect. For Edwards is a man who enjoys humiliating anyone who works for him — especially Oscar Muldoon, a figure soaked in flop sweat.

The trio visit a Spanish dive to catch Maria's dance routine, agree that she's a seedling superstar, and offer to plant her in Los Angeles. There she enjoys instant success, attended by a series of personal travails. The worst of them is an inability to find love. She envies Harry's happy marriage to Jerry (Elizabeth Sellars), while the men in her own life offer nothing but misery. Edwards is an emotionally stunted figure, out for instant gratification. On a trip to Europe she abandons him for Alberto Bravano (Marius Goring), a South American wastrel who, it turns out, is only interested in acquiring another sex toy. At a gambling table Bravano goes on a losing streak and publicly blames Maria for his bad luck. Out of the crowd steps the gallant Count Vincenzo Torlato-Favrini (Rossano Brazzi), who offers his arm. At last Maria has found her Prince Charming.

Lamentablemente, things are not as they appear. On their honeymoon she discovers that the count has suffered a disabling war wound not unlike that of Jake Barnes in

Hemingway's *The Sun Also Rises*. Vincenzo is the last of his line, and Maria cannot bear the thought of the Torlato-Favrini line ending with her husband. An idea comes to her naïve mind and she spills it to Harry: she'll take a lover, get pregnant by him, then present Vincenzo with an heir. Harry warns Maria not to go any further with this lunatic plan. His caveat comes too late; the count, jealous, suspicious of his new bride and her background of numerous affairs, finds her with his chauffeur and kills them both. The pop opera ends as it began, with the group of mourners saying their farewells to the barefoot contessa.

Mank's dialogue alternated between bitchy and literate. An envious blonde cases Maria and mumbles, "She hasn't even got what I've got." Replies Jerry, "What she's got you couldn't spell, and what you've got, you used to have." When Maria observes that it's difficult to believe she's living in this day and age, Harry looks around at the displays of grandiose wealth and power: "What makes you think we're living in this day and age?"

But when the film was released, few cared about the smart banter. Columnists (and then the general public) considered the movie a celluloid guessing game. Was Maria

Vargas a portrait of Rita Hayworth? Were the other characters also taken from real life? Was Bravano the Dominican playboy Porfirio Rubirosa? Was Kirk Edwards meant to be Howard Hughes, the oddball aviator, industrialist, and owner of RKO Pictures? Secrets are not long-lived in Hollywood; shortly after the picture wrapped Hughes heard about the Edwards role and threatened a major lawsuit. He was just eccentric enough to follow through, forcing Mank to make some quick postproduction alterations. TWA, Hughes's airline, provided a plane to fly film editor William Hornbeck across the Atlantic to rerecord bits of narration. In the process Edwards was changed from a "Texas tycoon" to a "Wall Street lion," and a sequence in which he imprisons Maria — said later to be based on an incident involving Hughes and Gina Lollobrigida — was eliminated.

All this tailoring came to very little. Mank had failed to do for the screen what he had done for the theater in *All About Eve*. The film might have been better received had it not run against another backstage drama, which opened at the same time around the country. It was a remake, and oddly enough Humphrey was a devotee of the original *A Star Is Born,* starring Janet Gaynor and Fredric March. Every year, on his birthday, he screened it with tears streaming down his face at the fate of Norman Maine, a onetime matinee idol down on his luck. Richard Brooks, who was present at many of the private showings, remembered that Bogie wept bitterly on each occasion. "He associated himself with the Fredric March character, with his downfall and being unable to pull himself together. That was the only time I saw Bogie cry." Asked why he was so obsessed with the film, Humphrey explained that he strongly identified with the Maine character: "I expected a lot more of myself, and I'm never going to get it." Some of this was the Scotch talking. But much of it was prompted by the feeling that he had squandered too much of his talent, and made too many unwise choices. There was no going back now; the films were all in the can and he was certainly not one to complain in public. If his career was less than it should have been, so be it. He could still take pride in half a dozen classics of the American cinema. How many other actors could say the same? And yet no matter how many times Humphrey saw *A Star Is Born,* the Norman Maine scene prompted a melancholia he couldn't dismiss or explain away as the self-pity of an aging drunk.

The remake of the March-Gaynor movie featured a knockout song, "The Man That Got Away" by Harold Arlen and Ira Gershwin, and a bravura turn by Judy Garland, backed by the poignant performance of James Mason. Garland used up all the raves that season. One writer was unkind enough to retitle *Contessa* "A Star Is Stillborn." The other reviews were gentler but rarely more than tepid. In the *New York Herald Tribune* Otis L. Guernsey spoke for them all: "This movie has style in some places, and a certain flamboyance, but the level of its human drama is routine."

Humphrey knew he had turned in a sharp, credible performance as Dawes, a burned-out case seeking one last chance. But he also knew that this was Ava's film, not his. Future prospects were ominous. He was in his midfifties, and there were inklings that from now on he would be relegated to character parts — much as Edward G. Robinson had been in *Key Largo: Why not second billing? At fifty-three I was lucky to get any billing at all.*

Humphrey was not introspective by nature, and looked for compensation in the usual places — the bottle, the family, the pals who liked to drink as much as he did. The trouble was that grain alcohol could only go so far in elevating his spirits. When he was drunk enough, he would sit at a restaurant and complain that nobody sent him good scripts anymore, and that he was going to "go back to the boat and pack it in." On occasion the children could lighten his mood, but he didn't understand them very well. Leslie was only two; Stephen was five. When he spoke about his son to a friend, he confessed, "I guess maybe I had the kid too late in life. I just don't know what to do about him. But I love him. I hope he knows that." His fourth marriage was going well enough, yet he still paid visits to the increasingly realistic Verita Thompson. According to her memoir, "Bogie and I continued seeing each other because we wanted to, but after the birth of Stevie the talk of divorce all but ended, and with Leslie's birth, it ended completely." Friends managed to divert him from time to time, but they couldn't produce another *Maltese Falcon* or *Casablanca* or *African Queen.* So there he was in 1954, in harness but dissatisfied with his professional status, a restive husband and father, feeling a bit more tired these days, seeking something he couldn't quite put his finger on. Was this the Big Fadeout, the way so many superstars had ended — in neglect and regret and obscurity? He didn't want to think about it. It was too damn sad.

CHAPTER 8
STORM-TOSSED BY FATE

I

Humphrey's melancholia made life difficult for those around him. Like most depressions, this one contained a great deal of anger, although the subject of Humphrey's rage was never expressed in so many words. It had to do with diminishing respect from the new studio heads, with a lack of challenging film roles, and with something far more inexorable and demoralizing: increasing age. With these distresses in the back of his mind, even lighthearted subjects became weighted with sadness. When a friend asked if he had picked out a good prep school for his son, for example, Humphrey snapped, "Hell, no! I'll be dead by then." The remark was not meant as prophecy, just as a grim declaration. You went through life as two people, the mature, unyielding leading man — and the guy with thinning hair, diminishing teeth, and an overfondness for liquor,

398

Chesterfields, and outrageous remarks. It was a collision course with reality, but that's who you were, and that's the way it was going to be.

This pugnacious attitude did nothing to gratify Humphrey's wish for one more great movie, one more memorable performance. He had his own gang of intimates, but some of the important people in the industry started to give him a wide berth, unsure of how steady Humphrey was these days. Would he be as difficult on the set as he was at a restaurant table? Would he come up with one of those astonishing star turns, or would he just try to get by? For that matter, could he still remember his lines?

Humphrey had picked up a lot of detractors recently; it wouldn't have hurt to spend a little time with studio chiefs, reminding them of his virtues. But he was too proud to beat his own drum, and retreated to the company of like-minded colleagues — actors, singers, and writers who had played the game in order to stay viable in the movie business, and who disliked themselves for doing it. In 1955, some twenty of them chartered a flight to Las Vegas to catch Noël Coward's act at the Desert Inn. The leader was Frank Sinatra, and the manifest included the Bogarts, the David Nivens, Sid and Judy Luft, scenarist George Axelrod and his wife, producer Charles Feldman and model Capucine, songwriter Jimmy Van Heusen and actress Angie Dickinson, agent Irving Lazar and actress Martha Hyer, and inevitably, Prince Mike Romanoff and his Princess Gloria.

The prince was emblematic of his surroundings. Harry Gerguzin had passed from Bolshevik Russia to the United States, where he spent time in orphanages, got arrested for various misdemeanors in New York City, journeyed to Paris and London, where he plunged into more trouble (Scotland Yard had him down as "a rogue of uncertain nationality"), toured the capitals of Europe, and went back to New York, nourishing big dreams all the way. But in the New World the only job he could find was pressing pants in the back of a Brooklyn tailoring establishment. Amid the clouds of steam, an inspired idea came to him. Overseas, Harry had seen many a White Russian aristocrat reduced to driving a cab or waiting on tables. Why not leave New York, where there were too many other immigrants from the Pale? Why not go west, start fresh, put on airs, and claim to be a Slavic nobleman? He was fluent in several languages, including English, which he spoke with a bogus Oxonian intonation. If he claimed to be Prince Michael Dimitri Alexandrovich Obolensky-Romanoff, nephew of Tsar Nicholas II, who was there to say nay?

Nowhere in America could Harry have found so hospitable a climate. The Napoleonic (five-foot, five-inch) émigré was right at home in Hollywood, where pretenders have always been as much a part of the town as palmettos. In 1939, backed by actors and directors, "Prince Michael," sporting a Marine crew cut and a civilian smile, opened Romanoff's in Beverly Hills. The imperial *R* was emblazoned on the front door. The prince was the restaurant's boniface, maître d', chess maven, raconteur, and lender of money to those down on their luck. His place caught on straightaway, not least because most movie people had come from humble backgrounds and reinvented themselves. They knew a pretender when they saw one and they liked his style. Humphrey, who made a habit of lambasting phonies, gloried in the company of the most blatant imposter of them all. He had his own booth near the door, where he met friends, consumed his customary lunch of a cheese omelet washed down with Scotch, and, when things quieted down, played high-level chess with the prince. By 1947, Romanoff's had become a required tourist stop, like Schwab's drugstore or the Walk of Fame. In the film *Miracle on 34th Street,* Kris Kringle is hauled before a psychiatrist for insisting he's the authentic Saint Nicholas from the real North Pole. The doctor dismisses Kringle's claim as a harmless fantasy. Why, he goes on, thousands of people have similar delusions, living completely normal lives in every other respect. "A famous example is that fellow — I can't think of his name. For years, he's insisted he's a Russian prince." Is the man in an institution? inquires Kringle's boss. "No. He owns a famous restaurant in Hollywood."

Now, as the Hollywood cronies sat back in their banquettes at the Desert Inn in Vegas, they consumed whiskey and mixed drinks, loudly cheering Noël Coward's renditions of favorites like "Mad Dogs and Englishmen," "I'll See You Again," and "Uncle Harry's Not a Missionary Now." Humphrey, Lauren, Prince Michael, Judy, and all the others raised glasses to the singer's health. Then they drank to their own health. Then to the health of absent friends. Then they began the cycle all over again. Somewhere along the way, the prince took a close look at Humphrey. "Bogart," he concluded, "is a first-class person with an obsessive compulsion to behave like a second-class person." The roistering went on for four days. Contemplating the multiple hangovers, listening to the groans and promises of sermons and soda water from now on, Lauren informed them that they looked "like a god damn rat pack."

The sobriquet stuck. The members of the pack formalized their roles, as if they were all in the same movie. Frank Sinatra was named Pack Master; Judy Garland, First Vice President; Lauren Bacall, Den Mother; Sid Luft, Cage Master; Irving Lazar, Recording Secretary; Nathaniel Benchley, Historian; and Humphrey Bogart, Rat in Charge of Public Relations. Joe Hyams's syndicated column quoted Humphrey on the purpose of the organization: "The relief of boredom and the perpetuation of independence." To underline that phrase, Benchley designed a letterhead for Pack stationery. It showed a rat gnawing a human hand — presumably the one that fed it. Beneath the drawing was the legend "Never Rat on a Rat," an oblique reference to the blacklist days of the previous decade. Most of the Rats had a celebrity that reached beyond Hollywood. Singly they had always been given space in the papers and time on television. Soon, all around the globe, the Pack would enjoy a notoriety larger than the sum of its parts. They made the most of it, wisecracking, mocking tradition, appearing drunk, or pretending to be drunk, whenever a camera was around.

But not everyone was a fan. Columnist Hedda Hopper tried to wangle invitations to the group's parties; she was refused entrance. Of course she wrote disapprovingly of the Pack; predictably this added to public curiosity. The more reclusive and insular they were, the more Humphrey & Co. got space in newspapers, with breathless reportage about the glamorous names who had turned their backs on fame. Before long the Pack's activities were the subject of articles in European papers, something that irritated nonfans like the conservative movie star William Holden, who had disliked Humphrey since *Sabrina*. He complained that as a film star he represented America, and that his job was made difficult when he journeyed overseas. Foreigners were forever asking him about the Rats. "In every barrel there's bound to be a rotten apple," he assured them. "Not all actors are bad. It may sound stuffy and dull, but it is quite possible for people to have social intercourse without resorting to a Rat Pack." Naturally the Pack delighted in such antagonists, thumbing their noses at Holden and anyone else they considered stuffy and dull. They maintained a tight insularity, barring all but a few iconoclastic guests from either end of the sexual scale. The unabashedly gay Clifton Webb, a colleague from Humphrey's days on Broadway, was admitted. So was Mickey Rooney, MGM's much-married juvenile. In general the Pack avoided any interviewer they couldn't control. Edward R. Murrow, seemingly the most independent newsman in America, was ideal for Humphrey's purpose.

It was said around the network that there were two Murrows, the High Ed and the Low Ed. The High Ed confronted Senator Joe McCarthy in March 1954, on *See It Now* ("We cannot defend freedom abroad by deserting it at home"). The Low Ed hosted the weekly program *Person to Person,* paying calls on overexposed celebrities like Marilyn Monroe, heavyweight champion Rocky Marciano, pianist Wladziu Liberace, and, in September 1954, the Bogart family. If audiences expected lip from the guest they were disappointed. The politesse was prearranged. Scrutinizing the TV monitor in New York, Murrow saw what millions of watchers did: a slender middle-aged man in polo shirt, jacket, and slacks, with his pretty, intelligent wife, informally dressed in blouse and pants. Humphrey was asked softball questions about his career on the stage and in film; Murrow inquired about the gold bracelet Lauren wore on her wrist. She showed off the little charm, a tiny whistle commemorating her line in *To Have and Have Not*. Then the Bogart children were brought on to win viewers over and reinforce the image of Humphrey as a reformed rogue, a man whom you could now trust with your nubile daughter or your little grandchildren. He and Murrow smoked away, but drinking was not mentioned. Reviewing the show, *Variety* called the Bogarts "a literate, witty, engaging couple," and in her column Louella Parsons praised Humphrey as seen on TV: "The 'bad boy' is becoming a very sedate citizen of the town."

One of Louella's typical effusions, but Humphrey *was* beginning to assume a greater responsibility as a father and husband. At the end of 1954 he sold Santana Productions to Columbia Pictures for one million dollars. His financial manager, Morgan Maree, showed him the check. Humphrey borrowed it for the afternoon, temporarily abandoning his anti-Hollywood stance, waving the little piece of paper around to friends lunching at Romanoff's. He got a kick out of those seven figures, but the joy swiftly wore off. He had no intention of buying some ridiculously extravagant car or boat or house. As far as Humphrey was concerned, the money wasn't really his. It was a legacy, something for Lauren and Stephen and Leslie. "An actor lives in a world of anxiety and insecurity," he told his friend Joe Hyams. "He can't spread his big-money years over a lifetime like a businessman. He has to grab the bundle while he can. It's his only defense." Spoken like a man whose own father had left him with his debts, outstanding IOUs that Humphrey honorably paid to the last cent. That would never happen to Stephen and Leslie. Humphrey made a copy of the million-dollar check, and hung it on the wall of his den. The house was proof that Humphrey Bogart was a good provider. The check reminded visitors that he always would be.

II

The racking cough could no longer be masked; on several occasions scenes had to be held up until Humphrey regained his breath after an attack. The lines under his eyes and around his mouth had deepened severely in the last year. He also appeared to be suffering from "smoker's skin," a grayish pallor, accompanied by pronounced lines under the eyes and around the mouth. Cigarette consumption was something he rationalized: without butts he would gain weight; besides, they were part of his image. Drinking was more fun to talk about. Scotch, he blithely informed a reporter, "is a very valuable part of my life." It was all very well for him to joke about his habits, but he could see the results in the mirror, and they were not reassuring. In the small hours he reflected on some bitter truths: Humphrey Bogart, the most durable of the old superstars, was now a hard-to-cast leading man slipping from first place and hungry for a job. Happily, even if he was losing his teeth and hair, his timing was still intact. At this dark moment, Paramount made an offer he couldn't refuse.

In 1955 Alfred Hayes's *The Desperate Hours* was running on Broadway. The drama starred the veteran Karl Malden as Daniel Hilliard, head of a family held hostage by the gunman Glenn Griffin, played by a gifted young actor named Paul Newman. The year before, Humphrey had tried to purchase the property. But Paramount had outbid Santana. Resigned to the situation, he shrugged: "If I can't buy it at least I can be in it." The role of Griffin was ideal for him. It would have been unthinkable to cast other stars of his generation in the part. Cary Grant, Gary Cooper, Henry Fonda, Spencer Tracy, and the rest had played nice guys for most of their careers. Although James Cagney and Edward G. Robinson were still capable of projecting narrow-eyed villainy, they were seeking to change their images. Cagney had gone back to hoofing in the musical *The Seven Little Foys,* where he would impersonate George M. Cohan for the second time, and Robinson had signed to play the Hebrew leader Dathan in Cecil B. DeMille's upcoming remake of *The Ten Commandments.*

Humphrey had the field all to himself. He was twenty-five years older than Newman, but the desperado could be any age, and Humphrey intended to play him as a more mature, and therefore more threatening, Duke Mantee. He also had another idea about casting: what if Spencer Tracy played Daniel Hilliard? The two men hadn't been in a film together for more than twenty years. He and Spence loved to kid each other from adjoining booths at Romanoff's; when passersby asked Humphrey who was the best film actor in America, he pointed to himself but added that Tracy was a close runner-up. Spencer would say the same thing, putting his own name first and Bogart's second.

Initially Tracy showed some interest, but when it came time to commit he signed instead for the lead in *Bad Day at Black Rock*. Fredric March took the role. Humphrey shrugged off the disappointment and got to work. The director of *Desperate Hours* was William Wyler, a demanding, expert craftsman who had guided Humphrey through *Dead End* eighteen years earlier. He kept to a tight schedule, accommodating the Bogart contract, which specified that his workday ended at 6:00 p.m. but getting every erg from his star — and from the supporting cast — until the lights went off. *Desperate Hours* had a pounding, suspenseful plot, and a lineup of superb actors. Humphrey's fellow outlaws were played by Dewey Martin as Griffin's handsome and unlucky younger brother and Robert Middleton as a moronic sociopath. The ur-middle class Griffin family (the exterior of the house was later used for the 1950s and '60s TV series *Leave It to Beaver*) was headed by March and the veteran actress Martha Scott. Mary Murphy played their attractive adolescent daughter, Gig Young her fiancé, Richard Eyer her bratty brother. Arthur Kennedy was the deputy sheriff who tracks the villains to their lair.

Wyler and Joseph Hayes, who had written the novel, the play, and the film script, were faced with an insoluble dilemma. The black-and-white movie, filmed in wide-screen VistaVision, needed to be "opened up" with exterior scenes. But in doing so it would lose the tight, claustrophic atmosphere that had made *Desperate Hours* so suspenseful as a book and as a theater piece. To emphasize the human drama Wyler shuttled between the innocent and the malevolent, concentrating on faces that registered hostility and fear. But the dialogue and the characters often seemed at odds. Martin tries to make a move on the winsome Murphy, but never steps out of line ("I taught you everything you know," says the older brother. "Yeah," Martin admits, "everything except how to behave in a house like this"). Middleton is all blather and no action. Bogart threatens Fredric March with his customary authority — "If you pull anything, Hilliard, I'll let you watch me kick the kid's face in" — but he tolerates the boy's annoying behavior until the sadism seems histrionic, something out of a paperback thriller. So does the finale. After a plot twist, Daniel Hilliard confronts Griffin. Now he has the upper hand, and holds a gun on the brute who has terrified his family. Griffin dares him to shoot, certain that this middle-class househusband hasn't got murder in him. Hilliard disagrees: "I got it in me. You put it there." A good line, but not quite believable. Though the reviews for *Desperate Hours* praised the actors and the direction, almost all of them addressed the subject of credibility, and almost all of them had a point. What worked on the stage seemed hokey on the screen. Hilliard's dilemma wasn't agonizing, it was only melodramatic; the confrontation of good folk and malefactors wasn't terrifying, it was only histrionic.

The movie didn't thrive at the box office, which prompted Humphrey to blame the disappointment on Momism. That word was coined by Philip Wylie in his 1942 screed *Generation of Vipers,* but it got a new life when the book was republished in 1955: "When we agreed upon the American Ideal Woman, the Dream Girl of National Adolescence, the Queen of Bedpan Week, the Pin-up, the Glamour Puss — we insulted women and disenfranchised millions from love. Thus we made Mom. The hen-harpy is but the Cinderella chick come home to roost:

the taloned, cackling residue of burnt-out puberty in a land that has no use for mature men or women." According to Humphrey, if *Desperate Hours* didn't turn out to be the expected box office bonanza, well, "maybe it was because of the dignity label on the film — they didn't let people know it was a gangster film. Maybe it's because of Mom-ism these days, and no one cares if Pop is in danger of having his head bashed in." Maybe. But it was more likely that audiences wanted to see Pop in a new light, the way he was in *The Caine Mutiny,* or *The African Queen,* or even *Beat the Devil.* What they didn't want to see anymore was Humphrey Bogart in a Humphrey Bogart picture.

III

Very little time lapsed between *The Desperate Hours* and the next Bogart film, financed and distributed by Twentieth Century Fox. *The Left Hand of God* had once been the property of Warner Bros., and Fox production chief Darryl Zanuck sought to rework the script to fit the star. "We should take more advantage of the Humphrey Bogart type," he wrote in a memo to the script-writer. The dialogue was "written a trifle too much like a straight leading man. He should be more cynical, hard-boiled and a trifle more bitter." And it was done.

Humphrey and director Edward Dmytryk had meshed well in *The Caine Mutiny;* no period of adjustment was required when they began working on *Left Hand.* The film was based on a novel by William Barrett and adapted by Alfred Hayes, but it was clearly a province of Graham Greeneland. In wartime China, a Roman Catholic priest, Father Jim Carmody, shows up in a remote mountain village. The cynical, hard-boiled, bitter cleric joins the efforts of missionaries Beryl Sigman (Agnes Moorehead), her husband, David (E. G. Marshall), and their recently widowed nurse, Anne Scott (Gene Tierney). Before long the priest and the nurse find themselves attracted to each other. She is ashamed of her feelings; he is uncomfortable about his. For Carmody is not a priest after all; he's an American soldier of fortune, a pilot on the run from his ex-boss, corrupt warlord Mieh Yang (Lee J. Cobb).

In the 1950s Caucasian actors were still playing Asians, as they had in the 1930s and '40s when Peter Lorre was the Japanese detective Mr. Moto, and Sidney Toler was the Chinese sleuth Charlie Chan. Marlon Brando would impersonate Sakini, Okinawan narrator of *The Teahouse of the*

August Moon, so it was not unusual for Cobb to play Yang, it was merely appalling. His bullet head shaven, Cobb lumbers around, throwing the picture off balance. Toward the finale, when Yang confronts Jim and they roll dice for the future of the village, the drama slides into unintentional farce. Still, *Left Hand*'s lack of distinction could not wholly be blamed on Cobb. Gene Tierney's elegant carriage and exquisite face — "a fortune in cheekbones," as the columns had it — had made her a luminary. Over the course of a decade she had worked for some of the most celebrated directors in Hollywood, including Ernst Lubitsch, John Ford, Rouben Mamoulian, and Otto Preminger. But during many of those productions she suffered through attacks of severe depression. They had occurred and reoccurred since she gave birth to a child with serious disabilities. In 1943, then married to designer Oleg Cassini, she was ecstatic to learn that she was pregnant. During a visit to the Hollywood Canteen to raise money for GIs she contracted rubella (German measles). The infant, Antoinette Daria, was born prematurely, suffering from deafness, partial blindness, and severe mental retardation. Years later a woman confessed that though she had come down with German measles, she had broken quarantine to come to the canteen that night. She spoke to her idol, impulsively hugged her, and disappeared into the crowd. Tierney's autobiography, *Self-Portrait,* recalls that moment, and its result. After Antoinette's birth, she wrote, "I didn't care whether ever again I was anyone's favorite actress." On the set of *Left Hand* she kept blowing lines, retreating into herself, sometimes breaking into tears. Humphrey, who had seen a sister in the throes of mental illness (post-partum depression), warned the studio bosses that Gene was sick and needed help. "They assumed I was a trouper," the actress wrote, "and was aware how much had been invested in the film and would not let them down. They suggested that Bogart be kind and gentle. He was nothing less. His patience and understanding carried me through the film." Before it wrapped she consulted a doctor. When *Left Hand* was done, she flew to New York and checked into Harkness Pavilion, beginning a long and agonizing period of therapy. Tierney's instability rarely affected her on-camera radiance, but her timing was off for most of the picture, and the romance of Anne and Jim never jelled.

Fox publicists had no idea how to promote

the film. Humphrey had walked through his part, obviously miscast as a bogus father figure. If the part made him uncomfortable, the taglines for *Left Hand* gave him the creeps: "The strangest covenant between God and man ever made!"; "He profaned the cloth he wore! She fought against a forbidden relationship!" The United States Conference of Catholic Bishops took no offense; it rightly wrote the picture off as trivia: "The conflict between pilot and bandit has some interest but the priestly masquerade and the romantic feelings it arouses in a mission aide are pure Hollywood hokum." Professional reviewers showed the same disregard. Although *The New Yorker* praised Humphrey as an actor who "maintained over the years a singularly decent standard in his work for Hollywood," the magazine had little use for his latest effort. Other critics put the movie down as an "unconvincing demonstration of the ennoblement of a renegade" and one with a questionable moral: "If a young woman falls in love with a priest, she should not give up hope of marrying him and living happily ever after. It will probably turn out, after all, that the priest is really just some nice hardened criminal in disguise." The Bogart who could always spot a poseur had lost his way. Partly it was because he felt increasingly ill, short of breath, beset by coughing episodes that could go on for five minutes at a time. He had no inclination to weigh alternatives, to think things through. And partly it was because he had an almost pathological desire to keep working, a need that had nothing to do with money, or even with reputation, a need as urgent as his craving for cigarettes.

IV

Less than a genius, more than a foreman, Michael Curtiz had collected seven Academy Award nominations and one Oscar over the course of three decades. Curtiz's Homeric wrangling with Jack Warner had come to an unpleasant end; these days he was freelancing for any studio that would pay his salary. Paramount hired him to direct the adaptation of a Broadway hit, *We're No Angels,* itself an adaptation of a French stage comedy. Humphrey had already been signed; so had a cast of bright supporting actors, including Aldo Ray, Peter Ustinov, Joan Bennett, Basil Rathbone, and Leo G. Carroll. The names Curtiz and Bogart were forever associated with one of the most memorable American films of all time, *Casablanca,* and Paramount had reason to believe that *Angels* could become another classic. It even had a preliminary treatment by Julius Epstein, one of the writers on *Casablanca.*

By rehearsal time, however, many changes had been wrought in the adaptation of Sam and Bella Spewak's play. The new script was written by Ranald MacDougall, best known for scenarios of the drama *Mildred Pierce* (also directed by Curtiz) and the Clifton Webb babysitting farce *Mr. Belvedere Rings the Bell.* In a way, MacDougall's résumé foreshadowed the flaws to follow. Curtiz was known for wit rather than exaggerated comedy, and Bogart had not engaged in slapstick and heavy banter since his days on Broadway. Ustinov and Ray could handle all sorts of comic situations, but they were relatively new to the game; the others had made their reputations in drama.

The presence of Joan Bennett echoed an earlier experience in Humphrey's career. Back in 1941, in *The Maltese Falcon,* he had acted opposite Mary Astor, who was still smarting from a highly publicized sex scandal involving the playwright George S. Kaufman. Excerpts from her diary were printed in the papers, and the divorce received additional coverage, all of it lascivious. Although Mary was the subject of

419

whispering on the *Maltese Falcon* set, Humphrey took no part in it. Off-screen he continued to play the gentleman, never mentioning Astor's steamy past. Now he was cast opposite Bennett, also the subject of a tabloid scandal. In 1951 her husband, producer Walter Wanger, had followed his wife and her agent, Jennings Lang, to a parking lot. Convinced they were having an affair, he shot Lang in the thigh and groin. From his hospital bed, Lang protested that the only relationship he and Bennett had was "strictly business." Wanger's lawyer invoked the insanity defense, insisting that the producer had been suffering from a nervous collapse due to severe financial setbacks. Bennett remained loyal during her husband's four-month incarceration. She read a prepared statement to the press: "I never dreamed a marriage that has been as successful as ours for twelve years would ever be involved in so unhappy a situation. Knowing Hollywood as I do, knowing how good, wholesome, and sincere, by far and away a majority of motion picture people are, I want to express my deep regret that this incident will add to the erroneous opinion entertained by so many."

The speech seemed a dignified defense of her marriage at a painful time, but it was much more than that; she was fighting for her professional life — in vain, as things turned out. Bennett went on the studios' moral blacklist and made only five movies in the decade that followed. She was to summarize her downfall in nine words: "I might as well have pulled the trigger myself." One of those films was *We're No Angels.* Her appearance was due to heavy lobbying by Humphrey on her behalf. The Wangers had no Pack status, but they were Holmby Hills neighbors; the Bogarts knew them socially, and Humphrey thought it unjust for a studio to punish Joan for Walter's lunacy. He "made the stand," the actress recalled gratefully, "to show what he thought of the underground movement to stamp out Joan Bennett." The part was not large, and Paramount executives were feeling expansive that day. They allowed her to play a housewife whose home is invaded by three nefarious escapees from Devil's Island.

The trio — Joseph, Albert, and Jules (Bogart, Ray, and Ustinov) — call on the Ducotels (Carroll and Bennett), politely volunteering to fix their leaky roof — and incidentally seeking to hide from the police until a boat comes to take them to Paris. As they work, they make plans to slay the family of shopkeepers, pocketing everything they can lay their hands on. But eavesdropping reveals that the Ducotels are experiencing financial setbacks. Moreover, their daughter, Isabelle (Gloria Talbott), is having trouble with her faithless fiancé (John Baer) and his ruthless father (Rathbone). The convicts are touched by the situation. In a few arch lines they go from desperate to lovable — a setup known in show business as kitchy-koo with an anvil:

JOSEPH: You guys act like you don't want to cut their throats.

JULES: Well, speaking for myself I'd just as soon not.

ALBERT: After all, it might spoil their Christmas.

JOSEPH: I don't care how nice they are, they're not going to soften me up. We're escaping, and this is our only chance. We came here to rob them and that's what we're gonna do — beat their heads in, gouge their eyes out, cut their throats — as soon as we wash the dishes.

For reasons known only to him, Curtiz abandoned his usually deft touch in favor of an elephantine coyness. Saints in the guise of sinners, the escapees induce their poisonous pet snake, Adolphe, to bite Isabelle's intended and his father. Not satisfied with murder, they find an acceptable young man for the *jeune fille en fleur* before voluntarily returning to Devil's Island. At the fadeout halos appear over their heads — and over the cage holding Adolphe. It was too much for reviewers. The *New York Times* called *We're No Angels* "a shrill, misguided picture that should have been a honey." *Time* said the "over-whimsical" film suffered because of Curtiz's inability "to decide whether he is reading from a fairy tale or a police blotter. Bogart plays his role pretty straight; Aldo Ray is disconcertingly elfin for an alleged sex fiend; and Ustinov's mugging seems overdone." Nearly every paper remarked on the inappropriate choice of the screen-expanding VistaVision for an intimate family picture. It was true, as some acknowledged, that the male lead had a chance to parody his tough guy roles of the past, but this was old news; Humphrey had done that in *All Through the Night,* released in 1942. In those palmy days, though, he was on the rise, waiting for *The Maltese Falcon* to vault him to the top of the marquees. There were no such prospects now. All that mattered from here on was the job.

Forget the salary and the celebrity that might — or might not — go with it. In this town nothing had really changed. If you were working and you knew your lines, you were a professional. If you were loafing, you were a bum.

V

In March 1955, the Academy Awards were dispensed at the RKO Pantages Theater. Humphrey was nominated for his performance as Captain Queeg in *The Caine Mutiny*. The last time he and Marlon Brando had been up against each other was 1951. Marlon was nominated for *A Streetcar Named Desire*, Humphrey for *The African Queen*. This time matters were reversed. Marlon earned his first Oscar for *On the Waterfront*, which received eight nominations overall. Yet Humphrey's influence could be felt throughout the evening. Edmund O'Brien won Best Supporting Actor for his work in *The Barefoot Contessa*; Billy Wilder was nominated for Best Director, Hal Pereira and Walter Tyler for Art Direction, and Sam Comer and Ray Moyer for Set Direction for *Sabrina*; Stanley Roberts for Best Screenplay and Max Steiner for Best Score for *The Caine Mutiny* — all of them Bogart films.

Two months later Humphrey did something strange: he appeared in a television drama. He had never liked the medium; it tended to chew up actors and spit them out. Maybe it was OK for young performers beginning their careers, but the TV studio's unforgiving lights were not for a man of advancing years. "I look awful on television," he told a reporter. "Every pore on my face can be seen on those home screens. And you can imagine what I look like on sets with bad reception." But NBC's high-toned *Producers' Showcase* lured Humphrey with an irresistible offer: if he said yes, Lauren would play the female lead. Except for radio shows, the Bogarts hadn't performed together in ten years. Added to this was the allure of the role: he'd be reprising Duke Mantee in *The Petrified Forest.* Humphrey needed some luck right about now, and surely the play that put him on the map in 1935 would bring him good fortune in 1955. And so, on Memorial Day, Humphrey and Lauren appeared in a ninety-minute adaptation of the Maxwell Anderson opus. Broadcast in prime time, the teleplay co-starred Henry Fonda as Alan Squier. Lauren played the innocent Gabriella. *The Desperate Hours* had featured

Humphrey as a kind of Duke Mantee in middle age; he had no trouble doing a variation for *Showcase*. Fonda registered well as the faded intellectual. Lauren, however, was too urbane and throaty for the part that helped launch Bette Davis. It was difficult to believe her as an unsophisticated child of the desert. Delbert Mann, who would win an Oscar for his direction of *Marty,* cleverly deemphasized the male roles and shielded Lauren with flattering close-ups. The protection came at a price. *Petrified Forest* was a dated work that needed all the help it could get. For maximum effect Duke had to be a continual presence, a representative of inexorable fate affecting everyone he came across. Instead, Mann kept him out of sight for significant portions of the program. When Duke did have a big scene, the little screen undid him. He came across as tired and possibly ill, the face seamed by more than a life of crime. Television critics, most of them new to the job, pointed out the program's deficiencies but regarded them as secondary; what counted was the singular Bogart style. The *Times* praised Humphrey's performance as "cold, vicious and convincingly peremptory." Few actors could "suggest so much evil so quietly." *Variety* said that *Producers' Showcase* was exactly that, offering Bogart "at his best, a tough gunman capable of murder, snarling delight at the way his captives must obey his orders, and animal-instinctive in the ways of self-preservation."

After this television debut, Humphrey received a cluster of offers. Would he like to do another play on TV? How about a weekly adventure series on film? Neither choice met with his approval. To the former option, he said, "Suppose I had laryngitis, suppose I just wasn't feeling up to par. I turn in a bad performance and the critics rap me. I just don't like the idea of a one-shot." A regular series had even less appeal: "I'd sooner dig ditches." On a visit to Hollywood, Helen Hayes suggested a return to his original venues. According to A. M. Sperber, who interviewed Hayes three years before her death, Humphrey wasn't even willing to do a play in Los Angeles, much less on Broadway. "You know what would happen?" he asked the first lady of the American theater. He didn't wait for her reply. "These bastards would all go out in the lobby and say, 'So that's what's come to us as a big, big star — a big important actor. . . . That's what's been posing as a great big performer?' No, I couldn't do that."

It was feature films or nothing. In 1956

Humphrey announced the formation of Mapleton Pictures, whose products would be distributed by Allied Artists. The new company planned to buy hot properties, providing its CEO with roles that would otherwise go to younger stars. He needed those parts. Money and status had been his for a long time, but they were not enough to assuage an almost pathological desire to work, to go somewhere in the morning, to learn lines, to play a character whose name was not Humphrey Bogart.

Mapleton's first movie would be based on a crime series, *Underworld U.S.A.,* then being serialized in the *Saturday Evening Post.* Humphrey and Lauren planned to be reunited on the big screen for that one, as well as for the adaptation of *Melville Goodwin, U.S.A.,* John P. Marquand's novel about an army general and the baroness of a newspaper syndicate. Before those could get under way, he was contract-bound to appear in an adaptation of *The Harder They Fall,* a novel Budd Schulberg called his "black valentine to the sweet science of boxing." The film would be distributed by Columbia. Jerry Wald, who had been involved with six Bogart films at Warners, was set to produce; Rod Steiger and Nehemiah Persoff were given big parts. Those names set off alarms. In Humphrey's lexicon, Actors Studio graduates were defined as slackers with bad wardrobes. He suddenly chose to forget that he had set the pattern of sartorial impudence long before they arrived on the scene. (David Niven once asked his sailing companion how he could keep such a tight ship and such a neat home and then show up for a formal dinner unshaven, wearing an unpressed tweed sport coat. "The point I'm making," Humphrey told him, "is that if I choose to show up unshaven and stinking, it's nobody's business but mine, and nobody gets hurt but me." Marlon Brando could not have been more succinct.)

Now Humphrey would be face-to-face with an uncomfortable confluence of talents. Schulberg had written *On the Waterfront,* which had totally eclipsed *The Caine Mutiny* at the Oscars. In *Waterfront,* Steiger had played Brando's brother, and Nehemiah Persoff a beetle-browed cutthroat. They would be the only actors ever to work with both Marlon and Humphrey. The idea of sharing the screen with those two gave Humphrey many a bad night; he made no secret of his contempt for members of the "scratch your ass and mumble" school. But he was a professional, not a bum, and resolved to see it through.

The "dailies" — the takes that were run at the completion of each day's filming — showed Humphrey looking tired and ill-used. Few bothered to comment on his appearance; boxing pictures were always about down-and-dirty types, sellouts who surround pugs on their way up and on their way down. Here, Eddie Willis is a disillusioned journalist weary of being underpaid for telling the truth. He's ripe for the plucking, and boxing promoter Nick Benko (Rod Steiger) makes him an offer he can't refuse. For 10 percent of the gate, Eddie will hype Toro Moreno (Mike Lane), an obscure Argentinian heavyweight. Once Eddie succumbs to his blandishments, Nick guides "the Giant from the Andes" through a series of fixed fights. All along, Eddie serves as Toro's enabler, convincing the press, and the naïve Giant himself, that the overgrown boy is a legitimate contender. In one bout Toro manages to kill his opponent — a man so damaged by previous adversaries that one vigorous jab is enough to finish him. Eddie knows his client actually has "a powder puff punch and a glass jaw," but he goes along and gets along until the big man is ranked Challenger Number One. At the championship bout, Nick and his cohort place their bets against Toro, watch the carnage from the front row, and take home the big money.

From the opening moments of the film, self-revulsion shows on Eddie's face and in his body language. But his conscience has been chloroformed, and all along he makes no attempt to right the wrongs he has abetted. Near the end, though, when the scarred and bruised Toro can barely speak through his broken jaw, the journalist does awaken to what has been done to him, and to the ruined boxer. Eddie takes his own dishonest earnings, fills the fighter's ham hands with dollars, and sends him home to South America. This is only the beginning of the Willis redemption. With the encouragement of his forbearing wife, Beth (Jan Sterling), he inserts a sheet of paper in his typewriter and begins a book that will tell the truth about professional boxing and the racketeers who run it.

The Harder They Fall was obviously based on the career of Primo Carnera, a circus strongman from Italy who fought in the 1920s and 1930s, between the heydays of Jack Dempsey and Joe Louis. At the time the heavyweight division was controlled by mobsters Frankie Carbo and Blinkie Palermo, who brought "the Ambling Alp" along through a series of questionable fights. Primo finally fought an honest one against champion Max Baer, who knocked him down eleven times in eleven rounds. Not long afterward, Carnera learned that his manager had stolen most of his money.

The film gained its punch from that sorry history — and from the presence of retired fighters with welted faces, among them Jersey Joe Walcott and Baer himself. Persoff, as Benko's corrupt bookkeeper, and Harold Stone, as an honest sportswriter, were vital assets. But it was Lane's pathos, Steiger's snarling intensity, and Humphrey's tattered antihero that put the story across with the force of a blow to the solar plexus. Humphrey needled Steiger throughout; still, they enjoyed each other, and the younger man got a particular kick out of watching the older one when he got going. At one point in the filming Humphrey read a news story about Darryl F. Zanuck. The producer was advocating a search for new acting talent, unfamiliar faces, and names who would be tomorrow's superstars. That was all Humphrey needed. In his view there was nothing wrong with Hollywood's established actors: "What they want are new Bogarts, Coopers, Gables and Stewarts — at seventy-five dollars a week!"

To put Zanuck in his place, and anyone else who was thinking along those lines, he ran an ad in *Variety* satirizing the Tabs and Rocks and Tonys and other male starlets. A photo showed "Nails" Bogart in a sweatshirt standing with "Spike" Baer in a suit with bow tie and "Tack" Walcott in slacks, sweater, and leather fedora. The headline read THE OLDEST ESTABLISHED PERMANENT NEW FACES NOW AVAILABLE. Aline Mosby, a reporter for United Press International, sought Humphrey out for an interview, and found him getting his hair trimmed. While the barber snipped, he gave her enough quotes to get the town talking. "New faces," he snarled. "Why don't they lift the old faces? The studios are full of hot air. Every couple of years the studio heads say this. If they're going to make new stars, why haven't they made them by now?" Later he elaborated on the theme. Many of these young men had been picked up for screen tests from street corners and filling stations. "Shout 'Gas!' around the studios today, and half the young male stars will come running."

Of course Humphrey knew that exaggeration is the royal road to attention. But at the root of his arguments was the very real fear of disregard. He had seen it happen too often: the hard climb up, the few years of disproportionate rewards, and then the slide to obscurity. Everyone in Hollywood knew the joke about the three stages of fame: (1) Get me John Gilbert. (2) Get me a John Gilbert type. (3) Who is John Gilbert? Would they be saying the same of Humphrey Bogart someday?

The dailies didn't give Humphrey any reason to cheer. There was nothing wrong with his acting — he still had the same authority and gritty masculinity. But the image was dispiriting. He looked even wearier and more afflicted then he did on television. His eyes were watery and his toupee wouldn't fool a blind man. He thought the critics would kill the film. They didn't. Reviews for *The Harder They Fall* were generally approbatory, and sometimes more than that. By that time, however, Humphrey had little interest in the box office receipts, the critical assessments, or the next assignment. He was about to get involved in a much larger battle, and the odds were stacked against him.

VI

While lunching at Romanoff's, Humphrey happened to run into another Oscar winner, Greer Garson. In the middle of their conversation he doubled over with a coughing fit. Alarmed, Garson insisted that he consult her doctor, Dr. Maynard Brandsma, an internist at the Beverly Hills Clinic. Humphrey tried to put off the appointment, she kept pushing, and he gave in. "I should have realized at once," Lauren was to write, "that the mere fact that he'd consented to go was an indication of something serious."

It was very serious. Doctor Brandsma did a bronchoscopy, reaching down into Humphrey's esophagus, and the results showed some disturbing results. "It still didn't seem ominous to us," Lauren wrote, more like "an infection of some kind." Because Humphrey found it painful to swallow, his weight, never more than 170 pounds, had dropped to 155. Frank Sinatra offered the Bogarts the use of his house in Palm Springs and they went on a brief vacation, assuming the "infection" would heal under the sun. It did not. When they returned Humphrey visited the clinic for more tests. They showed the presence of malignant cells. An operation was mandatory and ought to be done at once. Humphrey appealed to Dr. Brandsma: There was a movie he and Lauren wanted to make. How about postponing the op until they finished *Underworld U.S.A.*? Responded the doctor, "Not unless you want a lot of flowers at Forest Lawn." He saw his patient wavering, and went on: "We were lucky to catch it so early — it's not often that we can in that area."

So that was it. Humphrey told a friend, "I was never sick a day in my life, and now I have the feeling I'll be in intensive care from now on." Another friend, British journalist Alistair Cooke, once wrote of the renegade Rick Blaine in *Casablanca:* "More than any other character he was to play, this one fitted Bogart's own like a glove." Cooke was wrong. The postoperative Humphrey had lost his distinctive diction and his unique compact energy. He could still be a husband, father, and friend. But his acting career was done. From here on, only one role was open to him: a cancer patient hiding his pain in order to put his friends and family at ease. *That,* as it turned out, was the hand-in-glove part, the one that most closely befit his temperament and moral stance.

VII

The irony was that outside the hospital the world was enjoying a false spring. Polls said President Dwight Eisenhower would be a shoo-in for reelection. He had done what he had promised to do: end the war in

436

Korea. His secretary of defense, Charles Wilson, had become notorious for a statement uttered during a Senate hearing. Asked whether he could make a decision contrary to the interests of the company he once headed, Wilson replied that he could do so in the abstract, but couldn't imagine such an occasion "because for years I thought what was good for General Motors is good for the country." The quote inspired Al Capp, the author and illustrator of "Li'l Abner," to create the plutocratic General Bullmoose, who spouted such aphorisms as "Don't do anything crooked unless it's legal." Yet Wilson had slashed the military budget, and shortly afterward the economy began to boom. During this good time Dr. Jonas Salk developed a vaccine that proved effective at immunizing children against polio. In the USSR the new leader, Nikita Khrushchev, was about to list, in some detail, the mass murders and other crimes of Joseph Stalin, thereby creating at least a temporary thaw in the Cold War.

Battered by an expanding television schedule and shrinking profits, the film industry still refused to think small. *Giant* was not only the name of a Warner Bros. epic starring James Dean and Elizabeth Taylor; it also addressed the way movies were heading. Paramount would distribute Cecil B. DeMille's remake of *The Ten Commandments* and King Vidor's version of Tolstoy's *War and Peace,* starring Audrey Hepburn and Henry Fonda. Twentieth Century Fox presented *The King and I,* one of the biggest musicals ever produced. Mike Todd's *Around the World in Eighty Days,* shown in a wide-screen process called Todd-AO, had more than forty cameo roles; the actors filling them included George Raft, Peter Lorre, Frank Sinatra, and Edward R. Murrow, all of whom had touched Humphrey's life one way or another. The major studios had heard the bell tolling for years, but they were still active. None of them were going quietly into that good night.

Humphrey watched it all from the sidelines, wishing vainly that he could be a part of the action. Sadly, he and Lauren took the children aside. She remembered telling them that "Daddy had to have something removed from his throat — it wasn't serious but he'd be away for a couple of weeks. Steve naturally didn't understand. Leslie, being three and a half, certainly didn't. How could they when even we didn't?" The operation was the best money could buy at the time, but the time was not propitious for victims of esophageal malignancy. Methods of detection were inaccurate, and laser surgery lay more than ten years in the future. Two months after his fifty-seventh birthday, Humphrey checked into Good Samaritan Hospital in Beverly Hills. On March 1, 1956, a radical procedure began. It went on for nine hours. The esophagus was entirely removed, along with two lymph nodes and a rib. The vagus nerve, which controls digestion, was cut. Humphrey's stomach was attached to his gullet; food would have a shorter way to travel, he would fill up rapidly — too rapidly — and would never really enjoy eating again. The scar from the operation was more than three feet long, running from shoulder to waist.

Recovery was excruciating. At one point Humphrey coughed his stitches loose and they had to be resewed; he had no appetite, and he was in constant pain, alleviated by telegrams, flowers, and visits from friends. John Huston showed up, full of his patented bonhomie and assurance. "He'll be fine, just fine," he told Lauren. Bogie would be ideal for a film he had in mind, an adaptation of a Kipling novel. "We'll make *The Man Who Would Be King* yet." Fred Astaire and John Wayne, stars he scarcely knew, phoned in. The superagent Irving Lazar, who was terrified of illness, came by. A perennial opponent sent a wire: DEAR BOGIE, KNOW YOU WILL BE YOUR GOOD SELF IN THE VERY NEAR FUTURE. MY THOUGHTS ARE WITH YOU FOR A SPEEDY RECOVERY. REGARDS, JACK WARNER. For all of Jack's solicitude, however, he was strictly business. The Warners film that was to have reunited Humphrey and Lauren, *Melville Goodwin,* was coldly retitled *Top Secret Affair* and recast with Kirk Douglas in the lead role and Susan Hayward as his love interest.

Precisely the opposite occurred at Columbia. Harry Cohn was the most detested of the old Hollywood moguls. (Indeed, when he died the following year a crowd of some two thousand went to the cemetery, prompting one of the attendees to murmur, "Give the people what they want and they will go out for it.") Yet Harry was extremely fond of Humphrey and Humphrey of him, possibly because Humphrey liked to play thugs, and Harry was the real thing. In a rare benign gesture Cohn kept *The Good Shepherd* on Columbia's production schedule and saw to it that press releases regularly went out, announcing that the C. S. Forester sea story would be Bogart's next picture. Humphrey told one of his pals he would beat cancer because Cohn kept calling him about getting back in harness, and "you know that tough old bastard wouldn't call if he thought I wasn't going to make it."

Surgery was only the first part of Humphrey's ordeal. He had to undergo X-ray treatments that left him nauseated and chemotherapy that weakened his constitution. "When a man is sick," recalled Dr. Brandsma, "you get to know him. You find out whether he's made of soft wood or hard wood. I began to get fonder of Bogie with each visit. He was made of very hard wood indeed." Humphrey convinced himself that the treatments were working, and in that optimistic spirit he started smoking again, this time filtered Chesterfields. Save for the time spent in the hospital, his liquor consumption never stopped.

In the previous two years Humphrey had made eight films. Now he was at home every day, all day, and the rumor mills began to grind overtime. Friends brought Humphrey the news he didn't hear on the radio or read in the columns. It was all bad: he was dying, the countdown had begun, a burial plot had been picked out. Dorothy Kilgallen, the Hearst columnist who thrived on distress, real or imagined, wrote that Humphrey Bogart had been moved to the eighth floor of Memorial Hospital, where he was fighting for his life. There was no Memorial Hospital

441

in Los Angeles, and Humphrey leapt on her misinformation. He got hold of the editor of the *New York Journal-American,* Kilgallen's home paper, and shouted into the phone, "Do I sound as if I'm fighting for my life? God damn it, don't you check your stories? You just allow that bitch to print *anything.*" He hung up exhausted but vindicated. A retraction followed.

After years of playing character leads, Humphrey had reverted to the part he knew best — the Raymond Chandler male "who is neither tarnished nor afraid." Chandler elaborated on this in his essay "The Simple Art of Murder." Such a figure "must be, to use a rather weathered phrase, a man of honor. He talks as the man of his age talks, that is, with rude wit, a lively sense of the grotesque, a disgust for sham, and a contempt for pettiness." Humphrey filled that description as if it had been written with him in mind. Joe Hyams suggested an official tongue-in-cheek denial — something on the order of "I'm down to my last martini" or "I'm fighting to keep my head above the press." But Humphrey wanted to write his own material this time, and he came up with a three-hundred-word open letter to the press. It not only displayed a rude wit, but a lively sense of the grotesque and a profound disgust for sham.

"I have read," the statement began, "that both lungs have been removed; that I couldn't live another half-hour; that I was fighting for my life in a hospital which doesn't exist out here; that my heart has stopped and been replaced by an old gasoline pump from a defunct Standard Oil station." He was just getting warmed up. "I have been on the way to practically every cemetery you can name from here to the Mississippi — including several where I am certain they only accept dogs." The indisposition was explained in layman's terms. "I had a slight malignancy in my esophagus. So that some of you won't have to go into the research department, it's the pipe that runs from your throat to your stomach. The operation for the removal of the malignancy was successful, although it was touch and go for a while whether the malignancy or I would survive."

In conclusion, all he needed was "thirty pounds in weight which I am sure some of you can spare. Possibly we could start something like a Weight Bank for Bogart and believe me I'm not particular which part of your anatomy it comes from.

"In conclusion, any time you want to run a little medical bulletin on me, just pick up the phone and, as they say in the Old Country — I'm in the book."

Decades later, oncologist Albert B. Lowenfels examined Humphrey Bogart's medical records. Despite the fact that the patient was treated with all the therapeutic measures then available, wrote the doctor, his "operation must be considered palliative." What he meant was that a cure was very unlikely — less than 4 percent of esophageal cancer patients survived for more than a year during the 1950s. The physicians at Good Samaritan had two objectives: (1) to excise the cancer tissue, in the knowledge that they were probably too late to get it all, and (2) to relieve suffering. Although their efforts were heroic, they failed on both counts.

During the postoperative period Humphrey dropped in at Romanoff's. Nicholas Ray, who had directed *Knock on Any Door* and *In a Lonely Place,* watched with grim wonder as his friend tried to choke down some food. "One could hear the Romanoff sanddab hit the bottom of Bogie's stomach, so he softened the creature's fall with a pool of scotch and beer, and settled a haze of Chesterfield smoke around it." Occasionally

444

Humphrey took the wheel of the *Santana*. In happier days, his boat was a haven, a place free from the stress of filmmaking and everyday life. Now it was a sad reminder of what used to be. One afternoon, Claire Trevor and her husband, producer Milton Bren, came aboard for a visit. She saw how emaciated he looked, and made the mistake of giving him a motherly pat on the arm. "Leave me alone and get off my boat," he snapped. "I don't want any sympathy." Hyams remembered the incident. "When they left he said he was sorry he had spoken so harshly. After all, they were old friends. But dammit, he didn't want any sympathy — theirs or anyone else's. 'Milton will understand,' he said."

Two months later, in November 1956, Humphrey complained of acute soreness in his left shoulder. He and Lauren assumed that the hurt came from a pinched nerve; these were frequent after major surgery. That was not the case here. During Humphrey's brief return to the hospital, doctors found that the malignancy had spread. Lauren was taken aside by one of the attending physicians and told what the families of cancer patients were usually told at such a time: Everything is being done. As long as the patient's alive there's a chance. Research is being conducted all the time — a cure could suddenly appear. After all, one day there was no penicillin, next day there was.

Humphrey was allowed to go home. He moved slowly, agonizingly, and had no interest in food. His weight kept going down. Yet he remained alert to what was going on around him. The preceding year, Lauren had starred in *Designing Woman* opposite Gregory Peck. *Written on the Wind,* in which she co-starred with Rock Hudson, had just opened in New York theaters. The first was a romantic comedy about the fashion business, the second a soap opera about the lives and loves of an oil-rich brother and sister. Lauren was to remember her husband stretched out on a chaise reading the reviews, "and his saying, 'I wouldn't do too many of these.' His standards were as high as ever." He remained aware of his wife's roving eye. She had been infatuated with Adlai Stevenson, and then with the conductor-composer Leonard Bernstein. With deliberate coolness he warned her, "Lenny has too many things to do in his life to be a satisfying mate. You'd probably have a great time for a weekend, but not for a lifetime." There were rumors about a fling with Sinatra. Humphrey responded as Lauren thought he would: "I knew that Bogie

— how ever much he loved me — would put up with flirtation," she wrote in her memoir. "But if I ever really did anything, he would leave me. He valued character more than anything, and he trusted mine — I knew that and it kept me in check."

Because he shaved every morning with an electric razor, he saw what was happening to him; the eyes bright with pain, exceedingly large in the diminished face, the body growing leaner and weaker. One afternoon as Stephen and Leslie played in the bedroom, he appealed to Lauren, "Don't have them in here too often, Baby." The idea was to have the kids remember their father in better days, not as a drained and humiliated husk watching them from a chair.

Ever the chess player, Humphrey moved into endgame as Christmas came around. His hairdresser, Verita Thompson, had remarried. She heard about her former lover's indisposition and dropped by to pay her respects to a dying man. "He was losing weight so fast that I could hardly believe it," she wrote sadly. "I died inside every time I put his toupee on him, he was so skeletal." He needled her nonetheless, and then, in a sudden quixotic gesture, offered to leave her the *Santana*. She smiled, thanked him, and refused. John Huston stopped by with

Morgan Maree, who had managed Humphrey's money in the old days. In the course of their first drinks, Humphrey suddenly burst out, "Look, fellas, come clean. Am I going to make it? Tell me the truth." With a booming voice of assurance, Maree said, "Of course you are, Bogie. We're not kidding you." Huston understood that he was lying, and approved. Lauren "didn't want Bogie to read in the paper that he was going to die, so everyone who knew him put the best face on they could."

It was not good enough. Humphrey was, above all things, a realist. He made arrangements to take care of his sister Pat, who had been in and out of institutions for episodes of manic depression, and had his lawyer draw up a will leaving stipends to his secretary and his cook. The bulk of the estate would be divided between Lauren and their children, Stephen and Leslie, in the form of trust funds. That way, he told a friend, the money would be out of the reach of fortune hunters.

Humphrey had been able to walk on his own until December. Dressed in slacks and a red smoking jacket, he managed to get himself downstairs every evening to receive the special friends Lauren invited for a drink, usually between 5:00 and 7:00 p.m.

But as the disease moved into the final stages, he was forced to make his way around in a wheelchair. He weighed a little more than eighty pounds. The dumb-waiter was turned into a makeshift elevator; a butler lifted him from the wheelchair onto a stool, and the contraption brought him up and down as desired. Fighting for breath, he took hits from two large green oxygen tanks, one upstairs and one downstairs — yet another indignity to be borne, along with the injections of nitrogen mustard to delay the progress of the malignant cells, along with the crescent-shaped receptacle for his sputum, along with the frequent vomiting of blood. Lauren refused to accept the inevitable until three of Humphrey's physicians came to the house and asked for a private audience. Dr. Brandsma spoke for them. "I'm sure you'd rather know the truth, wouldn't you? I'm sure you know already Bogie cannot last much longer. We don't know how he's lasted this long." She begged them for some sign that he might still recover. They shook their heads. It was just a matter of weeks, perhaps days.

The best Lauren could do was make her husband comfortable, confine visits of friends to a precious few, and pre-order the funeral arrangements. Clifton Webb paid a call and when he left the bedroom collapsed in moans and tears. Lauren begged him to be quiet so Humphrey wouldn't hear his cries of distress. Sam Goldwyn and William Wyler came to the bedroom. Jack Warner followed. He attempted to tell an amusing story and choked up. Afterward, Humphrey remarked to Lauren, "Jack's not a bad guy — he's just so uncomfortable with everyone. He has to make jokes to prove he's regular." The frequent visitors Katharine Hepburn and Spencer Tracy came by on Saturday, January 12, 1957. When they left, Spencer said, "Good night, Bogie." Returned Humphrey, "Good-bye, Spence." They knew what he meant. The odor of death was all around the room in the last days; no fumigant could disguise it. Dr. Brandsma did what he could to prepare the children. He took Stephen aside and informed him that his father was going to sleep soon, a sleep so deep that he wouldn't wake up. The eight-year-old listened without expression and abruptly ran out of the room. Lauren phoned Spencer Tracy and asked him to write a eulogy to be read at the memorial service. Spencer begged off; he thought he would be too emotional to deliver anything coherent. Lauren understood. She called John Huston and asked him. The director grimly agreed to do it. The countdown began. The next morning Lauren was preparing to take the children to Sunday school when Humphrey called out weakly, "Goodbye, kid. Hurry back." When she returned he was comatose. Later that day Stephen was taken in to see him. It was as the doctor predicted: his father was in a sleep from which he would not, could not, awaken. The boy kissed his father's cheek and went to his own room. At 2:25 the following morning, a nurse awakened Lauren. The terrible ordeal was over. She dialed David Niven with the news: "My darling husband is gone."

IX

Obituaries ran in the major newspapers of the world, from New York to Paris to Hong Kong to Melbourne to New Delhi and beyond, praising Humphrey Bogart as "a consummate actor," "the essence of toughness," "a hard-working professional," "a star who thrived on Broadway and [in] Hollywood," an actor who became "the perfect image of a man hunted by death," and "a man storm-tossed by fate."

On the morning of January 17, friends gathered at the All Saints Episcopal Church in Beverly Hills. More than two thousand fans stood outside, people who didn't know the deceased personally, but who felt some connection with him through the image he had so forcefully projected in more than seventy films. As they did, a cremation was taking place twenty miles away. The ashes would be put in an urn holding the tiny gold whistle Humphrey Bogart had given to Lauren Bacall thirteen years before. Humphrey had always been uncomfortable at burial ceremonies. He left word that his remains were to be scattered over the waves of the Pacific Ocean. To do so would have been illegal at the time, and so, fitting though a saltwater tribute would have been, the family arranged for a permanent niche at Forest Lawn. Friends would grumble about that option; one of them remembered that Humphrey had called the sumptuous cemetery "Disneyland for stiffs."

The church held some two hundred and fifty mourners. The group included drinking pals, sailing cronies, and the Hollywood elite. The sailors were particularly pleased with the glass-enclosed model of Humphrey's beloved *Santana,* a stand-in for the casket. A new generation of actors was knocking at the door, but the traditional leads had not yet lost their places. The male stars of the late 1940s were still big in the late 1950s, as evidenced by those in the pews. Charles Boyer attended, as did Gary Cooper, Louis Jourdan, Danny Kaye, James Mason, David Niven, Gregory Peck, Ronald Reagan, and Spencer Tracy. The veteran female stars included Marlene Dietrich, Joan Fontaine, Jennifer Jones, and Katharine Hepburn. Richard Brooks was there, along with fellow directors Nunnally Johnson, Billy Wilder, and William Wyler. Nearby sat the moguls Harry Cohn, David O. Selznick, and Jack Warner. A great many reminiscences were exchanged; it was remembered that the school dropout had been a reverse fake — someone who pretended to be uneducated and common, but who, as his friends testified, could recite from memory whole swaths of Plato, Pope, Ralph Waldo Emerson, and Shakespeare. Nunnally Johnson smartly summarized the deceased: "Bogart thought of himself as Scaramouche, the mischievous scamp who sets off the fireworks, then nips out." Joe Hyams, friend and biographer, had his own bemused take: "It seems likely that in death Bogart has come close to his own rigorous test of fame. 'You're not a star,' he once said, 'until they can spell your name in Karachi.' "

The ceremony was appropriately spare and ecumenical. The Reverend Kermit Castellanos read the Twenty-third Psalm ("Yea, though I walk through the valley of the shadow of death I will fear no evil"), as well as Tennyson's poem of setting out to sea as a metaphor for death, "Crossing the Bar" ("Twilight and evening bell / And after that the dark! / And may there be no sadness of farewell, / When I embark . . ."). Music by Humphrey's favorite composers, Bach and Debussy, filled the air.

John Huston came forward to deliver his eulogy. The tall man spoke in a distinctive papery baritone: "Himself, he never took too seriously — his work most seriously. He regarded the somewhat gaudy figure of Bogart, the star, with amused cynicism. Bogart, the actor, he held in deep respect. . . ." Huston went on to describe the fountains of Versailles, where a sharp-toothed pike keeps the carp active so that they never get complacent and fat. "Bogie," he said with a wicked smile, "took rare delight in performing a similar duty in the fountains of Hollywood." He concluded, "He was endowed with the greatest gift a man can have: talent. The whole world came to recognize it. . . . We have no reason to feel sorry for him — only for ourselves for having lost him. He is quite irreplaceable." It was a poignant and effective envoi. The director of *The Maltese Falcon* and *The African Queen* expressed what everyone knew — the departed was indeed sui generis, the most perversely attractive actor in the history of cinema. Yet even Huston underestimated the enduring image of the man. For as the wet-eyed mourners went up the aisles and out into the Southern California sunshine, it was not the beginning of the end of Humphrey Bogart's reputation. It was the end of the beginning.

CHAPTER 9
BREATHLESS

I

In the early 1950s the Brattle Theater in Cambridge, Massachusetts, tried something old. Like many another venue for productions of Shakespeare, Chekhov, and Shaw, the Brattle had become a film house in the early 1950s. But it was a film house unlike any other. It had a rear-screen projector, rather than the standard setup that beamed movies on a screen above the audience. And it had owners who believed that the past could be more alluring than the present. In 1953, for example, while neighboring movie theaters showed Esther Williams in *Million Dollar Mermaid* and Walt Disney's animated *Peter Pan,* the Brattle opened its season with Alfred Hitchcock's 1938 thriller, *The Lady Vanishes,* and *My Little Chickadee,* a 1940 comedy starring W. C. Fields. On April 19, 1957, three months after the Bogart memorial, the theater ran the fifteen-year-old *Casablanca.*

Final exams were coming up at neighboring Harvard, and students needed a break from the strain of cramming. Warners' morality play in the desert, complete with Nazi villains, compromised refugees, and a love triangle, provided a perfect escape at an ideal time. Imbued with romantic agony, the undergraduates identified with Rick Blaine's noble misery as he forsook Ilsa for the Greater Good. Again and again they returned to the Brattle, wearing trench coats and dangling cigarettes from their lower lips, singing "La Marseillaise," shouting lines of dialogue on cue.

The cult spread to campuses around the country. Other Bogart films joined *Casablanca* as college favorites. If Rick Blaine led the way, Sam Spade, Philip Marlowe, Dix Steele, Fred C. Dobbs, and Billy Dannreuther were not far behind. Dannreuther, in fact, became something of a celebrity thanks to Truman Capote's indefatigable self-promotion. The novelist enjoyed giving with one hand and taking with the other, but there was no ambiguity in his Bogart endorsement. After the star's death he wrote a tribute, recalling the way he had divided the world into two kinds of people: professionals and bums. To Humphrey, "the bum true-blue was any fellow who shirked his job, was not, in meticulous style, a 'pro' in his work. God knows he was." With all the drinking and needling, Bogart understood that discipline was the better part of artistic survival, and because of that, "he lasted, he left his mark."

Another actor did not come off so well. "The Duke in His Domain" was a detailed and malicious portrait of Marlon Brando. Published in *The New Yorker* in November 1957, Truman's hatchet job occasioned commentary on both coasts. Brando threatened to sue for defamation of character, and Capote became the subject of countless interviews. The judo expert rarely failed to mention *Beat the Devil,* a film that was reappraised, given a number of revivals, and started on its way from loser to camp classic.

Capote's praise of Humphrey whetted the public appetite for more encomiums. They were not long in coming. Although her name was linked to Frank Sinatra's during the last months of Humphrey's life and for more than a year afterward, and although she married Jason Robards Jr. (the marriage lasted from 1961 to 1969), Lauren Bacall remained the keeper of the flame. Bogart was "the only man I have ever known who truly and completely belonged to himself," she wrote. "His convictions about life, work and people were so strong they were unshakeable. Nothing — no one — could make him lower his standards, lessen his character." He possessed "the greatest gifts a man could have: respect for himself, for his craft," and "integrity about life as well as work."

Actors who had worked with Humphrey spoke out. Rod Steiger likened him to "the master sergeant who had brought the platoon through the jungle. You respected the wars he had been through, and his ability to survive. He was a gentleman, an artistic soldier."

David Niven remembered his friend as "quite alarming to meet, for the first time, with his sardonic humor and his snarl that passes for a smile. It took me a little while to realize that he had perfected an elaborate camouflage to cover up one of the kindest and most generous of hearts." Niven's was a story told over and over again, a portrait of a man who hated to let the world know of his sensitivities and charitable impulses. As they all noted, he would often turn his back on a down-at-heels actor in public, then quietly send him a generous check.

Two ladies spoke of Humphrey as much

more than a sexual presence; to them he was what the old-time producers called a *mensch,* literally Yiddish for "man," but signifying much more than that — an individual who always comes through, whose actions are as reliable as his words. Katharine Hepburn recalled Humphrey as "one of the biggest guys I ever met. He walked straight down the center of the road. No maybes. Yes or no. He liked to drink. He drank. He liked to sail a boat. He sailed a boat. He was an actor. He was happy and proud to be an actor." And lauding her co-star in *Maltese Falcon* and *Across the Pacific,* Mary Astor wrote: "There he is, right there on the screen, saying what everyone is trying to say today, saying it loud and clear. 'I hate hypocrisy. I don't believe in words or labels or much of anything else. I'm not a hero. I'm a human being. I'm not very pretty. Like me or don't like me!' "

Joseph Mankiewicz was more intellectual. A great reader (as was Humphrey), he offered a literary speculation: Bogart's attitude reflected "a sadness about the human condition. He had a kind of eighteenth-century, Alexander Pope nature. I think he would have made a superb Gatsby. His life reflected Gatsby's sense of being an outsider."

The journalists and writers joined in. Gossip columnist Earl Wilson offered an admiring description in *The Show Business Nobody Knows*. Humphrey "lived the year around in a world of make-believe, false faces, and toupees, but he remained a realist who could stare you down and say, 'Now let's cut the crap and have a drink.' "

Humphrey, as most of his friends acknowledged, was two Bogarts, the rough-hewn knight of the cinema, and the real-life aristocrat who came on like a tough guy. Max Lerner, Wilson's *New York Post* colleague, appreciated Humphrey's act, "mainly because most of us, in our actual lives, have so little chance to thumb our noses and consign the fakes, the stuffed men and the hollow men to hell."

Alistair Cooke described Humphrey as a character who might have come from a Graham Greene novel — a disappointed saint and a sanctified sinner. The Bogart he knew was "a much more intelligent man than most of his trade, or several others, a touchy man who found the world more corrupt than he hoped: a man with a tough shell hiding a fine core. He transmuted his own character into a film persona and imposed it on a world impatient of men more obviously good."

And Beat Generation novelist John Clellon Holmes (*The Horn*) observed that Humphrey Bogart is "not merely Sam Spade in *The Maltese Falcon* or Rick in *Casablanca.* Sometimes a hero, sometimes a villain, he is always suspicious of sentiment, verbosity, and cheap idealism. He was Bogey to us; we knew his style and attitudes as well as we knew our own; and he taught us something about the world we would inherit that was no less contagious than what Hemingway taught us." Still, that style and those attitudes could hardly be expected to outlast the decade. After all, every other Hollywood celebrity had been subject to the whims of time and fashion. As it turned out, though, Bogart was immune.

II

On December 10, 1957, forty-four-year-old Albert Camus accepted the Nobel Prize for Literature. In his biography of the French-Algerian author, Herbert Lottman comments, "Albert Camus was seen as a moral guide for the postwar period. He was also a very likeable hero, looking even younger than his years, dapper in his Humphrey Bogart trench coat (looking very much a Bogart clone, and enjoying the notion when told so)." Having personified Ernest Hemingway's solitary figure ("A man alone ain't got no bloody f—ing chance") and Raymond Chandler's contemporary knight-errant ("Down these mean streets a man must go who is neither tarnished nor afraid"), the Humphrey Bogart character was now seen as an example of the tough-minded existentialist as Camus had defined him ("vulnerable but obstinate, unjust but impassioned for justice, doing his work without shame or pride in view of everybody, not ceasing to be divided between sorrow and beauty . . .").

This was only the start of an appreciation that developed into idolatry. Only a few weeks after the Bogart obituary had been printed in *L'Express* and *Paris Soir,* France's predominant film theorist, André Bazin, weighed in with an essay, "The Death of Humphrey Bogart," in *Cahiers du Cinéma.* We must not confuse Bogart's acting style, he wrote, with the one "made fashionable by Marlon Brando prior to James Dean." The behavior of those actors was "intended to be unforeseeable." Bogart *was* foreseeable. That was his strength. He would always be a man who exhaled "distrust and weariness, wisdom and scepticism: Bogie is a stoic." In a corrupt world he kept his own code of honor, without the consolations of religion or social approval. In the end, the kind of man Bogart portrayed over and over again "is not defined by his accidental respect, or his contempt, for bourgeois virtues, by his courage or his cowardice, but above all by this existential maturity which gradually transforms life into a stubborn irony at the expense of death."

The emerging generation of French actors and directors had always been attracted to American B movies, but did not always go public with their approval. After many of those features were dubbed *films noir,* and after Bazin gave Humphrey his imprimatur, the *homages* began in earnest. In 1960, Jean-Luc Godard, another contributor to *Cahiers,* went from theorist to director. His debut, *Breathless,* initiated the *nouvelle vague,* the new wave of French cinema, by using jump cuts, handheld camera work, and iris in-and-out shots — and by starring the twenty-six-year-old unprepossessing yet strangely attractive Jean-Paul Belmondo. He played Michel, a car thief whose gestures mimic the Bogart style from the incessant cigarette to the classic facial tics. Should anyone in the audience miss the allusions, Michel stares reverentially at a poster of *The Harder They Fall* and murmurs "Bogie" before starting out on a doomed criminal enterprise with the American expatriate Patricia (Jean Seberg), Godard's version of Bacall.

On the heels of *Breathless* came a film by Godard's younger colleague François Truffaut. "What Bogart did, he did better than anyone else," wrote Humphrey's admirer. "He was more threatening than anyone else, and he struck his blows better. When he sweated, you could have wrung out his shirts." Humphrey was obviously the man Truffaut had in mind when he created Charlie Kohler, the central character of *Shoot the Piano Player.* Charlie is played by Charles Aznavour, an unprepossessing/ attractive singer known as the Sinatra of France. As the plot develops, the pianist's real name is revealed as Edouard Saroyan. The reason he's so good at the keyboard is that he was once a serious classical performer. He abandoned that career after the suicide of his wife. To disguise his pain, Charlie affects a tough, chain-smoking, trench-coated façade even when dealing with hardened criminals, an M.O. that leads to his downfall. In a consideration of *Breathless* and *Shoot the Piano Player,* critic Pauline Kael saw that both films were "haunted by the shade of Bogart." Many more *nouvelle vague* movies would be obsessed by that shade. When those films unreeled at art houses in New York, Chicago, and Los Angeles, they granted Humphrey a renewed significance.

In 1964 *Time* sent a reporter to the Brattle, where the Bogart festival was now a hallowed tradition. A Blue Parrot room, named for Sydney Greenstreet's café in *Casablanca,* had been set up in the theater. Nearby a jukebox kept playing "As Time Goes By." "When Bogart lights a cigarette on the screen," the article stated, "girls respond with big, sexy sighs." Asked about the object of their affection, a Radcliffe student lamented the Age of Analysis: "Bogie is everything we wish Harvard men were," she said. "Bogie's direct and honest. He gets involved with his women but he doesn't go through an identity crisis every five minutes." Her friend observed that there was "something just so heroic about going to see something anti-intellectual the night before an exam. Like imitating Bogart's I-don't-give-a-damn attitude." Humphrey was, in brief, "the essence of cool."

That word deserves elaboration. "Cool" departed from its customary definition — a temperature closer to cold than to warm — in the 1930s. The new meaning came from African American sources and delineated a style, first in music and then in life itself. Cool jazz departed from the angular tempos and difficult harmonies of bebop. The long notes of Lester Young; the elegant solos of trumpeter Miles Davis (who titled one album *The Birth of the Cool*); the arrangements of Gil Evans and Gerry Mulligan, which stayed "inside" the melody — all featured a pure tone and an unemotional approach. In time "cool" turned into a description of all those who separated themselves from the herd, aloof, proud, unwilling to accede to the demands of fashion and status. The co-eds of a rising generation, turned off by self-absorbed Ivy Leaguers, saw the man in the trench coat as their beau ideal: mature, elusive — cool. Their male counterparts saw what was going on. They started to wear clothes in the Bogart mode; after that it was only a short step to copying his manner. Where others gushed, Vincent Sherman, who had directed Humphrey in *Crime School* and *All Through the Night,* held a wry view of the Bogart cult. "You know something? If Bogie knew that he had become a god, you know, for the modern generation of young people, he would have said, 'Oh, cut the crap.' "

Or would he? For all his scoffing at Tinseltown and Celluloid City, for all the put-downs of old-time producers and the rising generation of actors, Humphrey was quietly — and sometimes not so quietly — proud of his trade, of what he had accomplished in it, of his ability to catch a part of American life and put it into his pictures. In an unguarded moment, he gave a terse and accurate self-appraisal: "I'm a professional. I've done pretty well, don't you think? I've survived in a pretty rough business." Chances are he would have been pleased to be the essence of cool.

III

In the mid- to late 1960s Humphrey Bogart films receded from dormitory chat. Undergraduates had more pressing matters to discuss. For more than a year they were in shock following the assassination of the young president, John F. Kennedy. That heartbreaking catastrophe seemed to use up all the oxygen in the room. They recovered their balance when Lyndon Johnson, stepping in for the fallen leader, excited them with his endorsement of the Voting Rights Act, a culmination of the civil rights movement. But only a few years later he infuriated them by stepping up the Vietnam War, subjecting them to the draft. That conflagration, coupled with the tragedy of three voter-registration workers murdered in Mississippi, and the assassinations of Martin Luther King, Malcolm X, and Bobby Kennedy, pushed all thoughts of entertainment aside.

It wasn't until the late 1960s that the drug-and-bike escapades of *Easy Rider* grabbed the attention of young moviegoers, along with the crime melodrama of *Bonnie and Clyde* and the adolescent hysteria of *The Graduate.* The "beach-blanket" films produced by a new studio, American International, played into the youthquake that made an icon of Elvis Presley, established rock 'n' roll as the expression of the age, and quite literally changed the face of American cinema. New stars arose: Jack Nicholson, Gene Hackman, Al Pacino, Robert De Niro, Dustin Hoffman. Unfamiliar directors also made their marks in this period, among them Mike Nichols, Arthur Penn, Stanley Kubrick, and Woody Allen. Humphrey Bogart had been reduced to a verb by the time the 1960s got going. To "bogart" was to hold on to a joint of marijuana with all four fingers and a thumb, the way Humphrey often held a cigarette — but without passing it on to others. There was even a song on the *Easy Rider* sound track called "Don't Bogart Me." It seemed likely that Humphrey would be remembered (if at all) as an antique personality, someone from a bygone era, like Wallace Reidl or Richard Dix. Ironically, it was Allen who turned things around, bringing his generation back to Humphrey with *Play It Again, Sam.*

Allen's wistful comedy opened on Broadway in February 1969 and played for 453 performances. It became a film in 1972, with virtually the same cast — Allen as Allan Felix, a neurotic, recently divorced film critic; Tony Roberts and Diane Keaton as Dick and Linda Christie, Allan's best friends; and most notably, Jerry Lacy as the ghost of Humphrey Bogart. The film opens with the finale of *Casablanca,* when Rick Blaine nobly gives his letters of transit to Ilsa, the love of his life, and her heroic husband, Victor Laszlo. Allan gazes in wonder at his ideal, a man who never has any trouble with the opposite sex. Allan is the diametrical opposite; his liaisons are always cringe-making and usually end after one catastrophic date. After one wrenching episode, Humphrey's shade appears in his classic trench coat, puffing his omnipresent cigarette. "Forget all this fancy relationship stuff," he advises in Humphrey's wise, sibilant tone. "The world is full of dames. All you got to do is whistle."

The shade proceeds to teach Allan a few things about women and how to handle them.

HUMPHREY: Move closer to her.
ALLAN: How close?
HUMPHREY: The length of your lips.

During the course of instruction, Allan and Linda find themselves falling in love. This is Allan's most successful affair — indeed, his only successful affair. But the neurotic film buff is too burdened with guilt to carry on with his best friend's wife. At the finale, with noble gravitas he gives her back to Dick, à la *Casablanca*.

HUMPHREY: That was great. I guess you won't be needing me anymore. There's nothing I can tell you now that you don't already know.
ALLAN: You're not too tall and kind of ugly, but I'm short enough and ugly enough to succeed on my own.

Before the ghost vanishes, he offers his famous salute:

HUMPHREY: Here's looking at you, kid.

From *Play It Again, Sam* the Bogart mystique reentered popular culture with a new vigor. Suddenly Humphrey seemed to be everywhere. *Bogart Slept Here,* directed by Mike Nichols, never quite made it to Broadway. A small theater in Los Angeles presented another play, *When Bogart Was.* In it, two drifters in New York City fantasize about the actor on the set of *The Treasure of the Sierra Madre.* Gerald Duchovnay's *Humphrey Bogart: A Bio-Bibliography* mentions *A Kiss Is Just a Kiss,* an off-Broadway play dealing with Humphrey's failed marriages to Helen Menken and Mayo Methot, as well as *Bogart: The Good Bad Guy,* a London revue that turned Ezra Goodman's friendly memoir into a musical. In addition, Humphrey's name was dropped in more than twenty songs, from Bertie Higgins's "Key Largo" to Murray McLauchlin's "What Would Bogie Do?"

Bogart-themed bistros, taverns, and bars sprouted up all across the United States, and even in Mexico. Most were unimaginative recreations of the *Casablanca* set, replete with ceiling fans and waiters in rumpled white linen suits. But there were a few that played up Humphrey's image, among them Bogart's American Restaurant in Raleigh, North Carolina, Bogart's Chophouse of Tinely Park, Illinois — and Pizza

Humphrey Bogart in Veliko Tarnovo, Bulgaria.

Thomasville Furniture unveiled its Bogart Collection in the late 1990s. According to the ad copy, Humphrey "believed that true class could not be imitated or taught." You either had it or you didn't, and Bogart had it in overplus. The collection presented close to a hundred pieces, including the Trench Coat Chair, the Santana Sofa, and the Contessa Banquette.

On more than a dozen websites devoted to the memory of Humphrey Bogart, all sorts of merchandise is currently offered for sale. Fans and scholars can buy DVDs and videotapes of more than fifty Bogart movies, as well as a tape recording of Humphrey's appearance on the *The Jack Benny* program, and audiotapes of old radio shows. There are T-shirts with likenesses of Humphrey and Lauren, as well as garments bearing some favorite (and sometimes inaccurate) Bogart quotes: "The problem with the world is everyone is a few drinks behind"; "Play it again, Sam"; "When you're slapped, you'll take it and like it"; "I stick my neck out for nobody." *Bogie,* a brilliantly drawn adult comic book, is obtainable in French and English. There are five-foot-high likenesses of Humphrey in his traditional coat, Bogart-style fedoras, drawings, caricatures, still photographs and posters of Bogart movies from *The Petrified Forest* to *The Harder They Fall.*

But these are only the outward symbols of the star's pervasive influence. The character he had played so effectively in so many features began to pop up in retro mysteries and pulp crime novels. In 1939 novelist John O'Hara sadly noted, "George Gershwin died today, but I don't have to believe it if I don't want to." Writers seemed to feel the same way about Humphrey Bogart. They didn't have to believe he was gone if they didn't want to, and they didn't want to. It was as if they couldn't tolerate a world bereft of Humphrey's wounded arrogance and mordant backchat. So they brought him back, treating his character as if he were still alive, still running his café, or his private-eye office, or mining gold, or running a ship — any vocation at all, as long as he could still be counted on to entertain the world, and perhaps save it in the process.

Humphrey was referenced in Neil Simon's Broadway play *Lost in Yonkers:* "You come in here acting like you're Humphrey Bogart or somethin.' Well, you're no Humphrey Bogart." He has been mentioned on all sorts of television shows, from *M*A*S*H* to *Law* *and Order.* In *Bogie,* a TV "biodrama," Humphrey was impersonated by Kevin O'Connor. The show provided a fever chart of the Battling Bogarts, as well as a more subdued account of Humphrey and Lauren during the first weeks of their courtship.

In movies Humphrey was imitated by the British star Albert Finney in *Two for the Road* and *Gumshoe* and mimicked by Robert Sacchi in *Sam Marlowe, Private Eye,* adapted from *The Man with Bogart's Face.* Sacchi, said the *New York Times,* "who has been doing a Bogart look-alike turn on college campuses, shows considerable acting skill in the title role, although his hopes for future employment in films would seem to be limited."

Humphrey (along with Peter Lorre) was given a send-up in *Brown Sugar,* a hip-hop film. Two African American promoters, Chris (Mos Def) and Dre (Taye Diggs), argue about their latest scheme:

CHRIS: I'm not the Humphrey Bogart in this. I'm the Peter Lorre. I'm the sidekick character. You're the Humphrey Bogart . . .

DRE: Don't be dissin' Humphrey Bogart, man.

CHRIS: Why not?

DRE: 'Cause he's Humphrey Bogart!
He's the man. Yo, he was fightin' a war.
That's what they did back then.

IV

The image and reputation of Humphrey Bogart would be expected to run through popular culture. But rather unexpectedly, they worked their ways into high culture as well. Nobel laureate V. S. Naipaul was asked about the importance of cinema during his childhood in Trinidad and afterward. The writer replied, "Without the movies I would have died." When he saw the old features on television, he especially admired "the rich tones you get in black and white." Among his indispensables? "I must say *High Sierra* with Humphrey Bogart and Ida Lupino. My God, I've seen it so often! It is my favorite film." This was more than the chatter of a movie buff. In his 1959 novel, *Miguel Street,* Naipaul introduces a character named Bogart. The year that *Casablanca* was made, says the narrator, Humphrey's "fame spread like fire through Port of Spain and hundreds of young men began adopting the hardboiled Bogartian attitude." Naipaul's 1962 nonfiction book, *The Middle Passage,* offers more commentary on Humphrey's social influence: "When Bogart, without turning, coolly rebuked a pawing Lauren Bacall, 'You're breathin' down mah neck,' Trinidad adopted him as its own. 'That is man!' the audience cried."

John Berryman's Pulitzer Prize–winning poetry collection, *Dream Songs,* mentions "Bogart's duds." Scores of other bards refer to Bogart. *The Faber Book of Movie Verse* offers many poems about him, ranging from Norman Rosten's "Nobody Dies Like Bogart" to Lee L. Berkson's "Bogey." Kenneth Tynan was fascinated with Humphrey Bogart, a man he had actually met only once. The British theater critic and impresario (*Oh! Calcutta!*) read the obituaries and essays and found them wanting. Eventually he filed his own discerning, if snobbish, essay. With seeming effortlessness, he noted, Humphrey could transfer the essence of himself to cinema. "And what was that essence? I trace it back to Seneca, of whom Bogart may not have heard." The tragedian flourished in the first century A.D., and "what he preached and put into his plays was the philosophy known as Stoicism. It meant: accept the fact of transience, don't panic in the face of mortality, learn to live with death. This sums up the Bogart stance." On film Humphrey frequently died; in his first thirty-four pictures he was shot in twelve and electrocuted or hanged in eight. " 'We're wrong in looking *forward* to death,' says Seneca, 'in great measure it's past already. Death is master of all the years that are behind us.' And Bogart's voice told us as much. Even in the most flippant context, it carried with it a bass note of mortality."

Scholar and novelist Umberto Eco (*The Name of the Rose*) had his own view of Humphrey and what he brought to pictures. In *Travels in Hyperreality* he cites *Casablanca* as a prime instance of the cinema of semiotics — the interrelation of symbols and language. The film arrives with hidden meanings that drive its narrative: "It is not until *To Have and Have Not* that Bogie plays the role of the Hemingway hero, but here he appears 'already' loaded with Hemingwayesque connotations simply because Rick fought in Spain." Peter Lorre trails reminiscences of Fritz Lang; Conrad Veidt's German officer emanates a faint whiff of *The Cabinet of Dr. Caligari*. Thus *Casablanca* became a cult movie "because it is not one movie. It is 'movies.' And this is the reason it works, in defiance of any aesthetic theory." And Robert Coover, one of the most inventive novelists of his generation (*The Universal Baseball Association, The Origin of the*

Brunists) took his own turn at *Casablanca* in a short story collection, *A Night at the Movies.*

And still it was not enough. Inevitably, there were books *about* Bogart himself. Three memoirs show how elusive he was, even to those to whom he was close. Lauren Bacall's *By Myself,* later expanded to *By Myself and Then Some,* offers some affectionate glimpses of the Bogarts' lives and careers without giving too much away. In her debut film she was a virgin playing a woman with cat's eyes and a slinky manner no man could resist — least of all her co-star. Director Howard Hawks ordered her "to approach a scene as a man would. He wanted insolence, and he wanted a man in control." This was to be the hallmark of her style from then on; she would never be an Ilsa who asked Rick to do the thinking for both of them. Lauren Bacall was the brainy and sexy New Woman, and this she remained on-screen and in marriage. On the surface it was an odd combination; the poor Jewish girl who had an aristocratic bearing, and the WASP surgeon's son who always seemed to have slept on the sidewalk the night before. They made several films together, but Lauren never again displayed the winning effrontery of *To Have and Have*

Not. The reason is revealed in *By Myself:* upon marrying, she "immediately became part of Bogie's generation." Leaping more than two decades, she could no longer be the fresh, sexy kid with chips on both shoulders. *By Myself* won a National Book Award in 1980 and was generally well received. Yet there were those who remained unimpressed. The British *Guardian,* for example, mocked the author's superficial name-dropping: "Cole Porter, for instance, was a 'fairly small, very neat' man and the food at his house was 'incredibly good, immaculately served. . . .' Only when on the subject of Bogie does she really get going, and then her adoration for him, cloying as caramel, tends to blur the man himself, so that he when he is drunk or feeling neglected, he comes over as pathetic and self-pitying."

Lauren makes much of her husband's insistence on marital fidelity. To be sure, he was married four times. But, according to her account, he was serially faithful until the final, miserable days with Mayo when a nineteen-year-old ingenue hove into view. So the appearance of Verita Thompson's *Bogie and Me* in 1982 came as something of a shock. Thompson's unverified account recalls a thirteen-year love affair of Humphrey and his hairdresser–wig maker, broken off by mutual consent when she remarried. The star is quoted at length, particularly when the subject gets around to Lauren's penchant for social climbing. "When we first met," Humphrey tells Verita, "she talked like a goddamn dead-end kid — all deze, dem, and doze. I had to teach her English, for God's sake, and before I knew it she was trying to go high-hat on me with her society stuff!" Though the book met a chilly critical reception, Verita remained a tireless self-promoter for the rest of her life — she died in 2002 at the age of eighty-nine. Hollywood studios showed no interest in adapting her book; she had better luck running a piano bar called Bogie and Me in New Orleans. There she informed customers that Humphrey "called me Pete, introduced me as his 'secretary and mistress' because, he said, 'That'll throw 'em off; they'll think it's a rib.' He kidded me constantly. He was a sweet guy, a fascinating guy and oh, darlin', did we have fun!"

Of greater interest is the memoir by a man who knew Humphrey for the shortest time. Stephen Humphrey Bogart was eight years old at the time of his father's death. Yet as he was to write in *Bogart: In Search of My Father,* it was only after his second marriage and the birth of two children that he "began to pull from my shoulder a chip the size of Idaho that had been there since the death of my dad." After Humphrey's death, and the collapse of the Bacall-Sinatra romance, Stephen's mother abruptly sold the house and relocated the family, first to another part of Los Angeles, and then to London. "Now I was down one father, one school, one house, dozens of friends, and an entire state and country." It was a bewildering time for him, and the beginning of a decades-long rebellion. Like Humphrey, Stephen was kicked out of a couple of schools; unlike his father, he didn't care much for alcohol. Instead, the budding television producer sought refuge in cocaine, rebelling against the Bogart name, but also using it to advance his literary career. Stephen would write two mysteries featuring the Bogartesque shamus R.J. Brooks, who specializes in divorce business — gathering evidence to be used against adulterous husbands and wives. R.J. is not just another PI; his parents were movie stars back in the day. R.J. never did get along with his inattentive mother. But in *Play It Again,* she and her lover wind up dead and he feels compelled to investigate the twin slaying. Lest anyone miss the obvious connections, the paperback publisher paraphrased Sam Spade's lines about Miles Archer in *The Maltese Falcon:* "When your mother is murdered, you have to do something about it. It doesn't matter if you liked her or not. She was your mother and you have to do something." In *The Remake: As Time Goes By,* R.J. learns that Andromeda, one of Hollywood's production houses, intends to remake his parents' most famous film. Interviewed on the network news, he makes ominous comments about the studio. Shortly afterward, important Andromeda employees are knocked off. The police like Brooks for the murders. . . .

Whatever their underlying purpose, these books were offered to the public as entertainment rather than therapy. Not until 1995 did Stephen write a book that dealt with his father head-on. In it, he remembers that whenever people heard his surname they inquired, " 'Are you related?' And I'd say: 'Well, no, I'm not related. If I was related, I'd be living in his mansion, right? I was named after him. My parents were fans. I have a sister, Leslie. She's named after their daughter. That's what big fans they were.' "

He longed for someone from old Hollywood to tell him privately, "Bogie was great, but sometimes he was a prick, you know . . . and maybe show that the guy had some shortcomings so that I wouldn't have to live up to a legend." Stephen also longed for the dailiness of ordinary life, the Little League coaching, the split-level, the to-and-fro commute that most Americans do most of their lives. It was not to be an easy journey. Only at the age of forty-five, after he examined the peaks and troughs of his father's life, was the author free to be himself. Visiting Stephen Bogart in his finally achieved New Jersey suburban home, the *New York Times* observed that Humphrey's son "is neither the on-screen nor off-screen incarnation of Fred C. Dobbs, Rick Blaine, Duke Mantee, Charlie Allnut or Sam Spade, the anti-heroes of American film noir . . . and never wanted to be. He wanted to be, apparently, what he has struggled his whole life to become: the guy next door."

It was to be expected that family members would want their say. Since the early days of Hollywood, stars have always provoked memoirs from those who were closest to them, from *A Quite Remarkable Father,* an homage to Leslie Howard by his daughter, to *Mommie Dearest,* Christina Crawford's malicious portrait of her mother, Joan.

But here it was the others, the scholars,

historians, fans, and total strangers, who were unable to let go of Humphrey Bogart. They were determined to acknowledge his enduring cultural image — and in the process to enhance it. Some books attempted to summarize the private and public man. Gerald Duchovnay's *Humphrey Bogart: A Bio-Bibliography* briskly discussed Humphrey's childhood, went over his theatrical and cinematic careers, discussed the films, and listed an impressive number of articles on Bogart, film noir, and Hollywood's golden era. Not to be outdone, Ernest W. Cunningham presented what he called, rather grandly, *The Ultimate Bogart: All the Facts and Fantasies About the Quintessential Movie Tough Guy.* In addition to synopses of Humphrey's movies and marriages, the book was filled with amusing trivia. Before he became famous (and in two instances afterward) Humphrey was slain in a variety of picturesque ways. As a felon, he was gunned down in *Midnight, The Petrified Forest, Bullets or Ballots, Kid Galahad, King of the Underworld, The Roaring Twenties, Angels with Dirty Faces, Invisible Stripes, San Quentin, Virginia City, High Sierra, The Big Shot,* and *The Desperate Hours.* He was electrocuted in *The Return of Dr. X* and *You*

Can't Get Away from Murder. He was blasted out of the sky in *Body and Soul,* when the kaiser's men brought down his plane during World War I. During the next war he was slain by Nazis in *Passage to Marseilles* and by a Japanese officer in *Tokyo Joe,* and fatally wounded by a hand grenade in *Sirocco.* In addition he was mauled to death by a lion in *The Wagons Roll at Night* and beheaded by Mexican bandits in *The Treasure of the Sierra Madre.* No other movie star had given his life so many times on the way up.

Forty years after his death, two full-length biographies simultaneously appeared. Each offered a wealth of personal detail, accompanied by a historical overview. They were quite unlike the indulgent reminiscences of friends like Nathaniel Benchley (*Humphrey Bogart*), Ezra Goodman (*Bogey: The Good Bad Guy*), and Joe Hyams (*Bogie*). Or the scurrilous, allegedly tell-all volume, *The Secret Life of Humphrey Bogart: The Early Years (1899–1931),* by Darwin Porter. ("Learn at last," trumpeted the publisher, "what was really beneath the trenchcoat of America's most famous male movie star.") According to Porter, who used unsupported scuttlebutt by Bogart's old rival Kenneth MacKenna, Humphrey worked secretly for

Howard Hughes, procuring male prostitutes for the bisexual tycoon. The young actor was also allegedly involved with Bette Davis, Marlene Dietrich, Tallulah Bankhead, and Barbara Stanwyck. None of this was particularly convincing, and reviewers advised their readers to look elsewhere for real insights.

Ann M. Sperber's massive biography of CBS newsman Edward R. Murrow (*Murrow: His Life and Times*) was a finalist for the Pulitzer Prize in 1986. Her next subject was Humphrey. She devoted seven years to researching aspects of his personal life and acting career, interviewing nearly two hundred people along the way. But after she had accumulated a quarter ton of material, Sperber suddenly died of a heart attack in the winter of 1994. *Bogart,* a 675-page tome, was completed two years later by a collaborator she had never met: Eric Lax, Woody Allen's witty biographer. This unorthodox collaboration worked surprisingly well. Its man-behind-the-myth technique offered few surprises. But as the narrative traced Humphrey's professional and personal arcs it compiled a wealth of diverting anecdotes and incidents. Here is the confused child of quarreling parents, marked forever by his strong-willed mother and withdrawn and cantankerous father; here is the rebellious youth, the pretty-boy juvenile, the hard-drinking, chain-smoking abrasive character actor, the young Hollywood failure, the middle-aged Hollywood success, the husband as three-time loser, the romantic legend of Bogart and Baby, the accolades, the rise to superstar, the stoic last year, the stuff that dreams are made of.

What that great doorstop of a book lacked was a verdict. This was supplied by Jeffrey Meyers in his competing biography, *Bogart: A Life in Hollywood.* Meyers noted with some satisfaction that Humphrey Bogart "survived twenty-five years in Hollywood without a drug problem, a nervous breakdown, or a psychiatrist." Yet, as the biographer explains, the star of stars was more than a survivor. Meyers had previously written a biography of Ernest Hemingway, and noted the many similarities between Ernest and Humphrey. Both men came from well-to-do families; both had physician fathers who met bad ends — Clarence Hemingway committed suicide, Belmont Bogart destroyed himself with morphine addiction — and mothers who chose artistic vocations (Grace Hemingway was an opera singer and painter; Maud Bogart, as we have seen, a prominent illustrator). Both were political liberals, both men had four wives, both were overfond of alcohol, both were notorious for riding friends and foes alike. Humphrey referred to it as "needling"; Ernest called it "talking rough." Either man could spot a phony through lead walls.

But likenesses can be deceiving. James Cagney, who grew up in a poor, gritty New York neighborhood at about the same time the Bogarts were enjoying a life of indulgence, watched Humphrey in action on- and off-screen. "When it came to fighting," said Cagney, Bogart "was about as tough as Shirley Temple." Edward G. Robinson, Humphrey's fellow villain, felt somewhat the same way. He wrote, "For all his outward toughness, insolence, braggadocio, and contempt . . . there came through a kind of sadness, loneliness, and heartbreak (all of which were very much a part of Bogie the man). I always felt sorry for him — sorry that he imposed on himself the façade of the character with which he had become identified."

Cagney and Robinson, as well as many of their colleagues, took pains to distance themselves from the characters they played, and even from the industry that had made them headliners. Cagney, for example, lived geographically and psychologically as far from Beverly Hills as he could get, operating a hundred-acre farm on Martha's Vineyard. Robinson stayed west, but made certain that journalists knew that his was one of the most impressive private art collections in America, with works by Gauguin, Degas, Van Gogh, Matisse, and Picasso. Bogart, on the other hand, was a creature of Hollywood. His image was constructed by Warner Bros. and burnished by other film companies and most of all by Humphrey, who played the part of the surly paladin on screen and off for three decades. He had not begun that way; it was as if the juvenile lead of the 1920s had acted out the folktale of the man who puts on a mask, can't remove it, and eventually becomes the disguise.

Yet in the end, it is Humphrey who outpointed his contemporaries and outlasted them.

Why?

He wasn't better looking than Gary Cooper, or more lithe than Cagney, or more authoritative than Robinson, or jauntier than Cary Grant, or warmer than James Stewart, or more versatile than Spencer Tracy. Something else was at work here. In a characteristically discerning essay, film scholar and director Peter Bogdanovich analyzed Humphrey's durability: "He was a man who tried very hard to be Bad because he knew it was easier to get along in the world that way." In film after film he went from belligerent neutrality to reluctant commitment — from "I stick my neck out for nobody" to "I'm no good at being noble, but it doesn't take much to see that the problems of three little people don't amount to a hill of beans in this crazy world." By the finale, if he was asked why he sacrificed himself he might say, "Maybe 'cause I like you. Maybe 'cause I don't like them." Of course, Bogdanovich continued, "it was always 'maybe' because he wasn't going to be that much of a sap, wasn't making any speeches, wasn't going to be a good guy. Probably he rationalized it: 'I'm just doing my job.' But we felt good inside. We knew better."

Take It and Like It, Jonathan Coe's coffee-table-book tribute, borrows its title from a line Sam Spade delivers to Joel Cairo after the little man has been slapped by Brigid O'Shaughnessy. The British journalist concludes that "arguments over Humphrey's personal qualities will continue to recede helplessly into history," but the fact remains that "nobody walks out of one of the great Bogart movies without having seen something that uplifts and enriches." His films and his career "teach us a strategy, and a very wholesome one, for dealing with life at its best and its worst. Take it and like it."

In *Bogie,* another lavishly illustrated volume, film historian Richard Schickel adds that Humphrey "perfectly embodied some of the simple, admirable qualities once held to distinguish the American character," among them "a capable self-sufficiency and a refusal to be pushed around." As an actor he was "authoritative, professional, and secure. In his life as well as his screen persona, Bogie was his own man."

These detailed, posthumous appraisals were on the money. And still something was missing. It had to do with the larger theme of American masculinity. In the years since Humphrey's death, both the definition and the image of the male role had drastically changed. Once upon an epoch the nuclear family was dominant, the husband/father was the main provider, his actions prescribed by tradition. As a leader, as a breadwinner, as a husband and lover, he was expected to look and speak and behave in a certain manner. Humphrey defined that figure, and it accounted for his eminence in the 1940s and '50s.

But the mainstream of American life has

completely changed in the ensuing decades. Feminism; gay rights; androgynous models; the metrosexual man, straight but interested in fashion — all were co-opted by Hollywood. By the rules of history, Humphrey Bogart should have become obsolete, a faded image totally obscured by new faces and fresh interpretations of the male role.

Instead, he became more prominent, looming larger as we moved away from his epoch. For what he offered was more than a re-creation of movies past, where men were men and women were unemployed. His masculinity was not swagger, but its opposite — a quiet, bitter recognition of reality and the way in which it had to be acknowledged, approached, and, on occasion, opposed: *Down these mean streets a man must go who is neither tarnished nor afraid.* As American life coarsened, as flamboyance and the desire to "let it all hang out" elbowed reticence out of the way, as reality shows replaced scripted dialogue and shouting became a substitute for political debate, the curt, stiff-lipped men that Humphrey Bogart represented on-screen, and the sharp-witted individual that he was off-screen, took on a meaning far beyond sentiment. They stood for values that certain men and women — most of them far too

young to remember him in his heyday —
remembered and romanticized.

CHAPTER 10
THE GREATEST GIFT

I

Some forty years after his death, Humphrey Bogart attained a summit no other actor had ever reached. The American Film Institute ranked him as the Greatest Male Star in cinema history. The honors were only beginning. In 1997 *Entertainment Weekly* designated Humphrey the Number One Movie Legend of all time. That year the United States Postal Service issued a stamp bearing his likeness. At a ceremony in Hollywood Lauren Bacall and her children, Stephen and Leslie, heard an announcement from Tirso del Junco, chairman of the USPS board of governors: "Today, we mark another chapter in the Bogart legacy. With an image that is small and yet as powerful as the ones he left in celluloid, we will begin today to bring his artistry, his power, his unique star quality, to the messages that travel the world."

495

Nine years later, Lauren and Stephen again stood side by side, this time in the rain, on Manhattan's Upper West Side. As they watched, a portion of 103rd Street between Broadway and Amsterdam Avenue was officially named Humphrey Bogart Place. "Bogie would never have believed it," Lauren told a group of city officials and onlookers huddling under umbrellas. The block where Humphrey grew up had changed considerably since the days of Belmont and Maud Bogart. That brownstone was now the property of the city's housing authority, part of a low-income housing development known as the Douglass Rehabs. But the bronze plaque gleamed through the wet weather, as if it were adorning a town house on the Upper East Side, where Dr. Bogart would surely have settled if he had been practicing medicine in the late twentieth century. After the ceremony, all the attendees mounted the steps and traced the letters with their fingers:

THIS SITE IS THE CHILDHOOD HOME OF
HUMPHREY DeForest Bogart
1899–1957

Mr. Bogart lived at this site from the time
he was born until 1923. During a film

career that spanned almost 30 years and 75 films, Mr. Bogart became not only a mythical American hero but a popular culture icon known worldwide.

"He was endowed with the greatest gift a person can have: talent. The whole world came to recognize it."

JOHN HUSTON

II

In the summer of 2008, *New York Times* columnist Sharon Waxman remarked on an extraordinary sociological shift. hollywood's HE-MEN ARE BUMPED BY SENSITIVE GUYS, read the headline. For her detailed analysis Waxman quoted Debra Zane, a prominent casting director. "They are always looking for the macho man," she stated, "but they are pulling from this other group, who are strong but more overtly sensitive and more emotionally available, because that's what there is right now." Zane noted a shortage of the "man's man." Always in demand, they were "in short supply. And why is that? I don't know. . . ."

Waxman had some ideas. The softer-edged actors, she wrote, may reflect "a more feminized American society, the rise of the metrosexual male and the absence, until recently, of war and true hardship in the last two decades of American life." She interviewed a group of movie veterans. They contrasted the unlined and unfinished countenances of present-day stars and "the generation of actors who came out of the Depression or wartime, when hardship could be read in the faces of stars like Humphrey Bogart. . . ."

Variety followed up that story with one of its own. "Where have the manly movie stars gone?" asked columnist Anne Thompson. "Not so long ago, Hollywood's male stars were men's men. Think Humphrey Bogart. . . ." As masculine archetypes, the younger actors failed to impress her; Johnny Depp was "fey" in his *Pirates of the Caribbean* series, Brendan Fraser (of the Mummy films) was "goofy." Tom Cruise appeared to be "out of his league" in mature parts, and comic-book superheroes Brandon Routh (Superman), Edward Norton (the Incredible Hulk), and Tobey Maguire (Spider-Man) were all "boy-men." Director Frank Miller agreed with Thompson. "Hollywood is great at producing male actors," he complained, "but sucks at producing men." Searching for someone to play *The Spirit,* he interviewed scores of candidates and "found them all too much like boys." Somehow, American actors seemed unable to demonstrate a wide-screen virility. "When we want a tough guy," observed Jim Gianopulos, a co-chairman of Fox, "we go to Russell Crowe, Hugh Jackman [both Australian] or Colin Farrell [an Irishman]."

Harvey C. Mansfield, a conservative professor of government at Harvard, set down his views in the deliberately controversial *Manliness,* lamenting the lack of male role models like Humphrey Bogart. In *Casablanca,* for example, Rick's character "was confident and cynical — cool before 'cool' was invented." As Mansfield saw it, our society has adopted "a practice of equality between the sexes that has never been known before in all human history." In his eyes this was a sign of unrest, and possibly of things much more dire. Without a restoration of old values, the entire social structure was up for grabs. For manliness "restores order at moments when routine is not enough, when the plan fails, when the whole idea of rational control by modern science develops leaks."

Others chimed in, among them Guy Garcia, whose book *The Decline of Men* insisted that in the United States, postmodern males are "caught between the desire to conform to a kinder, gentler masculinity and a competing urge to swing from the trees and bring home a fresh kill for dinner." The shelf of lamentations widened to include Michael Chabon's *Manhood for Amateurs,* James Gilbert's *Men in the Middle,* Kathleen Parker's *Save the Males,* and Dr. Lionel Tiger's *The Decline of Males.*

It was all too much for columnist James Wolcott. In *Vanity Fair* he decried the "pathos, self-recrimination, and pathological dysfunction" of his fellow men. For him, the primary threat to the psychological well-being of most men wasn't "sexual or pop-cultural but economic, the fear that a single swing of the ax could render one destitute and undo everything one has attempted to build."

There is some validity to these economic and sexual observations. The trouble is that they're not new. Times have proved difficult in the first decade of the new millennium, with a chaos of bankruptcies and unemployment reaching 10 percent. But back in the early 1930s one in four Americans was unable to find work. From the corner office to the waterfront, everyone walked on eggs. Conditions were so dire that most Americans considered themselves a paycheck away from poverty, and versions of the "one ax" phrase were repeated around kitchen tables and factories across the country. The psyche of the American male was thought to be so lacerated it might not survive the Depression intact. During those years Humphrey, as apprehensive as any other workingman whose job was on the line, wasted no time on self-pity. He was too busy trying to stay afloat in a harsh, unforgiving company town. He became particularly adept at playing individuals under stress. Audiences, similarly afflicted, felt that he understood them and they made him a star.

As for that beleaguered American male: it's true that women now outnumber men at American law schools, and that there are more female senators and Supreme Court justices than ever before. Yet only 16 percent of the U.S. House and Senate are female, and of the Fortune 500 companies, 84 percent of the CEOs are male. The male ego is something else: that has been fragile for generations. Back in 1977 literary critic Wilfrid Sheed observed, "The prodigious success of *Life with Father* — a play about a late Victorian patriarch whose self-esteem has to be fostered like a house plant by the rest of the family — should have told us something." *Life with Father* opened at the end of the Depression, in 1939, the year that Humphrey appeared in *The Roaring Twenties.* It closed 3,224 performances later, in 1947, when he was filming *The Treasure of the Sierra Madre.*

Between these terminals, feminism grew in stature and power. Humphrey was no stranger to the movement. Maud Bogart had been a vigorous proponent; mother and son witnessed its progress from the days of the suffragettes to the epoch of Rosie the Riveter. If Humphrey felt threatened, however, he never let it show in his work, and his popularity among women remained untouched by social evolutions.

So there must be an additional key to Bogart's forward march through the epochs of the Great War, Prohibition, the Roaring Twenties, the Depression, the New Deal, World War II, the postwar euphoria of the 1950s, and on to the present day. That key has little to do with the battle of the sexes, the economic upheavals of the new millennium, or the country's current moral tone. Here it is:

The principal reason there never will, never *can,* be another Humphrey Bogart glares from the screens of every multiplex. When Humphrey began acting in films, demographics were irrelevant: everyone went to the picture show. Adolescent actors like Mickey Rooney and Deanna Durbin had their moments, but there were few teenage movies as such. Those under twenty were deemed insignificant, and in any case had no economic power. Studios produced films for the adults who controlled the purse strings. It didn't matter if the actors were heading toward middle age; so was a large part of the audience. Ergo, when a forty-two-year-old Bogart finally achieved leading-man status in *The Maltese Falcon,* he felt right for the role.

The move toward youthful male stars began in the early 1950s, when the U.S. Supreme Court ordered the studios to divest themselves of the film theaters they owned or controlled. Just as they were losing the power of "block booking" — dictating what features movie houses could show — television began to eat away at the potential audience. Then came the baby boomers. The suburbs grew, and with them came malls, smaller film houses, and drive-ins. Each year the filmgoing audience grew younger, with attendance shifting toward unmarried twentysomethings and teenagers. The remaining studios tried all sorts of gimmicks — imports, VistaVision, Todd-AO, Cinemascope 3-D, and so on. Humphrey continued to star, but the mature audience was drifting away. "It soon became a chicken-and-egg thing," maintains a Paramount executive. "The grownups said, 'If you'd make adult movies we'd come back to the theater.' And we said, 'If you'd come back to the theater we'd make adult movies.' Neither side budged, and one day it went past the point of no return." From then on, if films were going to turn big profits, the producers had to look elsewhere. As the statistics show, they did exactly that. Today, these are the twenty highest-grossing films in American history:

1. *Avatar (2009)* $2,728,713,460
2. *Titanic (1997)* $1,848,201,268
3. *The Lord of the* $1,119,110,941
   Rings: The Return
   of the King (2003)
4. *Pirates of the* $1,066,179,725
   Caribbean: Dead
   Man's Chest
   (2006)
5. *Alice in* $1,014,078,021
   Wonderland
   (2010)
6. *The Dark Knight* $1,001,921,825
   (2008)

7. *Harry Potter and the Philosopher's Stone (2001)* $974,733,550

8. *Pirates of the Caribbean: At World's End (2007)* $960,996,492

9. *Harry Potter and the Order of the Phoenix (2007)* $938,212,738

10. *Harry Potter and the Half-Blood Prince (2009)* $933,959,197

11. *The Lord of the Rings: The Two Towers (2002)* $925,282,504

12. *Star Wars Episode 1: The Phantom Menace (1999)* $924,317,558

13. *Shrek 2 (2004)* $919,838,758

14. *Jurassic Park (1993)* $914,691,118

15. *Harry Potter and the Goblet of Fire (2005)* $895,921,036

16. *Spider-Man 3 (2007)* $890,871,626

17. *Ice Age: Dawn* $884,784,626
    of the Dinosaurs
    (2009)
18. *Harry Potter* $878,643,482
    and the Chamber
    of Secrets (2002)
19. *The Lord of the* $870,761,744
    Rings: The Fel-
    lowship of the
    Ring (2001)
20. *Finding Nemo* $867,893,978
    (2003)

Not one of these features can be considered a purely "adult" film. They have been enjoyed by grown-ups, of course, but the target audience was a young one. With good reason. A recent survey by the Morgan Cinema Network measured moviegoing by age. Of those in the 14–17 category, 54 percent had been to the cinema during the previous month. During the same time period, the percentages declined by age cohort. Of those 18–24, 48 percent saw a movie during the previous month, those 25–34, 31 percent, 35–49, 29 percent. Of the filmgoers 50 and over, only 24 percent had seen a film during the previous four weeks.

Small wonder, then, that producers keep coming up with products that border on the puerile — and with boy-men to star in them.

Truth be told, though, in their rush to please the crowds, they have overlooked the obvious. Enormous political, ethnic, and psychological shifts in the U.S. population have occurred since Humphrey Bogart's final performance, but his unique amalgam of integrity and rue has not gone out of style. It has just gone out of American cinema. This disconnect is one of the main reasons why adults go elsewhere for emotional and aesthetic satisfaction.

The current vulgarity of American dialogue and conduct has become a favorite subject of sociologists and historians. On occasion, they cite Humphrey's rough-hewn persona and barroom misbehavior as early signs of the disintegration to follow. Actually, everything we know about him indicates that he would be dismayed by the present-day Hollywood products, by the headline-grabbing stars who trash hotel rooms, and by the starlets who manage to make scurrilous headlines just before the opening of their newest films. The big gap between the professional and the bum was very clear to him, and he wanted above all to be considered a pro. Unlike too many A-list celebrities, he aimed his barbs at the prominent; his kindnesses went to the powerless. He helped Fatty Arbuckle and Peter Lorre when they were in extreme need, defiantly hired people on the studio blacklist, aided Joan Bennett and Gene Tierney when they were in distress, and quietly donated to a long list of charities. He was courteous to women and straightforward to men, and when he made a promise he kept it. The latter was a rare thing in Hollywood; no wonder that a sense of disappointment registered so strongly in his performances and in his life.

Those in search of the Bogart style will have a hard time finding it in movie theaters. Today it flourishes elsewhere: in the principled action of individuals uncomfortable with compromise and conformity, in classic fiction, in the theater. And, of course, in old films — the kind that are still being bought and rented, or shown on channels like Turner Classic Movies, where Humphrey Bogart festivals attract millions of viewers every year.

From time to time columnists dub some young actor the new Clark Gable, the new Jimmy Stewart, the new Marlon Brando. No one claims to have discovered the new Humphrey Bogart. With good reason. There was nothing like him before his entrance; there has been nothing like him since his exit. In one of the great show business paradoxes, Humphrey vanished more than five decades ago, and yet audiences have never allowed him to fade away. Even now — perhaps *especially* now — we need the genuine article too much to let him out of our sight.

THE CREDITS

During the 1920s and '30s, most leading actors got their starts in the theater. But few could approach Humphrey Bogart's long apprenticeship. As we have seen, he began working on Broadway in 1922, broke away for an unsatisfactory try at a film career in 1930, resumed stage work in 1931, and continued until 1936, when his cinematic career finally gained traction.

BROADWAY PLAYS

1922

Drifting. Playhouse Theater; limited engagement.

Up the Ladder. Playhouse Theater; limited engagement.

Swifty. Playhouse Theater; limited engagement.

1923

Meet the Wife. Klaw Theater; 232 performances.

1924

Nerves. Comedy Theater; 16 performances.

1925

Hell's Bells. Wallack's Theater; 120 performances.
Candle Searchers. Music Box; 332 performances.

1927

Saturday's Children. Booth Theater; 310 performances.
Baby Mine. Chanin's 46th Street Theater; 12 performances.

1928

A Most Immoral Lady. Cort Theater; 106 performances.

1929

The Skyrocket. Lyceum Theater; 11 performances.
It's a Wise Child. Belasco Theater; 378 performances.

1931

After All. Booth Theater; 20 performances.

1932

I Loved You Wednesday. Sam H. Harris Theater; 63 performances.

Chrysalis. Martin Beck Theater; 23 performances.

1933

Our Wife. Booth Theater; 20 performances.

The Mask and the Face. Guild Theater; 40 performances.

1934

Invitation to a Murder. Masque Theater; 37 performances.

The Petrified Forest. Broadhurst Theater; 181 performances.

HOLLYWOOD FEATURES

1930

A Devil with Women. Fox.

Up the River. Fox.

1931

Body and Soul. Fox.

Bad Sister. Universal.

Women of All Nations. Fox.

A Holy Terror. Fox.

1932

Love Affair. Columbia.
Big City Blues. Warner Bros.
Three on a Match. Warner Bros.

1934

Midnight. All-Star Productions.

1936

The Petrified Forest. Warner Bros.
Bullets or Ballots. Warner Bros.
Two Against the World. Warner Bros.
China Clipper. Warner Bros.
Isle of Fury. Warner Bros.

1937

Black Legion. Warner Bros.
The Great O'Malley. Warner Bros.
Marked Woman. Warner Bros.
Kid Galahad. Warner Bros.
San Quentin. Warner Bros.
Stand-In. Walter Wanger Productions.

1938

Swing Your Lady. Warner Bros.
Crime School. Warner Bros.
Men Are Such Fools. Warner Bros.
The Amazing Dr. Clitterhouse. Warner Bros.
Racket Busters. Warner Bros.
Angels with Dirty Faces. Warner Bros.

1939

King of the Underworld. Warner Bros.
The Oklahoma Kid. Warner Bros.
Dark Victory. Warner Bros.
You Can't Get Away with Murder. Warner Bros.
The Roaring Twenties. Warner Bros.
The Return of Dr. X. Warner Bros.
Invisible Stripes. Warner Bros.

1940

Virginia City. Warner Bros.
It All Came True. Warner Bros.
Brother Orchid. Warner Bros.
They Drive by Night. Warner Bros.

1941

High Sierra. Warner Bros.
The Wagons Roll at Night. Warner Bros.
The Maltese Falcon. Warner Bros.

1942

All Through the Night. Warner Bros.
The Big Shot. Warner Bros.
Across the Pacific. Warner Bros.
Casablanca. Warner Bros.

1943

Action in the North Atlantic. Warner Bros.
Thank Your Lucky Stars. Warner Bros.

Sahara. Columbia.

1944

Passage to Marseille. Warner Bros.
To Have and Have Not. Warner Bros.

1945

Conflict. Warner Bros.

1946

Two Guys from Milwaukee. Warner Bros.
The Big Sleep. Warner Bros.

1947

Dead Reckoning. Columbia.
The Two Mrs. Carrolls. Warner Bros.
Dark Passage. Warner Bros.

1948

The Treasure of the Sierra Madre. Warner Bros.
Key Largo. Warner Bros.

1949

Knock on Any Door. Columbia.
Tokyo Joe. Santana; released by Columbia.

1950

Chain Lightning. Warner Bros.
In a Lonely Place. Santana; released by Columbia.

1951

The Enforcer. Warner Bros.
Sirocco. Santana; released by Columbia.
The African Queen. United Artists.
Deadline — U.S.A. Twentieth Century Fox.

1953

Battle Circus. Metro-Goldwyn-Mayer.

1954

Beat the Devil. Santana-Romulus; released by United Artists.
The Caine Mutiny. Columbia.
Sabrina. Paramount.
The Barefoot Contessa. United Artists.

1955

We're No Angels. Paramount.
The Left Hand of God. Twentieth Century Fox.
The Desperate Hours. Paramount.

1956

The Harder They Fall. Columbia.

ACKNOWLEDGMENTS

Humphrey Bogart has been gone for more than fifty years. Today the job of measuring his influence falls more to the social historian than to the interviewer. For most of his contemporaries are no longer with us, and those who remain are likely to have clouded or guarded memories. So for the most part I relied on the guidance of librarians at the Sterling Library at Yale; the 42nd Street Library, the Lincoln Center Library, and the Century Association Library in New York City; and on the collections in private libraries in Los Angeles and San Francisco.

Still, there were a few people on both coasts kind enough to answer questions about show business past. The late Daniel Melnick recollected the personalities, places, and events of old Hollywood. The late Chuck Jones, responsible for some of the greatest Warner Bros. cartoons in the heyday of the studio, recalled Jack Warner "in all his two dimensions." During the years when I was *Time*'s cinema reviewer, I was able to glean information from John Huston, Bob Evans, and Bette Davis, who had much to say about moviemaking in the golden era of American film. In more recent times I was aided by Warren Adler, Dick Cavett, Christina Davidson, Josh Greenfeld, Miles Kreuger, Diane Ladd, Paul Maslansky, Jeff Melvoin, Will Shortz, Harry Stein, Elaine Stritch, Priscilla Turner, and Michael York, as well as the late Henry A. Grunwald, Ike Pappas, David Scherman, Alan Schneider, and Frank Scioscia. Jess Korman, a friend since our undergraduate days at NYU, has been extraordinarily knowledgeable and heartening. Elie Wiesel has always taken time from his crowded schedule to advise and encourage, as has my wise adviser and *copain* Myron Magnet. My colleagues at *Time* and afterward, Gerald Clarke, Paul Gray, John Leo, Lance Morrow, Roger Rosenblatt, Christopher Porterfield, and R. Z. Sheppard, provided unfailing wit and counsel, as well as lunch.

The sharp-minded editors of publications to which I contribute — notably Brian Anderson and his colleagues Paul Beston and Benjamin Plotinsky of *City Journal*, Myron Kolatch of the *New Leader*, and Erich

Eichmann of the *Wall Street Journal* —
aided me on more occasions than I can
count.

Again, as in so much of my previous work,
Christopher Stephens, proprietor of the
Riverrun bookstore in Hastings-on-Hudson,
was able to furnish all sorts of obscure
magazines, rare volumes, and printed
ephemera.

Invaluable research for *Tough Without a
Gun* was done by John Bennett of the
Sterling Library and Villette Harris, both of
whom have been with me on prior books,
and Karen Marston, a new and gifted colleague.

None of this would have been possible
without the persons who are also tough
without a gun, among them Peter Gethers
and Claudia Herr, my alert and demanding
editors at Knopf, and Kathy Robbins, a
most percipient adviser and representative.

As always, my immediate family — May,
Lili, and Ethan, Andy and Daniela, Lea and
Aly — have been models of forbearance and
support. Added to their contributions is the
encouragement given by a very special
person, Lynn Henson, who has paid her
dues in overplus. Limitless gratitude and
love to all.

BIBLIOGRAPHY

PRIMARY SOURCES

Bacall, Lauren. *By Myself.* Alfred A. Knopf, 1980.

Barbour, Alan G. *Humphrey Bogart.* Pyramid Publications, 1973.

Benchley, Nathaniel. *Humphrey Bogart.* Hutchinson, 1975.

Bogart, Stephen, with Gary Provost. *Bogart: In Search of My Father.* E. P. Dutton, 1995.

Brooks, Louise. *Lulu in Hollywood.* Alfred A. Knopf, 1982.

Cahill, Marie. *Humphrey Bogart: A Hollywood Portrait.* Smithmark, 1992.

Choppa, Karen, and Paul Humphrey. *Maud Humphrey: Her Permanent Imprint on American Illustration.* Schiffer, 1993.

Coe, Jonathan. *Humphrey Bogart: Take It and Like It.* Grove & Weidenfeld, 1991.

Cooke, Alistair. *Six Men.* Arcade, 1995.

Cunningham, Ernest. *The Ultimate Bogart:*

All the Facts and Fantasies About Humphrey Bogart, the Quintessential Movie Tough Guy. Renaissance Books, 1999.

Duchovnay, Gerald. *Humphrey Bogart: A Bio-Bibliography.* Greenwood Press, 1999.

Duncan, Paul, and James Ursini. *Movie Icons: Bogart.* Taschen, 2008.

Eyles, Allen. *Bogart.* Macmillan, 1975.

Gehman, Richard. *Bogart: An Intimate Biography.* Fawcett Gold Medal, 1965.

Goodman, Ezra. *Bogey: The Good Bad Guy.* Lyle Stuart, 1965.

Hanna, David. *Bogart: A Confidential Biography.* Norton, 1976.

Hyams, Joe. *Bogart & Bacall: A Love Story.* Warner Books, 1975.

———. *Bogie: The Biography of Humphrey Bogart.* New American Library, 1966.

McCarty, Clifford. *Bogey: The Films of Humphrey Bogart.* Citadel Press, 1965.

Meyers, Jeffrey. *Bogart: A Life in Hollywood.* Houghton Mifflin Company, 1997.

Michael, Paul. *Humphrey Bogart: The Man and His Films.* Bobbs Merrill, 1965.

Porter, Darwin. *The Secret Life of Humphrey Bogart: The Early Years, 1899–1931.* Georgia Literary Association, 2003.

Ruddy, Jonah, and Jonathan Hill. *Bogey: The Man, the Actor, the Legend.* Tower

Books, 1965.

Schickel, Richard, and George Perry. *Bogie: A Celebration of the Life and Films of Humphrey Bogart*. St. Martin's Press, 2007.

Sklar, Robert. *City Boys: Cagney, Bogart, Garfield*. Princeton University Press, 1992.

Sperber, A. M., and Eric Lax. *Bogart*. William Morrow, 1997.

Thompson, Verita, and Donald Shepherd. *Bogie and Me: A Love Story*. St. Martin's, 1982.

SECONDARY SOURCES

Agee, James. *Agee on Film: Essays and Reviews*. Wideview/Perigee, 1983.

———. *Agee on Film: Five Film Scripts*. Beacon, 1964.

Astor, Mary. *A Life on Film*. Delacorte, 1977.

Basinger, Jeanine. *The Star Machine*. Knopf, 2007.

Baxter, John. *Hollywood in the Thirties*. Paperback Library, 1970.

Behlmer, Rudy. *Inside Warner Bros. (1935–1951)*. Simon & Schuster, 1985.

Bergman, Ingrid, and Alan Burgess. *My Story*. Warner, 1995.

Berryman, John. *The Dream Songs*. Farrar, Straus and Giroux, 1969.

Bishop, Jim. *The Mark Hellinger Story: A*

Biography of Broadway and Hollywood. Appleton, 1952.

Bogdanovich, Peter. *Who the Hell's in It?: Conversation with Hollywood's Legendary Actors.* Ballantine, 2004.

Christopher, Nicholas. *Somewhere in the Night: Film Noir and the American City.* Free Press, 2007.

Clarke, Gerald. *Capote: A Biography.* Simon & Schuster, 1988.

Comery, Douglas. *The Hollywood Studio System.* St. Martin's, 1986.

Deutsch, Armand. *Bogie & Me: And Other Friends & Acquaintances from a Life in Hollywood & Beyond.* Putnam, 1991.

Duncan, Paul. *Film Noir.* Pocket Essentials, 2006.

Eco, Umberto. *Travels in Hyperreality.* Trans. William Weaver. Harcourt, 1986.

Fraser-Cavassoni, Natasha. *Sam Spiegel: The Incredible Life and Times of America's Most Iconoclastic Producer.* Simon & Schuster, 2002.

French, Philip, and Ken Wlaschin. *The Faber Book of Movie Verse.* Faber and Faber, 1995.

Friedrich, Otto. *City of Nets: A Portrait of Hollywood in the 1940's.* Norton, 1997.

Goldman, William. *Which Lie Did I Tell?:*

More Adventures in the Screen Trade. Vintage, 2000.

Goodman, Ezra. *The Fifty-Year Decline and Fall of Hollywood.* Simon & Schuster, 1961.

Grobel, Lawrence. *The Hustons: The Life & Times of a Hollywood Dynasty.* Cooper Square Press, 2000.

Hannsberry, Karen Burroughs. *Bad Boys: The Actors of Film Noir.* MacFarland, 2008.

Henreid, Paul, and Julius Fast. *Ladies' Man: An Autobiography.* St. Martins, 1984.

Higham, Charles, and Joel Greenberg. *Hollywood in the Forties.* Zwemmer, 1968.

Hirsch, Foster. *The Dark Side of the Screen: Film Noir.* Da Capo, 2008.

Howard, Leslie Ruth. *A Quite Remarkable Father: The Biography of Leslie Howard.* Harcourt, Brace, 1959.

Huston, John. *An Open Book.* Knopf, 1980.

Kaminsky, Stuart. *John Huston: Maker of Magic.* Houghton Mifflin, 1978.

Kanfer, Stefan. *A Journal of the Plague Years: A Devastating Account of the Era of the Blacklist.* Atheneum, 1973.

Kimmel, Michael S. *Manhood in America: A Cultural History.* Oxford University Press, 2006.

Kluger, Richard. *Ashes to Ashes: America's Hundred-Year Cigarette War, the Public*

Health, and the Unabashed Triumph of Philip Morris. Knopf, 1996.

Koch, Howard. *As Time Goes By: Memoirs of a Writer.* Harcourt, 1979.

Krutnik, Frank. *In a Lonely Place: Film Noir, Genre, Masculinity.* Routledge, 1991.

Lehman, Peter, ed. *Masculinity: Bodies, Movies, Culture.* Routledge, 2001.

Lloyd, Ann, and David Robinson. *Movies of the Forties.* Orbis, 1984.

Logan, Joshua. *Movie Stars, Real People, and Me.* Delacorte, 1978.

Long, Robert Emmet, ed. *John Huston Interviews.* University Press of Mississippi, 2001.

MacShane, Frank, ed. *Selected Letters of Raymond Chandler.* Dell, 1987.

Mast, Gerald. *Howard Hawks, Storyteller.* Oxford University Press, 1982.

Meyer, William R. *Warner Brothers Directors: The Hard-Boiled, the Comic, and the Weepers.* Arlington House, 1978.

Mordden, Ethan. *All That Glittered: The Golden Age of Drama on Broadway.* St. Martin's, 2007.

Naipaul, V. S. *The Middle Passage.* Random House, 2002.

Naremore, James. *More Than Night: Film Noir in Its Contexts.* University of California

Press, 1998.

Niven, David. *Bring On the Empty Horses.* Putnam, 1975.

———. *The Moon's a Balloon.* Dell, 1972.

Nolen, Scott Allen. *Warners Wiseguys: All 112 Films That Robinson, Cagney and Bogart Made for the Studio.* McFarland, 2008.

Parish, James Robert. *The Hollywood Book of Scandals.* McGraw-Hill, 2004.

Pettigrew, Terence. *The Bogart File.* Golden Eagle, 1977.

Pratley, Gerald. *The Cinema of John Huston.* Barnes, 1977.

Quirk, Lawrence, and William Schoell. *The Rat Pack: Neon Nights with the Kings of Cool.* Avon, 1999.

Ray, Nicholas. *I Was Interrupted: Nicholas Ray on Making Movies.* University of California Press, 1993.

Robertson, James. *The Casablanca Man: The Cinema of Michael Curtiz.* Routledge, 1993.

Robinson, Edward G., and Leonard Spiegelglass. *All My Yesterdays: An Autobiography.* Hawthorn, 1973.

Royce, Brenda Scott. *Lauren Bacall: A Bio-Bibliography.* Greenwood, 1992.

Sarris, Andrew. *You Ain't Heard Nothin' Yet: The American Talking Film; History & Memory, 1927–1949.* Oxford University

Press, 1998.

Schickel, Richard, and George Perry. *You Must Remember This: The Warner Bros. Story.* Running Press, 2008.

Sennett, Ted. *Warner Brothers Presents: The Most Exciting Years — from* The Jazz Singer *to* White Heat. Castle Books, 1971.

Shipman, David. *The Great Movie Stars: The Golden Years.* Little, Brown, 1995.

Silke, James. *Here's Looking at You, Kid: 50 Years of Fighting, Working, and Dreaming at Warner Bros.* Little, Brown, 1976.

Sklar, Robert. *Movie-Made America: A Cultural History of American Movies.* Vintage, 1994.

Thomson, David. *The New Biographical History of Film.* Random House, 2006.

Tierney, Gene, with Mickey Herskowitz. *Self-Portrait.* Wyden, 1979.

Trice, Ashton D., and Samuel A. Holland. *Heroes, Antiheroes and Dolts: Portrayals of Masculinity in American Popular Films, 1921–1999.* McFarland, 2001.

Tynan, Kenneth. *Profiles.* Harper Perennial, 1989.

Warner, Jack, with Dean Jennings. *My First Hundred Years in Hollywood.* Random House, 1967.

Wilson, Earl. *The Show Business Nobody*

Knows. Cowles, 1971.

Wylie, Philip. *Generation of Vipers: Newly Annotated by the Author.* Pocket Books, 1958.

Youngkin, Stephen D. *The Lost One: A Life of Peter Lorre.* University Press of Kentucky, 2005.

Zolotow, Maurice. *Billy Wilder in Hollywood.* Limelight, 1996.

SPECIFIC FILMS
The Maltese Falcon

Anobile, Richard, ed. *The Maltese Falcon.* Pan Books, 1974.

Behlmer, Rudy. *Behind the Scenes: The Making of . . .* Samuel French, 1990.

Cahill, Marie. *The Maltese Falcon.* Smithmark, 1991.

Ebert, Roger. *The Great Movies.* Broadway, 1992.

Layman, Richard, ed. *Discovering the Maltese Falcon and Sam Spade.* Vince Emery Productions, 2005.

Peary, Danny. *Cult Movies: The Classics, the Sleepers, the Weird, and the Wonderful.* Gramercy Books, 1998.

Zinman, David. *50 Classic Motion Pictures: The Stuff That Dreams Are Made Of.* Crown, 1970.

Casablanca

Francisco, Charles. *You Must Remember This . . . : The Filming of Casablanca.* Prentice-Hall, 1980.

Fredriksen, Mark. *An A to Z of Casablanca.* Adelphi, 1995.

Harmetz, Aljean. *Round Up the Usual Suspects: The Making of Casablanca — Bogart, Bergman and World War II.* Hyperion, 1992.

Lebo, Harlan. *Casablanca: Behind the Scenes.* Simon & Schuster, 1992.

Miller, Frank. *Casablanca: As Time Goes By: 50th Anniversary Commemorative.* Turner, 1992.

Osborne, Richard E. *The Casablanca Companion: The Movie Classic and Its Place in History.* Riebel-Roque, 1997.

Siegel, Jeff. *The Casablanca Companion: The Movie and More.* Taylor, 1992.

The African Queen

Behlmer, Rudy. *Behind the Scenes: The Making of . . .* Samuel French, 1990.

Hepburn, Katharine. *The Making of the African Queen: Or How I Went to Africa with Bogart, Bacall, and Huston and Almost Lost My Mind.* Knopf, 1987.

Viertel, Peter. *White Hunter, Black Heart.* Dell, 1987.

NOVELS FEATURING OR ABOUT HUMPHREY BOGART

Baxt, George. *The Humphrey Bogart Murder Case.* St. Martin's, 1995.

Block, Lawrence. *The Man Who Thought He Was Bogart.* No Exit, 1995.

Bogart, Stephen. *As Time Goes By.* Macmillan, 1996.

———. *Play It Again.* Macmillan, 1994.

Fenady, Andrew. *The Man with Bogart's Face.* Avon, 1977.

Walsh, Michael. *As Time Goes By: A Novel of Casablanca.* Warner, 1998.

ABOUT THE AUTHOR

Stefan Kanfer's books include *The Eighth Sin, A Summer World, The Last Empire, Serious Business, Groucho, Ball of Fire, Stardust Lost,* and *Somebody.* He was a writer and editor at *Time* for more than twenty years. He was also a primary interviewer in the Academy Award–nominated documentary *The Line King* and editor of an anthology of Groucho Marx's comedy, *The Essential Groucho.* A Literary Lion of the New York Public Library and recipient of numerous writing awards, Kanfer lives in New York and on Cape Cod.